Load Balance for Distributed Real-time Computing Systems

East China Normal University Scientific Reports
Subseries on Data Science and Engineering

ISSN: 2382-5715

This book series reports valuable research results and progress in scientific and related areas. Mainly contributed by the distinguished professors of the East China Normal University, it will cover a number of research areas in pure mathematics, financial mathematics, applied physics, computer science, environmental science, geography, estuarine and coastal science, education information technology, etc.

Published

Vol. 13 *Load Balance for Distributed Real-time Computing Systems*
by Junhua Fang (Soochow University, China),
Rong Zhang (East China Normal University, China) and
Aoying Zhou (East China Normal University, China)

Vol. 12 *Biological Language Model: Theory and Application*
by Qiwen Dong (East China Normal University, China),
Xiaoyang Jing (Yunnan University, China),
Aoying Zhou (East China Normal University, China) and
Xiuzhen Hu (Inner Mongolia University of Technology, China)

Vol. 11 *Probabilistic Approaches for Social Media Analysis:*
Data, Community and Influence
by Kun Yue (Yunnan University, China), Jin Li (Yunnan University, China), Hao Wu (Yunnan University, China), Weiyi Liu (Yunnan University, China) and Zidu Yin (Yunnan University, China)

More information on this series can also be found at https://www.worldscientific.com/series/ecnusr

(Continued at end of book)

East China Normal University Scientific Reports | Vol. 13
Subseries on Data Science and Engineering

Load Balance for Distributed Real-time Computing Systems

Junhua Fang
Soochow University, China

Rong Zhang
East China Normal University, China

Aoying Zhou
East China Normal University, China

World Scientific

NEW JERSEY · LONDON · SINGAPORE · BEIJING · SHANGHAI · HONG KONG · TAIPEI · CHENNAI · TOKYO

Published by

World Scientific Publishing Co. Pte. Ltd.

5 Toh Tuck Link, Singapore 596224

USA office: 27 Warren Street, Suite 401-402, Hackensack, NJ 07601

UK office: 57 Shelton Street, Covent Garden, London WC2H 9HE

Library of Congress Cataloging-in-Publication Data

Names: Fang, Junhua, author. | Zhang, Rong, author. | Zhou, Aoying, 1965– author.
Title: Load balance for distributed real-time computing systems / Junhua Fang,
    Soochow University, China, Rong Zhang, East China Normal University, China,
    Aoying Zhou, East China Normal University, China.
Description: New Jersey : World Scientific, [2020] | Series: East China Normal University
    scientific reports, 2382-5715 ; vol 13 | Includes bibliographical references.
Identifiers: LCCN 2020010946 | ISBN 9789811216145 (hardcover) |
    ISBN 9789811216831 (paperback) | ISBN 9789811216152 (ebook) |
    ISBN 9789811216169 (ebook other)
Subjects: LCSH: Electronic data processing--Distributed processing. |
    Computer capacity--Management.
Classification: LCC QA76.9.D5 F36 2020 | DDC 004/.36--dc23
LC record available at https://lccn.loc.gov/2020010946

British Library Cataloguing-in-Publication Data
A catalogue record for this book is available from the British Library.

For any available supplementary material, please visit
https://www.worldscientific.com/worldscibooks/10.1142/11709#t=suppl

Desk Editors: Herbert Moses/Steven Patt

Typeset by Stallion Press
Email: enquiries@stallionpress.com

East China Normal University Scientific Reports

Preface

Load Balance for Distributed Real-time Computing Systems

Streaming data have critical requirements on process efficiency as their value decreases as time goes by. Traditional database techniques cannot be applied easily to process stream data due to their characteristics of magnitude and continuity, which will fill up storage, leading to the development of DSPEs. Usually, the stream-oriented computation frameworks are deployed on large-scale clusters or cloud platforms. The computation tasks are sent to distributed machines in the form of graphic-like topology, and the pipeline model turns the output of the preceding step into the input of the next step. However, workload skewness and variance are common phenomena in DSPEs which always generate workload imbalance among parallel processing tasks and could affect processing performance greatly.

Although some research results have been integrated into real-time prototype systems and implemented in commercial applications, distributed stream processing still faces the following three main challenges: (i) lack of adaptive algorithms with high throughput and low latency, especially for complex operators, (ii) lack of elastic system scalability and (iii) the conundrum of usability assurance strategy. Based on these, this book aims to illustrate how to develop novel technologies to guarantee high performance and high availability for DSPEs with the best use of hardware resource in cluster, which is called resource sensitive. The main contributions of this book are summarized as follows: (i) proposing an efficient key-based load balancing strategy, (ii) decreasing the resource utilization for join operation by designing a new node organizing mechanism and (iii) exploring a fault-tolerant strategy for economical resource utilization on the premise of efficient data recovery. Overall, the key features of this book are summarized as follows:

- This book comprehensively analyzes the load balancing problem in distributed stream processing systems and explores a set of high-performance real-time processing schemes established on key-based balancing strategies the join-matrix model and fault-tolerant mechanisms.
- This book provides theoretical support for the proposed techniques. Through a rich set of experiments and comparisons with the other state-of-the-art techniques using both standard benchmarks and real datasets, this book comprehensively verifies the correctness and effectiveness of the proposed methods.
- This book provides researchers with an introduction to these fields by comprehensively classifying the current state of research, by describing in-depth techniques and methods, and by highlighting future research directions. Moreover, this book is also appropriately a reference book for researchers in the fields of distributed stream processing, parallel systems, cloud computing, etc.

About the Authors

Junhua Fang is a Lecturer with the Advanced Data Analytics Group at the School of Computer Science and Technology, Soochow University. Before joining Soochow University, he earned his Ph.D. degree from East China Normal University in 2017. He is a member of the China Computer Federation. His research focuses on distributed databases and parallel streaming analytics.

Rong Zhang is a member of the China Computer Federation. She received her Ph.D. degree in computer science from Fudan University in 2007. She joined East China Normal University in 2011 and is currently a Professor at the university. From 2007 to 2010, she worked as an expert researcher in NICT, Japan. Her current research interests include knowledge management, distributed data management and database benchmarking.

Aoying Zhou is currently Vice President of East China Normal University (ECNU) and the Founding Dean and Professor of the School of Data Science and Engineering. He received his Bachelor's and Master's degrees in Computer Science from Chengdu University of Science and Technology, China, in 1985 and 1988, respectively, and his Ph.D. degree from Fudan University, China, in 1993. Before joining ECNU in 2008, Aoying worked for Fudan University in the Computer Science Department for 15 years. He is the winner of the National Science Fund for Distinguished Young Scholars supported by the National Natural Science Foundation of China (NSFC), as well as the professorship appointment under the Changjiang Scholars Program of the Ministry of Education, China. He is now serving as a Vice Director of the Database Technology Committee of the China Computer Federation. Aoying has served as a member of the editorial boards of journals such as Chinese Journal of Computer, Data Science and Engineering and World Wide Web Journal, among others. His research interests include databases, data management and data-driven applications.

Contents

2.3 Preliminaries 17
   2.3.1 Problem formulation 20
   2.3.2 Optimization goals 23
2.4 Balance Algorithms with Key Granularity Integration . . . 23
   2.4.1 Basic algorithm 24
   2.4.2 Minimum table algorithm 30
   2.4.3 Minimum migration algorithm: Heuristic
       algorithm 31
2.5 Computational Complexity Optimization 32
   2.5.1 Compact representations of key space 34
   2.5.2 Discretization on calculating and state
       workload 34
   2.5.3 Mixed algorithm over compact representations . . . 37
   2.5.4 Extension to multi-dimensional load balance 38
2.6 Practical Verification and Study 40
   2.6.1 Environment setting 40
   2.6.2 Load skewness phenomenon 43
   2.6.3 Impact of algorithm parameters 44
   2.6.4 Multiple resources 55
   2.6.5 Throughput and latency 57
   2.6.6 Scalability 59
   2.6.7 Dynamicity 61
2.7 Summary 63

3. Workload Balance by Key Splitting   65
3.1 Motivation and Basic Idea 65
   3.1.1 Basic idea 65
   3.1.2 Motivation 70
3.2 Related Work and Literature 73
3.3 Preliminaries 76
   3.3.1 Key grouping 76
   3.3.2 Hybrid routing policy 77
   3.3.3 Definition of related terms 78
3.4 Cost Model Analysis 78
   3.4.1 Basic principle 79

List of Figures

Chapter 1

Chapter 2

Chapter 3

Chapter 4

Chapter 5

Chapter 6

List of Tables

Chapter 1

Introduction

1.1 Background and Motivation

1.1.1 *Application scenarios*

Data are time-sensitive in many areas, which means data are valuable only when they are in the "fresh" state. Therefore, data processing and analysis in a real-time manner meets a broad range of requirements. For instance, over the last decade, the ubiquitous GPS-embedded devices generated a large amount of trajectory data, which enabled a variety of LBS applications, e.g., car pooling [Trasarti *et al.* (2011); Zheng *et al.* (2013a)], navigation and tour planning [Li *et al.* (2018); Shang *et al.* (2014, 2016)]. As it represents the moving trace of an object, the trajectory has been commonly used as a basic ingredient for the calculation of location-based commercial and public services [Su *et al.* (2013, 2015); Sun *et al.* (2018)]. Among those applications, the distance measure between trajectories is a fundamental and necessary operation for calculating the similarity of entities' behaviors [Shang *et al.* (2018, 2017); Xie *et al.* (2017)]. Moreover, since most of the LBS applications require interactive responses from the users and the similarities are usually performed on the ongoing trajectories, it is necessary to handle the large-scale trajectory similarity in an online scenario.

Furthermore, applications based on graphs are ubiquitous and they are useful in capturing behavior involving interactions between entities. The growing scale and importance of graph data have driven the development of

numerous specialized graph processing systems [Gonzalez *et al.* (2014)].
Existing work mainly focuses on how to manage such a large amount of data
or develop a special computing architecture for these specific applications
[Zheng *et al.* (2013b); Shang *et al.* (2012); Yin *et al.* (2016)]. Furthermore,
in the majority of cases, the applications based on graphs data are time
sensitive since the data themselves carry the time dimension. Then one
of the major challenges in the area of big graph data processing is how
to handle such a structure in a real-time update manner, namely dynamic
graphs. Mobility traces, e.g., WiFi traces, Bluetooth traces, instant message
traces and check-ins, can also be modeled by graphs by applying some
sophisticated techniques [Tsourakakis *et al.* (2014); Ji *et al.* (2017)]. Due
to the inherent characteristics of the spatio-temporal data, their timestamp
is a necessary item; these kinds of data require more real-time processing
to explore their greater value.

In recent years, the research on Distributed Stream Processing Engines
(DSPEs), which is used for processing large-scale real-time data, has
become an indispensable part in the development of data science and big
data technology. However, the intrinsic characteristics of stream data, such
as continuity, dynamic nature and unpredictability, bring about great challenges in the design of a high-performance and high-availability DSPE.
This book focuses on the current issues in DSPEs, such as the lack of algorithms which produce a node-wise lightweight adaptive workload balance,
the high cost of resilient processing architecture and the high cost of fault
tolerance, and pursuing a win–win fusion strategy of load balancing and
fault-tolerance mechanism.

1.1.2 *Distributed stream processing engine*

A program in a DSPE, such as the topology in Apache Storm or Flink, can
be represented as a directed graph, whose vertex is an operator executing
user-defined functions, and each edge between two vertices represents a
data stream (a collection of key-value pairs called *tuples*) produced by an
upstream operator and consumed by a downstream operator. To maximize
the throughput of the stream processing system and improve the utilization
rate of the computation resource, the workload of a logical operator is
usually partitioned and concurrently processed by a number of threads,
known as *slots*.

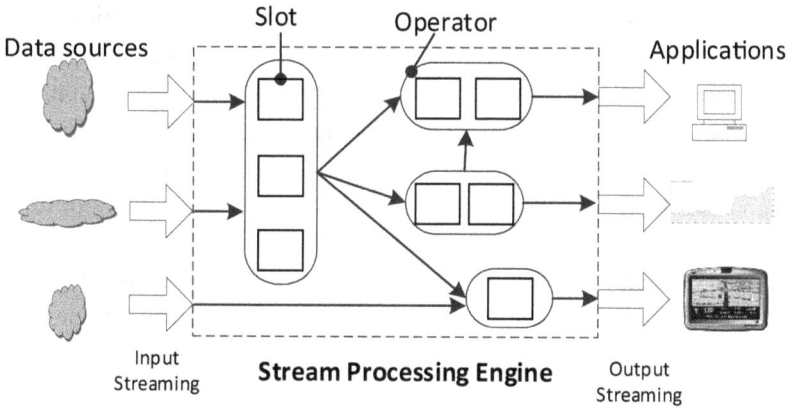

Fig. 1.1. Architecture of real-time processing system.

The high-level diagram of the DSPE architecture is shown in Fig. 1.1. Before each parallel processing slot implements its calculations, the primary slot of a DSPE is to decide how to distribute the incoming tuples among slots within the operation based on computational semantics. Key-based workload partitioning is now commonly adopted in DSPEs, such that tuples with the same key are guaranteed to be received by the same concrete slot for processing. This data partition manner is simple and practical, which models the incoming data and concrete slots as a mapping from a key domain to the running slots in the succeeding operator. In general, a hash function is used for such key-based workload partitions, and it incurs a cheap memory cost and a high computation efficiency. However, such a solution is vulnerable to workload variance, key skewness and a semantically complicated state. An intuitive solution is to explicitly assign the tuples based on a carefully optimized routing table, which specifies the destination of the tuples by a map structure on the keys. Although such an approach is more flexible on dynamic workload repartitioning, it is impractical due to its high operational cost on both memory and computation.

1.1.3 *Workload balance in a DSPE*

A data stream is an unbounded sequence of tuples with its intrinsic characteristics including continuity, dynamic and unpredictability. To maximize the throughput and improve the utilization rate of the computation resource, streams are usually processed in a parallel or distributed fashion. There-fore, a global execution plan is required so that the whole process can be divided into sub-tasks which are assigned to various workers. Such a plan is usually described by a directed graphical model (e.g., Storm [Toshniwal *et al.* (2014)], Heron [Kulkarni *et al.* (2015)] and Spark Streaming [Zaharia *et al.* (2013)]), in which a vertex denotes a computation operator and an edge denotes the data flow from one operator to another. Meanwhile, the workload of each computation operator is partitioned and concurrently pro-cessed by a number of threads, known as *tasks*, each of which processes the incoming tuples independently.

Besides, since each operation is performed by multiple task instances concurrently, the input tuples should also be distributed to the tasks evenly to ensure optimal throughput. Likewise, after a tuple is processed and emit-ted by one of the upstream task instances, the receiving downstream task instance should also be chosen wisely, which is achieved by a tuple-to-instance assignment function implemented as a mapping from the key domain of tuples to the task instance in the succeeding operator, such as *Fields grouping* in Storm. However, such a strategy may not perform as expected in distributed stream processing systems due to the lack of balancing on the homogeneous tasks within the same abstract operator. Fig. 1.2 shows an example illustrating the potential problem with such a

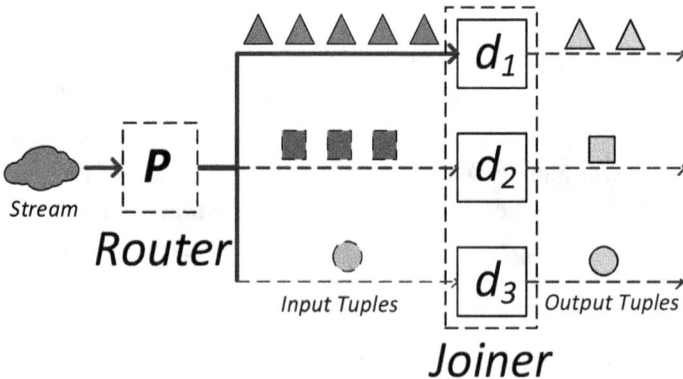

Fig. 1.2. The potential problem of workload imbalance within tasks in DSPE. *P* is the partition function in Router and tuples marked by different shapes indicate that they are assigned to different tasks.

strategy. In this example, there are three task instances running in a join operator, denoted by rectangles. Because of the distribution skewness on the input tuples, the number of tuples assigned to the first task instance is five times that assigned to the third task instance. Hence, regardless of how well the system allocates the tasks to available nodes for optimal computation resource utilization, the higher latency in the first task instance still dominates the total processing time of this operation, which slows down the whole process significantly.

1.2 Challenges, Research Issues and Basic Ideas

An operator is called a stateful operator if a memory buffer is required to cache the intermediate results, which are called states, of the keys appearing in the latest tuples. Basically, each state is associated with an active key in the corresponding task in a stateful operator. It, for example, can be used to record the counts of the words or recent tuples in the sliding window. Functions such as *random* or *round robin* are naturally load balanced among all the instances. However, this is at the price of other additional compensation operations to maintain the stateful information. For example, Nasir *et al.* (2015, 2016) designed a series of randomized routing algorithms to balance the workload of stream processing operators. Their strategy is based on the theoretical model and its variant of *power of two*, which evaluates two or more randomly chosen candidate destinations for each tuple and chooses the one with a smaller workload estimation. Their approach performs well for stateless operators in streaming processing, and a wide class of stateful operators, like counting, by introducing an aggregator to combine results of tuples sent to different working threads. For some stateful operators, e.g., join and median, the partial result is insufficient for simple aggregation, and almost all original tuples have to be forwarded to the aggregator for further processing.

The processing flow using a random routing strategy can be reflected by the example of Fig. 1.3. Given two data streams $S_1 = \{\tau_1, \tau_2, \tau_3, \tau_4\}$ and $S_2 = \{\tau_5, \tau_6\}$, each tuple τ_i in both streams has exactly the same join key. Therefore, the join result $S_1 \bowtie S_2$ contains eight pairs of tuples. By applying partial key grouping, $\{\tau_1, \tau_3\}$ and $\{\tau_2, \tau_4\}$ are sent to two processing instances d_1 and d_2, respectively. Similarly, τ_2 and τ_4 are processed by

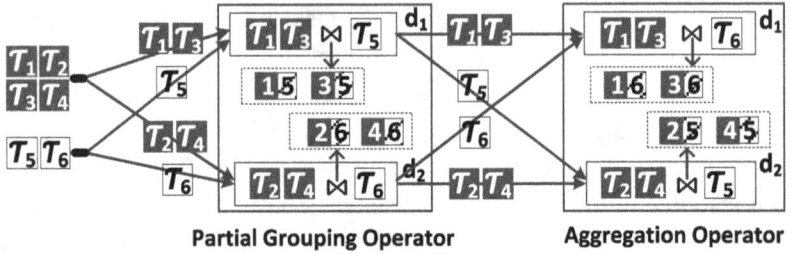

Partial Grouping Operator   **Aggregation Operator**

Fig. 1.3.   Example of partial key grouping used in join operator.

d_1 and d_2, respectively. These two instances d_1 and d_2 can only generate four pairs of join results based on the received tuples. They have to forward all these tuples to the merge operator in order to generate complete join results. Therefore, the communication cost of partial key grouping is doubled, while the merge operator has exactly the same workload that d_1 and d_2 have. The problems mentioned in both Figs. 1.2 and 1.3 imply that the most difficult problem of the partition function is how to ensure workload balance among tasks with state maintenance.

1.2.1   *Workload balance by key granularity integration*

Key-based workload partitioning is now commonly used in parallel stream processing, enabling effective key-value tuple distribution over worker threads in a logical operator. While randomized hashing on the keys is capable of balancing the workload for key-based partitioning when the keys generally follow a static distribution, it is likely to generate poor balancing performance when workload variance occurs on the incoming data stream. To handle workload balance with key granularity integration, a new key-based workload partitioning framework is a necessity, with practical algorithms to support dynamic workload assignment for stateful operators. The framework should combine hash-based and explicit key-based routing strategies for workload distribution, which specifies the destination worker threads for a handful of keys and assigns the other keys with the hashing function. We formulate the rebalance operation as an optimization problem in Chapter 2, with multiple objectives on minimizing state migration costs, controlling the size of the routing table and breaking workload imbalance among the worker threads. In spite of the NP-hard nature behind the optimization formulation, we carefully investigate and justify the heuristics behind key (re)routing and state migration, to facilitate fast response to workload variance with ignorable cost to the normal processing in the distributed system.

1.2.2 *Workload balance by key splitting*

Load balancing adjustment based on key as granularity has its own limitations such as clumsy balance activities or expensive network cost. Based on this, it is required to design a high efficient partition policy which can evenly distribute workload in a parallel shared-nothing stream environment so as to promise overall performance. In Chapter 3, we introduce a comprehensive cost model for the partitioning method, which makes a synthesis estimation of memory, CPU and network resource utilization. Based on cost model, we propose a novel load balancing adjustment algorithm, which adopts the idea of "Split keys on demand and Merge keys as far as possible", and is adaptive to different skewed workloads. Furthermore, we introduce how to combine the fault tolerance and workload balancing mechanisms in the DSPE to reduce the overall resource consumption while keeping the system interactive, scalable and highly available with high throughput. Based on the data-level replication strategy, the processing method can handle the dynamic data skewness and node failure scenario: during the distribution fluctuation of the incoming stream, the system rebalances the workload by selectively inactivating the data in high-load nodes and activating their replicas in low-load nodes to minimize the migration overhead within the stateful operator; when a fault occurs in the process, the system activates the replicas of the data affected to ensure the correctness while keeping the workload balanced.

1.2.3 *Workload balance for multi-stream θ-join*

Flexible and self-adaptive stream join processing plays an important role in a parallel shared-nothing environments. The join-matrix model is a high-performance model which is resilient to data skew and supports arbitrary join predicates for taking random tuple distribution as its routing policy. To maximize system throughputs and minimize network communication cost, a scalable partitioning scheme on matrix is critical. In Chapter 4, we present a novel flexible and adaptive partitioning model for a stream join operator, which ensures high throughput but with economical resource usage by allocating resources on demand. We first obtain the sample of each stream volume and processing resource quota of each physical machine, and generate a join scheme; then a migration plan generator decides how to migrate data among machines under the consideration of minimizing migration cost while ensuring correctness.

1.2.4 *Resource-sensitive workload balance scheme*

Join-matrix is a high-performance model on distributed stream joins and supports arbitrary join predicates. It can handle data skew perfectly since it randomly routes tuples to cells, where each stream corresponds to one side of the matrix. Designing partitioning scheme of the matrix is an important factor to maximize system throughputs under the premise of economizing computing resources, which are CPUs and Memories calculated on time. In Chapter 5, we introduce a flexible and adaptive partitioning scheme for stream join operator, which provides a highly efficient partition method to evenly distribute workload in a distributed and parallel manner. Specifically, a lightweight scheme generator is designed to generate a join scheme; a migration plan generator migrates data among machines under the consideration of minimizing migration cost while ensuring correctness, when streams change. Furthermore, we will present a general strategy to generate the processing scheme for a θ-join operator under dynamic stream changes at runtime, which achieves scalability, effectiveness and efficiency by a single shot.

1.3 Organization

The rest of this book is organized as follows. In Chapter 2, we present a key-based workload partitioning scheme and its majorization to make it more flexible and available, promising efficient resource utilization. In Chapter 3, we study data distribution methods for stream systems, which are based on the idea of "Split keys on demand and Merge keys as far as possible" to improve overall throughputs. In Chapter 4, we propose a flexible and adaptive model for distributed and parallel stream join processing. It inherits the characteristics of a traditional matrix model and allows irregular shaping of the matrix to allocate resources in demand, promising efficient resource utilization. In Chapter 5, we present an adaptive join processing scheme, which can adaptively change processing models to gain full advantage of key-based and matrix strategies. Then, we introduce case studies based on our proposed method in Chapter 6. Finally, we summarize the book in the last chapter.

Chapter 2

Workload Balance Adjustment among Parallel Processing Tasks under Key Granularity

2.1 Motivation and Basic Idea

As people pay more attention to the potential value in big data, real-time data analysis plays an increasingly important role in data analytic applications. A DSPE provides an effective solution which facilitates processing of massive data streams with low latency. Workload skewness and variance are common phenomena in DSPEs. When massive data streams flood into a distributed system for processing and analyzing, even a slight distribution change in the incoming data stream may significantly affect the system performance. Existing optimization techniques for stream processing engines are designed to exploit the distributed processor, memory and bandwidth resource based on the computation workload, but potentially render suboptimal performance when the evolving workload deviates from expectation. Unfortunately, workload evolution is constantly happening in real application scenarios (e.g., surveillance video analysis [Chen *et al.* (2005b)] and online advertising monitoring [Kutare *et al.* (2010)]). It raises new challenges for distributed systems in handling the dynamics of data streams while maintaining a high resource utilization rate.

In a distributed stream processing system, abstract operators are connected in the form of a directed graph to support complex processing logics. Traditional load balancing approaches in distributed stream processing engines attempt to balance the workload of the system, by evenly assigning

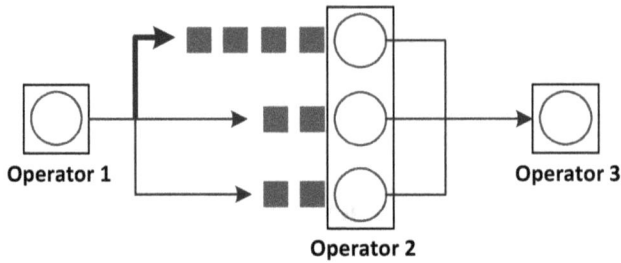

Fig. 2.1.   The potential problem of workload imbalance within operators in real distributed stream processing engine.

a variety of heterogeneous tasks to distributed nodes [Abadi *et al.* (2005); Xing *et al.* (2005, 2006); Ahmad and Cetintemel (2004); Khandekar *et al.* (2009)]. Such strategies may not perform as expected in distributed stream processing systems, because of the lack of balance in the homogeneous tasks within abstract operators. In Fig. 2.1, we present an example to illustrate the potential problems with such strategies. In the example, there are three logic operators in the pipeline, denoted by rectangles. There are three concrete task instances running in *operator 2*, denoted by circles. The number of incoming tuples to the first task instance is two times that of the second and third task instances due to the distribution skewness on the tuples. Because of the higher processing latency in the first task instance of *operator 2*, *operator 1* is forced to slow down its processing speed under backpushing effect, and *operator 3* may be suspended to wait for the complete inter-mediate results from *operator 2*. This example shows that load balancing among task instances within individual logical operators is more crucial to distributed stream processing engines to improve the system stability and guarantee the processing performance.

There are two types of workload variances in distributed stream pro-cessing engines, namely *long-term* workload shift and *short-term* work-load fluctuation. Long-term workload shifts usually involve distribution changes in incoming tuples driven by the trends in the physical world (e.g., a regular burst of tweets after lunch time), while workload fluctuations are usually short term and random in nature. Long-term workload shifts can only be solved by applying heavyweight resource scheduling [e.g., Fu *et al.* (2017)], which reallocates the computation resource based on the necessi-ties. Computation infrastructure of the distributed system may request more (or less) resource by adding (or removing) virtual machines or completely reshuffling the resource among logical operators according to computation demands. Such operations on the infrastructure level are inappropriate for short-term workload fluctuations, and usually too expensive and render sub-optimal performance when the fluctuation is over. It is thus more desirable to adopt lightweight protocols within the operators to smoothly redistribute the workload among task instances, minimize the impact on the normal processing and achieve the objective of load balancing within every logical operator. This chapter focuses on such a dynamic workload assignment mechanism for individual logical operators in a complex data stream processing logic against short-term workload fluctuations. Note that existing solutions to long-term workload shifts are mostly orthogonal to the mechanisms for short-term workload fluctuations, both of which can be invoked by the system optionally based on the workload characteristics.

Our proposal in this chapter is based on a mixed strategy of key-based workload partitioning, which explicitly specifies the destination worker threads for a reasonable number of keys and assigns all other keys with the randomized hash functions. This scheme achieves high *flexibility* by easily redirecting the keys to new worker threads with simple editing on the routing table. It is also highly *efficient* when the system sets the maximal size of the routing table, thus controlling the memory overhead and calculation cost with the routing table. Workload redistribution with the scheme is *scalable* and *effective* by allowing the system to respond promptly to the short-term workload fluctuation even when there are a large number of keys present in the incoming data stream. To fully unleash the power of the scheme, it is important to design a monitoring and controlling mechanism on top of the system, making optimal decisions on the routing table update to achieve intra-operator workload balancing. Recent work on PKG [Nasir *et al.* (2015, 2016)] is a sort of key splitting method which breaks the key-based operation semantic, meaning that there must be an additional processing stage right after a stateful operator, e.g., an aggregator, to ensure the correctness of the processing results. *Readj* in action [Gedik (2014)], although employing a similar workload distribution strategy, only considers migration of *hot* keys with high frequencies, which may have difficulty in load balancing by manipulating a bulky workload with hot keys only. Furthermore, Readj's computation complexity, i.e., the running time for generating a reasonable adjustment plan, is higher particularly when the applications experience dynamic scenarios, e.g., frequent changes of key distribution and scaling in/out of task instances. We break the limit in this chapter with a new solution for distributed systems to explore a much larger optimization space with all candidate keys for the routing table, thus maximizing the resource utilization with ignorable additional cost. Specifically, the technical contributions of this chapter include the following: (1) We design a general strategy to generate the partition function for data redistribution under different stream dynamic changes at runtime, which achieves scalability, effectiveness and efficiency in one shot. (2) We propose a lightweight computation model to support rapid migration plan generation, which incurs minimal data transmission overhead and processing latency. (3) We present a detailed theoretical analysis for proposed migration algorithms, and prove its usability and correctness; moreover, we extend the migration algorithms for multi-resource balance. (4) We implement our algorithms on Storm and provide extensive experimental evaluation for our proposed techniques by comparing with existing work using abundant datasets. We explain the results in detail.

The remainder of this chapter is organized as follows. Section 2.2 reviews a wide spectrum of related works. Section 2.3 introduces the overview and preliminaries of our problem. Section 2.4 presents our balancing algorithms to support our mixed workload distribution scheme. Section 2.5 describes the optimization techniques used in the implementation of our proposal. Section 2.6 evaluates performance of our proposals by conducting extensive experiments. Finally, we conclude our work in Section 2.7.

2.2   Related Work and Literature

Different from batch processing and traditional distributed databases [Dewitt and Gray (1992); Walton *et al.* (1991); Xu *et al.* (2008); Kwon *et al.* (2012); Gufler *et al.* (2012)], the problem of load balancing is more challenging in distributed stream processing systems because of the needs of continuous optimization. There are two common classes of strategies to enable load balancing in distributed stream processing systems, namely *operator-based* and *data-based*.

- **Operator-based** strategies generally assume that the basic computation units are operators. Therefore, load balancing among distributed nodes is achieved by allocating the operators to the nodes. In Borealis [Xing *et al.* (2005)], for example, the system exploits the correlation and variance of the workloads of the operators to make more reliable and stable assignments. Xing *et al.* (2006) observed that operator movement is too expensive for short-term workload bursts. This observation motivates them to design a new load balance model and corresponding algorithms to support more resilient operator placement. System S [Wolf *et al.* (2008)], as another example, also generates scheduling decisions for jobs in the submission phase and migrates jobs or sub-jobs to less loaded machines on runtime based on complex statistics, including operator workload and the priority of the applications. A common problem with operator-based load balancing is the lack of flexible workload partitioning.
- **Data-based** strategies allow the system to repartition the workload based on keys of the tuples in the stream, motivated by the huge success of MapReduce system and its variants. It is strongly related to elastic stream processing, which is a hot topic in both the database and distributed system communities. Such systems attempt to scale out the computation parallelism to address the increasing computation workload, e.g., Gedik *et al.* (2014) and Wu and Tan (2015). By applying queuing theory, it is possible to model the workload and expected processing latency, which can be used for better resource scheduling [Fu *et al.* (2017)]. When historical records are available to the system, it is beneficial to generate a long-term workload evolution plan to schedule the migrations in the future with smaller workload movement overhead [Ding *et al.* (2015)]. Note that all these systems and algorithms are designed to handle long-term workload variance. All these solutions are generally too expensive if the workload fluctuation is just a short-term phenomenon. The proposal in this work targets the short-term workload variance problem with minimal cost.

A number of research works focus on load balancing in distributed stream join systems. Elseidy *et al.* (2014) modeled the join operation with a square matrix, each side of which represents one of the input streams. One of the stream distributes its tuples by rows, while the other distributes its tuples by columns. Each cell contains the computation logic calculating the partial join results of tuples from the streams. To enable better elasticity, Lin *et al.* (2015) proposed a join-biclique model which organizes the clusters as a complete bipartite graph for joining big data streams. It proposes to deal with load imbalance by using different join algorithms. All these techniques are designed for join operators only, and therefore not directly extensible to general-purpose distributed stream processing.

In the rest of the chapter, we discuss limitations of four alternative solutions to intra-operator parallelism in distributed streaming processing.

- **Flux:** Shah *et al.* (2003) designed a widely adopted load balancing strategy for traditional distributed streaming processing systems. It simply measures the workload of the tasks, and attempts to migrate workload from overloaded nodes to underloaded nodes. One key limitation of Flux is the lack of consideration for the routing overhead. In traditional stream processing systems, the workload of a logical operator is pre-partitioned into tasks, such that each task may handle a huge number of keys but processed by an individual thread at any time. The approach proposed in this chapter allows the system to reassign keys in a much more flexible manner.

- **Consistent hash:** Karger *et al.* (1997) first discussed the dynamicity of the hash function when the output domain is extensible. They showed that it is likely to build such a hash function that the number of tuples moved across target bins of the hash outcome reaches the minimal lower bound in theory. This technique is now widely used in distributed systems, especially for data-intensive computation schemes with high overheads on workload reassignment. We argue that consistent hash may not be an optimal option to intra-operator parallelism in distributed stream processing. When the key domain is small or the number of target instances is large, randomized hash may not distribute the workload evenly because of the existence of relatively heavy keys. This phenomenon is demonstrated in our experimental results in Fig. 2.6.

- **Readj:** Gedik *et al.* (2014) proposed to resolve the stateful load balance problem with a small routing table, which is similar to our proposal. It introduces a similar tuple distribution function, consisting of a basic hash function and an explicit hash table. However, the workload redistribution mechanism used in *Readj* is completely different from ours. The algorithm in *Readj* always tries to move back the keys to their original destination by hash function, followed by migration schedules on keys with relatively larger workloads. Their strategy might work well when the workloads of the keys are almost uniform. When the workloads of the keys vary dramatically, their approach always fails to find a reasonable load balancing plan. The routing algorithms designed in this chapter completely tackle this problem, which presents high efficiency as well as good balancing performance in almost all circumstances.

- **Partial key grouping:** Nasir *et al.* (2015, 2016) designed a series of randomized routing algorithms to balance the workload of stream processing operators. Their strategy was based on the theoretical model and its variant of power of two, which evaluates two or more randomly chosen candidate destinations for each tuple and chooses the one with smaller workload estimation. Their approach performs well for stateless operators in streaming processing, and a wide class of stateful operators by introducing an aggregator to combine results of tuples sent to different working threads, e.g., counting. For some stateful operators, e.g., join and median, the partial result is insufficient for simple aggregation; almost all original tuples must be forwarded to an aggregator for processing.

2.3 Preliminaries

A DSPE deploys abstract stream processing logics over interconnected computation nodes for continuous stream processing. The abstract stream processing logic is usually described by a directed graphical model (e.g., Storm [Toshniwal *et al.* (2014)], Heron [Kulkarni *et al.* (2015)] and Spark Streaming [Zaharia *et al.* (2013)]), with a vertex in the graph denoting a computation operator and an edge denoting a stream from one operator to another. Each data stream consists of key-value pairs, known as *tuples*, transmitted over a network between computation nodes. The computation logic with an operator is a mapping function with an input tuple from upstream operators to a group of output tuples for downstream operators.

To maximize the throughput of stream processing and improve the utilization rate of the computation resource, the workload of a logical operator is commonly partitioned and concurrently processed by a number of

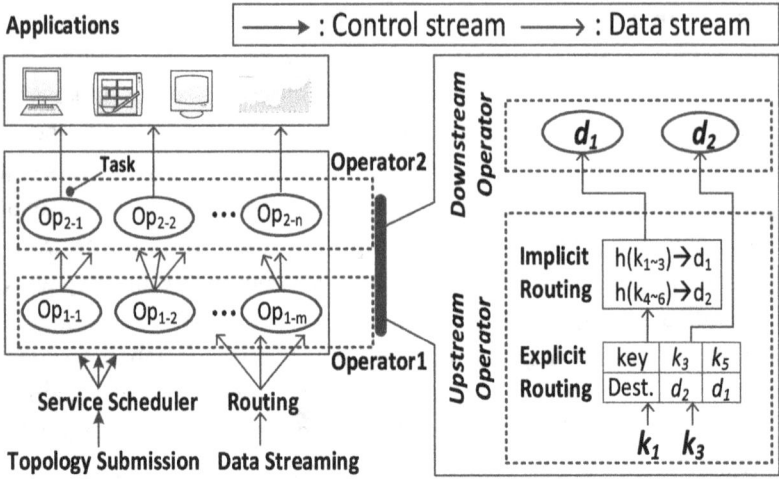

Fig. 2.2. Stream processing flow and the scheme of mixed routing with a small routing table and a hash function.

threads, known as *tasks*. In Fig. 2.2, we present an example topology with two logical operators, each of which independently processes the incoming tuples and then outputs the results to its downstream operator. Operator$_1$ (the upstream operator) is deployed as *m* parallel and distributed task instances with Operator$_2$ (the downstream operator) as *n* task instances. The upstream operator is aware of the concrete tasks and sends its output tuples to the tasks based on a global partitioning strategy [Toshniwal *et al.* (2014); Kulkarni *et al.* (2015)], such as *shuffle grouping* (tuples are dispatched to down-stream task instances in a round robin manner) and *field grouping* (tuples are dispatched according to the results of applying a unified hash function onto their keys). All concrete tasks within an operator process the incoming tuples independently and this means that the routing strategy determines the distribution of workload among the parallel processing instance tasks.

Key-based workload partitioning is now commonly adopted in dis-tributed stream processing engines, such that tuples with the same key are guaranteed to be received by the same concrete task for processing. The workload partitioning among concrete tasks is the model that maps tuples from key domains to running tasks in the successor operator. A straightfor-ward solution to workload partitioning is the employment of hash function (e.g., by consistent hashing), which chooses a task for a specific key in a random manner. Hash function aims to assign an equal number of keys to each task instance, neglecting the workloads corresponding to each key. As a result, by no means can hash function distribute total workloads among task instances in a balanced way, let alone when the key distribution is skewed or heavy-tailed. Another option of workload distribution is to explicitly assign the tuples based on a carefully optimized routing table, which specifies the destination of the tuples by a map structure on the keys. This is a simple way to handle key skewness and workload variances. However, there is no free lunch in the world. Each individual key has an assignment entry in the routing table, i.e., the size of the routing table is equal to the total number of distinguished keys. The number of distinguished keys is usually enormous, or probably increasing unboundedly in practice. In addition, each parallel processing task instance must maintain the same routing table and investigate every incoming tuple to determine the destination task instance. Such an enormous routing table must result in massive memory consumption and maintenance cost. For example, 10^7 entries in a routing table take up about 200 MB memory space[1] and for an upstream operator with 15 task instances, the total memory consumption approaches 3 GB (15×200 MB).

In this chapter, we develop a new adaptive workload partitioning framework based on a mixed routing strategy, expecting to balance the hash-based randomized strategy and key-based routing strategy. As shown in Fig. 2.2, a routing table is maintained in the system, but contains routing rules for partial keys only. When a new output tuple is generated for the downstream operator, the upstream operator first checks if the key exists in the routing table. If a valid entry is found in the table, the tuple is transmitted to the target concrete task instance specified by the entry, otherwise a hash function is applied on the key to deterministically generate the target task ID for the tuple. To determine the maximal routing table size, factors such as the amount of available resource, e.g., memory space, the size of key space and the change frequency of the key distribution shall be taken into account. By controlling the routing table with a maximal size constraint according to the incoming key domain, data dynamic and available resources, both the memory and computation cost of the scheme are acceptable, while the

---

[1]200 MB is the size of an explicit routing table with 10^7 entries whose *key* and *value* fields are both of integer types after serialization.

flexibility and effectiveness are achieved by updating the routing table in response to the evolving distribution of the keys.

Workload balancing between tasks from the same logical operator is crucial and it is the main problem that we aim to deal with. With the mixed routing strategy, we can solve the problem by focusing on the construction and update of the routing table with the constrained size, without considering the global structure of processing topology and workload. Hence, our discussion in the following Sections 2.4–2.5 focuses on one single operator and its routing table, while the techniques are obviously applicable to complex stream processing logics, as evaluated in the experimental Section 2.6.

2.3.1 *Problem formulation*

In our model, the time domain is discretized into intervals with integer timestamps, i.e., $(T_1, T_2, \ldots, T_i, \ldots)$. At the ith interval, given a pair of upstream operator U and downstream operator D, we use $\mathcal{U}$ and $\mathcal{D}$ to denote the set of task instances within upstream operator U and downstream operator D, respectively. We also use $N_U = |\mathcal{U}|$ and $N_D = |\mathcal{D}|$ to denote the numbers of task instances in U and D, respectively. A tuple is tuple $\tau = (k, v)$, in which k is the key of the tuple from key domain $\mathcal{K}$ and v is the value carried by the tuple. We assume N_U and N_D are predefined without immediate change. The discussion on dynamic resource rescheduling, i.e., changing N_U and N_D, is out of the scope of this chapter, since it involves orthogonal optimization techniques on global resource scheduling (e.g., Fu *et al.* (2017)). All notations used in the rest of the chapter are summarized in Table 2.1.

A key-based workload partitioning mechanism works as a mapping $F : \mathcal{K} \rightarrow \mathcal{D}$, such that a tuple (k, v) is sent to task instance $F(k)$ by evaluating the key k with the function F. Without loss of generality, we assume that a universal hashing function $h : \mathcal{K} \rightarrow \mathcal{D}$ is available to the system for general key assignment. A routing table A of size N_A contains a group of pairs from $\mathcal{K} \times \mathcal{D}$, specifying the destination task instances for keys existing in A. The mixed routing strategy shown in Fig. 2.2 is thus modeled by the following equation:

$$F(k) = \begin{cases} d, & \text{if } \exists \, (k, d) \in A, \\ h(k), & \text{otherwise.} \end{cases} \tag{2.1}$$

Table 2.1. Notations for key granularity adjustment.

Notations	Description
T_i	The ith time interval
U, D	Upstream, downstream operator
N_U, N_D	Numbers of task instances in U and D
$\mathcal{D}$	Instances set of downstream operator
(k, v)	Key-value pair on the data stream
k	Key of the tuple
v	Value of the tuple
d	Task instance in downstream operator
A	The routing table available to U
N_A	Number of entries in A
$c_i(k)$	Computation cost of all tuples with key k in T_i
$g_i(k)$	Frequency of key k in time interval T_i
$L_i(d, F)$	Total workload of task instance d under function F
$\bar{L}_i$	Average load of all instances in U in time interval T_i
$\theta_i(d, F)$	Load imbalance factor of task instance d
$\theta_{\max}$	Upper bound of imbalance tolerance
w	Number of time intervals
$S_i(k, w)$	Memory cost of key k with w time intervals at T_i
$\Delta(F, F')$	Keys with different destinations under F and F'
$M_i(w, F, F')$	Total migration cost by replacing F with F' at T_i

Therefore, workload redistribution is enabled by editing the routing table A with an assignment function $F(\cdot)$. In the following, we provide formal analysis on the general properties of the assignment function $F(\cdot)$.

- **Computation cost:** We use $g_i(k)$ to denote the frequency of tuples with key k in time interval T_i, and define the computation cost $c_i(k)$ by the amount of CPU resource necessary for all these tuples with key k in time interval T_i. Generally speaking, $c_i(k)$ increases with the growth of $g_i(k)$. Unless specified, we do not make any assumption on the correlation between $g_i(k)$ and $c_i(k)$, both of which are measured in the distributed system and recorded as statistics in order to support decision-making on the update of $F(\cdot)$. The total workload with a task instance

d in downstream operator D within time interval T_i is calculated by $L_i(d, F) = \sum_{\{k | F(k)=d, k \in \mathcal{K}\}} c_i(k)$.

- **Load balance:** Load balance among task instances of the downstream operator D is the essential target of our proposal in this chapter. Specifically, we define the imbalance indicator $\theta_i(d, F)$ for task instance d under assignment function F during time interval T_i as $\theta_i(d, F) = \frac{|L_i(d,F) - \bar{L}_i|}{\bar{L}_i}$, where $\bar{L}_i = \frac{1}{N_D} \sum_{d \in \mathcal{D}} L_i(d, F)$ is the average load of all task instances in $\mathcal{D}$. As it is unlikely to achieve absolute workload balancing with $\theta_i(d, F) = 0$ for every task instance d, an upper bound $\theta_{\max}$ is usually specified by the system administrator according to the resource utilization of the computing cluster and the dynamicity of input data flows, such that the workload of task instance d is approximately balanced if $\theta_i(d, F) \leq \theta_{\max}$.

- **Memory cost:** For stateful operators, the system is supposed to maintain historical information, e.g., statistics with the keys, for processing and analyzing newly arriving tuples. We assume that each operator maintains states independently on individual time interval T_i and only the last w time intervals are needed by any task instance. It means that the task instance erases the state from time interval T_{i-w} after finishing the computation on all tuples in time interval T_i. This model is general enough to cover almost all continuous stream processing and analytical jobs (e.g., stream data mining over sliding window). The memory consumption for tuples with key k in T_i is thus measured as $s_i(k)$, and the total memory consumption for key k is the summation over last w intervals on the time domain, as $S_i(k, w) = \sum_{j=i-w+1}^{i} s_j(k)$.

- **Migration cost:** Upon revision of assignment function F, a particular key k may be moved from one task instance to another. The states associated with key k must be moved accordingly to ensure the correctness of processing the following tuples with key k. The migration cost is thus modeled as the total size of states under migration. By replacing function F with another function F' at time interval T_i, we use $\Delta(F, F') = \{k \mid F(k) \neq F'(k), k \in \mathcal{K}\}$. The key state migration includes all the historical states within the given window w. Thus, the total migration cost, denoted by $M_i(w, F, F')$, can be defined as $M_i(w, F, F') = \sum_{k \in \Delta(F, F')} S_i(k, w)$.

2.3.2 *Optimization goals*

Based on the model of data and workload, we now define our dynamic workload distribution problem with the objectives of (i) load balance among all the downstream instances, (ii) controllable size on the routing table and (iii) minimization on state migration cost. These goals are achieved by controlling the routing table in the assignment function under appropriate constraints for performance guarantee. Specifically, to construct a new assignment function F' as a replacement for F in time interval T_i, we formulate it as an optimization problem, as follows:

$$\min_{F'(\cdot)} \ M_i(w, F, F')$$
$$\text{s.t.} \ \ \theta(d, F') \leq \theta_{\max}, \quad \forall d \in \mathcal{D}, \tag{2.2}$$
$$N_A \leq A_{\max},$$

in which F is the old assignment function and F' is the variable for optimization. The target of the program above is to minimize migration cost, while meeting the constraints on load balance factor and routing table size with user-specified bounds $\theta_{\max}$ and $A_{\max}$. While workload rebalance during the runtime improves the system performance in terms of processing throughput and latency, it incurs non-negligible costs that, during the rebalance procedure, the system has to stop processing in order to consistently and correctly maintain the internal states of the application. Because state migration is the most time-consuming step of the rebalance procedure, we believe that minimizing the migration cost is equivalent to minimizing the rebalance costs, as well as maximizing the performance gain.

2.4 Balance Algorithms with Key Granularity Integration

Since the optimization problem is NP-hard, there is no polynomial algorithm to find global optimum, unless P = NP. In the rest of the chapter, we firstly describe a general workflow for a variety of heuristics, such that all algorithms based on these heuristics follow the same operation pattern. We then discuss a number of heuristics with objectives on routing table minimization and migration minimization. A mixed algorithm is introduced to combine the two heuristics in order to accomplish the constraints in the optimization formulation with a single shot. Generally, the system follows the steps below when constructing a new assignment function F'.

- **Phase I (Cleaning):** It attempts to *clean* the routing table A by removing certain entries in the table. This is equivalent to moving the keys in the entries back to the original task instance assignment, as decided by the hash function. Different algorithms may adopt different cleaning strategies to shrink the existing routing table in F. Note that such a temporary removal does not physically migrate the corresponding keys, but just generates an intermediate result table for further processing.
- **Phase II (Preparing):** It identifies candidate keys for migration from overloaded task instances, i.e., $\{d|L(d) > L_{\max}\}$, where $L_{\max} = (1 + \theta_{\max})\bar{L}$. Different selection criteria, such as keys with highest computation cost first and largest computation cost per unit memory consumption first (concerning about migration cost), can be applied by the algorithm to select keys and disassociate their assignments from the corresponding task instances. These disassociated keys will be temporarily put into a candidate key set (denoted by C) for processing in the third step of the workflow.
- **Phase III (Assigning):** It reshuffles the keys in the candidate set by manipulating the routing table in order to balance the workloads. In particular, all algorithms proposed in this chapter invoke the Least-Load Fit Decreasing (LLFD) sub-routine, which will be described shortly, in this phase.

2.4.1 *Basic algorithm*

In this section, we introduce the LLFD subroutine, which will be applied by all the proposed algorithms in Phase III, based on the idea of prioritizing keys with larger workloads. The design of LLFD is motivated by the classic First Fit Decreasing (FFD) used in conventional bin packing algorithms. The pseudo codes of LLFD are listed in Algorithm 2.1.

Generally speaking, LLFD sorts the keys in the candidate set in a non-increasing order of their computation costs and iteratively assigns the keys to task instances, such that (i) it generates the least total workload (line 2) and (ii) it tries to adjust the key assignment, if the new destination task instance is overloaded after the migration (line 3). If such a key-to-instance

---

Algorithm 2.1 Least-Load Fit Decreasing Algorithm

---

input: key candidate C, task instances in D, imbalance tolerance factor
θ_{max}, key selection criteria ψ

output: A'

1: **foreach** k in C in descending order of $c_{i-1}(k)$ **do**
2:     **foreach** d in D in ascending order of $L_{i-1}(d)$ **do**
3:         **if** Adjust(k, d, C, θ_{max}) = TRUE **then**
4:             **if** $h(k) \neq d$ **then**
5:                 Add entry (k, d) to A'
6:                 Update $L_{i-1}(d)$; remove k from C; break;
7: **return** A'
8: **function** ADJUST(k, d, C, θ_{max})
9:     $L_{max} \leftarrow (1 + \theta_{max})\bar{L}_{i-1}$
10:    **if** $L_{i-1}(d) + c_{i-1}(k) < L_{max}$ **then**
11:        **return** TRUE
12:    **else if** $\exists \, \mathcal{E}$ selected by ψ and satisfying (i)-(iii) **then**
13:        **foreach** $k \in \mathcal{E}$ **do**
14:            Disassociate k from d
15:            Add k to C
16:        **return** TRUE
17:    **else**
18:        **return** FALSE

---

pair is inconsistent with default mapping by hashing (line 4), an entry (k, d) is then added to the routing table A (line 5). After each iteration, LLFD updates the total workload of the corresponding instance d and removes k from the candidate set (line 6). The iteration stops and returns the result routing table when the candidate set turns empty (line 7).

Basically, the algorithm moves the "heaviest" key to the task instance with minimal workload so far, which may generate another overloaded task instance (referred as "reoverloading" problem) if this key is associated with an extremely heavy cost. Consider the toy example on the left side of Fig. 2.3. There are two instances: d_1 is responsible for keys k_1, k_2 and k_5 with costs 7, 4 and 5, respectively, generating $L(d_1) = 16$, and d_2 is associated with keys k_3, k_4 and k_6 with cost 2, 1 and 1, respectively,

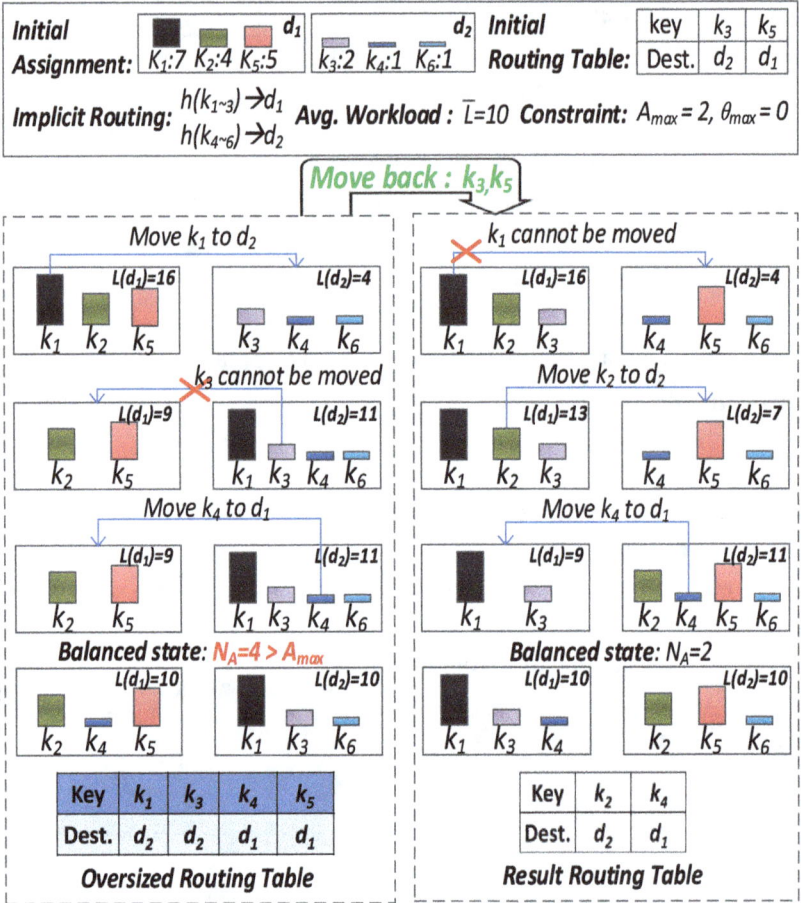

Fig. 2.3. A toy example illustrates how LLFD and MinTable work, where the heights of the bars indicate the amount of workloads corresponding to the keys. Each S_j with $j = \{1, 2, 3, 4\}$ is a running step in the algorithms. The entries in the initial routing table are $\{(k_5, d_1), (k_3, d_2)\}$, and the result routing tables are listed at the bottom. The left dotted box reflects the result by LLFD algorithm and right one is the result generated by MinTable with LLFD.

generating $L(d_2) = 4$. Suppose $\theta_{\max} = 0$, meaning that the total workloads on both instances are required to be equal (i.e., average workload $\bar{L} = 10$). It is clear that d_1 is overloaded and k_1, which incurs the largest computation cost, is expected to be disassociated from d_1. Although $L(d_1)$ decreases to 9, it is still larger than $L(d_2)$. Based on the workflow of LLFD, k_1 is assigned to d_2, only to overload d_2 as a consequence. To tackle the problem, we add a new function, called *Adjust*, to avoid the occurrence of such conflicts.

Specifically, if reoverloading does not happen after an assignment, i.e., $L_{i-1}(d)+c_{i-1}(k) \leq L_{max} = (1+\theta_{max})\bar{L}_{i-1}$, this assignment is acceptable and *Adjust* immediately returns a TRUE (lines 10–11). Otherwise (Lines 12–18), *Adjust* attempts to construct a non-empty key set (called *exchangeable* set and denoted by $\mathcal{E}$) by applying the selection criteria ψ (e.g., highest workload first). The *exchangeable* set must satisfy the following three conditions: (i) $\mathcal{E} \subseteq \{k'|F(k') = d\}$; (ii) $\forall k' \in \mathcal{E}, c_{i-1}(k') < c_{i-1}(k)$; and (iii) $L_{i-1}(d) + c_{i-1}(k) - \sum_{k' \in \mathcal{E}} c_{i-1}(k') \leq L_{max}$. Basically, (i) means that only keys originally associated with d are selected for disassociation, and (ii) tries not to choose a key with larger computation workload for disassociation, ensuring the decrease of the total workloads on instance d. Finally, (iii) ensures that instance d does not become overloaded after the assignment (Lines 13–15).

Recall the running example in which LLFD tries to assign k_1 to d_2, which makes d_2 overloaded. A TRUE is returned by *Adjust* because there exists an $\mathcal{E} = \{k_3\}$ satisfying constraints (i)–(iii). Therefore, k_1 is assigned to d_2, while k_3 is disassociated from d_2 and put into $\mathcal{C}$. Next, LLFD attempts to assign k_3 to d_1 because d_1 has less total workload at this moment. However, a FALSE (a red cross shown on the left side of S_2 in Fig. 2.3) is returned by *Adjust* because overloading occurs (since $L(d_1) + c(k_3) = 11 > L_{max}$) and no valid $\mathcal{E}$ exists, when neither of the two keys associated with d_1 (k_2 and k_5) has smaller computation workload than that of k_3, violating constraint (ii). After this failure, LLFD is forced to consider another option by keeping k_3 to d_2. Luckily, a TRUE is returned this time because a valid *exchangeable* set $\mathcal{E} = \{k_4\}$ exists. After disassociating k_4 from d_2 and putting it into $\mathcal{C}$, d_2 is responsible for k_1, k_3 and k_6 only; the keys with d_1 remain unchanged, and k_4 is now in $\mathcal{C}$. The algorithm does not terminate until $\mathcal{C}$ becomes empty, after k_4 is assigned to d_1, finally reaching perfect balance at $L(d_1) = L(d_2) = 10$.

In order to derive theoretic results about the LLFD algorithm, we first look at a more simplified key assignment algorithm, namely the Simple algorithm. We next derive a series of theoretic results based on the Simple algorithm. Lastly, we show how these results are applicable to the LLFD algorithm. The *Simple* algorithm works in the following way: At first, it disassociates and puts all the keys into the candidate set $\mathcal{C}$. Second, it sorts these keys in a descending order of the computation cost $c(k)$. Finally, it sequentially assigns each key to the instance with the least total workloads so far.

Lemma 2.1. *Given the instance set $\mathcal{D}$ of size N_D, key set $\mathcal{K}$ of size K and computation cost of each key $c(k)$, where keys are in a non-increasing order of their computation costs, i.e., $c(k_1) \geq c(k_2) \geq \cdots \geq c(K)$, if the perfect assignment exists, we have*

$$c(k_{qN_D+1}) \leq \frac{1}{q+1}\bar{L}, \quad q = 1, 2, \ldots, \left\lfloor \frac{K-1}{N_D} \right\rfloor. \tag{2.3}$$

Proof. Assuming $c(k_{qN_D+1}) > \frac{1}{q+1}\bar{L}$, then we have $c(k_1) \geq c(k_2) \geq \cdots \geq c(k_{qN_D+1}) > \frac{1}{q+1}\bar{L}$. This means that for keys from k_1 to k_{qN_D}, each instance can at most be associated with q of them. In conclusion, any instance that is associated with the $(qN_D + 1)$th key will generate workloads larger than $\bar{L}$, which contradicts the assumption of the existence of the perfect assignment. $\square$

Lemma 2.2. *Given the instance set $\mathcal{D}$ of size N_D, key set $\mathcal{K}$ of size K and computation cost of each key $c(k)$, where keys are in a non-increasing order of their computation costs, i.e., $c(k_1) \geq c(k_2) \geq \cdots \geq c(K)$, if the perfect assignment exists and $c(k_1) < \bar{L}$ (the computation cost of any individual key is smaller than the average workload of task instances), we have $K \geq 2N_D$.*

Proof. This is straightforward given that (i) the perfect assignment exists and (ii) the computation cost of any individual key is smaller than $\bar{L}$ because, for each instance, there must be at least two keys assigned to it. $\square$

Lemma 2.3. *Given the instance set $\mathcal{D}$ of size N_D, key set $\mathcal{K}$ of size K and computation cost of each key $c(k)$, where keys are in a non-increasing order of their computation costs, i.e., $c(k_1) \geq c(k_2) \geq \cdots \geq c(K)$, if the perfect assignment exists and $c(k_1) < \bar{L}$, we have*

$$\theta_{\max} \leq \frac{1}{3} \cdot \left(1 - \frac{1}{N_D}\right), \tag{2.4}$$

where $\theta_{\max} = \max_{d \in \mathcal{D}}(\frac{L(d) - \bar{L}}{\bar{L}})$.

Proof. We prove by considering the worst case (in terms of load imbalance) where (i) the $(2N_D + 1)$th key has the largest possible computation cost $c(k_{2N_D+1}) = \bar{L}/3$, according to Lemmas 2.1 and 2.2; (ii) keys after the $(2N_D + 1)$th have equal amount of computation costs, denoted by ε, which are very close to zero; and (iii) the remaining workloads, i.e., $\sum_{k \in \mathcal{K}} c(k) - \frac{1}{3}\bar{L} - \varepsilon(K - 2N_D - 1)$, all concentrate on the first $2N_D$ keys and are evenly distributed, summarized as follows:

$$c(k_i) = \begin{cases} \dfrac{N_D\bar{L} - \frac{1}{3}\bar{L} - \varepsilon(K - 2N_D - 1)}{2N_D} & \text{for } i = 1, 2, \ldots, 2N_D; \\[2ex] \dfrac{1}{3}\bar{L} & \text{for } i = 2N_D + 1; \\[1ex] \varepsilon & \text{for } i > 2N_D + 1. \end{cases}$$

Let $\varepsilon \to 0$, we have $L_{\max} = \max_{d \in \mathcal{D}} L(d) = c(k_i) + c(k_j) + c(k_{2N_D+1}) \leq \frac{4}{3}\bar{L} - \frac{\bar{L}}{3N_D}$, where $\forall i \neq j, i, j \in \{1, 2, \ldots, 2N_D\}$. Note $L_{\max} = c(k_i) + c(k_j) + c(k_{2N_D+1})$ is because according to the Simple algorithm, there is no chance for the keys after the $(2N_D + 1)$th to be assigned to the instance with workload of amount $L_{\max}$. This completes the proof according to our definition of $\theta_{\max}$. □

Theorem 2.1. *Given the instance set $\mathcal{D}$ of size N_D, key set $\mathcal{K}$ of size K and computation cost of each key $c(k)$, where keys are in a non-increasing order of their computation costs, i.e., $c(k_1) \geq c(k_2) \geq \cdots \geq c(K)$, if the perfect assignment exists and $c(k_1) < \bar{L}$, LLFD always finds a solution resulting with balancing indicator $\theta(d, F)$ no worse than $\frac{1}{3}(1 - \frac{1}{N_D})$ for any task instance d.*

Proof. According to Algorithm 2.1, it has a larger search space than that of the Simple Algorithm, and is devoted to finding the assignment with more balanced workloads among instances, i.e., $\theta(d, F) \leq \theta_{\max} \leq \frac{1}{3} \cdot (1 - \frac{1}{N_D})$, which is proved in Lemma 2.3. □

LLFD can produce a well-balanced adjustment because the number of keys is more than the number of instances and the load for the tails in skew data distribution is significant. Practically, the statement of Theorem 2.1 gives an estimate or hint on the worst case of workload imbalance among task instances in real implementation. Based on the experimental results presented in a later Section 2.6, we find out that our proposed algorithms achieve perfect workload balance in all the experiment settings and the bound given by Theorem 2.1 is validated.

2.4.2 Minimum table algorithm

The general workflow described above is essentially effective in guaranteeing load balance constraints, e.g., the LLFD sub-procedure. To address the optimizations on routing table minimization and migration cost minimization, we discuss two heuristics, namely MinTable and MinMig in this section.

In order to minimize the routing table size, in Phase I, all entries in routing table A are erased. The highest computation workload first criterion, which emphasizes the computation cost, is used for the second and third phases, so that a minimal number of entries are added into the new routing table A' during the key reassignment and load rebalance process. A detailed pseudo code description can be found in Fang *et al.* (2017).

The two toy examples in Fig. 2.3 demonstrate how MinTable helps to achieve a smaller routing table while keeping load balance constraints fulfilled. The example on the left side of Fig. 2.3 initially has two entries in the routing table, i.e., (k_3, d_2) and (k_5, d_1). LLFD is directly applied to achieve absolute load balance $L(d_1) = L(d_2)$, but resulting in *an oversized* routing table with four entries at the end. In contrast, before applying LLFD, the example on the right side of Fig. 2.3 moves back k_3 and k_5 (i.e., cleaning the routing table). Finally, it results in a routing table with only two entries. Although the removal of keys from the routing is *virtual* only, it increases the possibility of key migrations. Therefore, there is no cleaning run in the first phase at all. To characterize both computation and migration costs, we propose the *migration priority index* for each key, defined as $\gamma_i(k, w) = c_i(k)^\beta S_i(k, w)^{-1}$. Its physical meaning is straightforward, that is, a key with larger computation cost per unit memory consumption has a higher priority to be migrated. The weight scaling factor β is used to balance the weights between these two factors under consideration. Consider k_1 and k_2 in Fig. 2.3 and assume window $w = 1$. We have $c(k_1) = S(k_1, w) = 7$ and $c(k_2) = S(k_2, w) = 4$. If we give equal weights to both $c(k)$ and $S(k, w)$, i.e., $\beta = 1$, then $\gamma(k_1, w) = \gamma(k_2, w) = 1$. When we assign more importance to migration cost, i.e., $\beta = 0.5$, k_2 gains higher priority for migration. In addition, β also affects the size of the result routing table, i.e., the larger the β, the smaller the size of the routing table. The largest $\gamma_i(k, w)$ first criterion, which is aware of both computation and migration costs, is used during both key reassignment (Phase II) and the load balance process (Phases III) in order to minimize the bandwidth used to migrate the states of keys (e.g., the tuples in sliding window for join operator).

2.4.3 *Minimum migration algorithm: Heuristic algorithm*

Based on the discussion on heuristics, we discover that there are trade-offs between routing table minimization and migration cost minimization. Therefore, we propose a mixed algorithm to intelligently combine the two heuristics, MinTable and MinMig, in order to produce the best-effort solutions toward our target optimization in Eq. (2.2).

The basic idea is to properly mix MinTable (Phase I) and MinMig (Phases II and III). In the first phase, the mixed strategy *moves back n* keys, which are selected from A, based on the smallest memory consumption $S_{i-1}(k, w)$ first criteria. The other two phases simply follow the procedure of MinMig, in which the largest $\gamma_i(k, w)$ first criteria are used to initialize candidate key set C, applied by LLFD in the last phase. For the Mixed algorithm, the most challenging problem is how to pick up the number of keys for back moves, i.e., $n \in [0, N_A]$, during the cleaning phase. Actually, MinTable and MinMig work on two extremes of the spectrum in this step, such that $n = N_A$ in MinTable and $n = 0$ in MinMig.

Obviously, brute force search (named as $Mixed_{BF}$) could be applied to try with every possible $n = 1, 2, \ldots, N_A$, with the optimal n^* returned after evaluating the solution with every n. Alternatively, we propose a faster heuristic in Algorithm 2.2. It only tries a small number of values, which are the amount of table entries overused in the last trial (line 11). The trial starts from $n = 0$ (line 3, same as MinMig) and stops when it results in an updated A' of acceptable size, i.e., $N_{A'} \leq A_{max}$ (lines 12–13). Note that the efficiency of the algorithm is much better than $Mixed_{BF}$, although it may not always find the optimal n^* as $Mixed_{BF}$ does. Obviously, the size of the result routing table by the mixed algorithm is no smaller than that of the MinTable approach. Similarly, the migration cost of the result assignment function is no smaller than that of the MinMig approach. However, mixed algorithm is capable of hitting good balance between the heuristics, as is

---

Algorithm 2.2 Mixed Algorithm

1: $\eta \leftarrow$ smallest memory consumption $S_i(k, w)$ first.

2: $\psi \leftarrow$ largest $\gamma_i(k, w)$ first, where $\gamma_i(k, w) = \frac{c_i(k)^\beta}{S_i(k, w)}$

3: $n \leftarrow 0$

4: $A_{backup} \leftarrow A$

5: **do**

6:     $A \leftarrow A_{backup}$

7:     Phase I: According to η, select n keys from A and *move back* the keys, and

8:     $N_A \leftarrow N_A - n$

9:     Phase II: According to ψ, select and disassociate keys from each of the overloaded instances, put them into $\mathcal{C}$

10:     Phase III: $A' \leftarrow$ LLFD $(\mathcal{C}, \mathcal{D}, \theta_{\max}, \psi)$

11:     $n = N_{A'} - A_{\max}$ $\triangleright$ $N_{A'}$ is updated in Phase III based on the value of N_A (Line 7 in Alg. 2.1)

12: **while** $n > 0$

13: **return** A'

---

proved in our empirical evaluations. Furthermore, as Mixed takes the LLFD algorithm as its basic idea, the balance status generated by the Mixed is not worse than the balance status produced by the LLFD algorithm.

2.5 Computational Complexity Optimization

In this chapter, we discuss some techniques applied to improve the implementation efficiency of our proposed algorithms. At first, we describe the overall workflow of the distributed stream processing engine integrated with the runtime workload rebalance mechanism. Second, we introduce the compact representation and value discretization on statistical information of keys. Third, we present the adaptation of the mixed algorithm over the compact representation. Finally, we discuss how to extend the proposed mechanism to multiple resources.

The overall working mechanism of the rebalance control component, as is implemented in our distributed stream processing engine, is illustrated in Fig. 2.4. In the figure, each operation step is numbered to indicate the order of its execution.

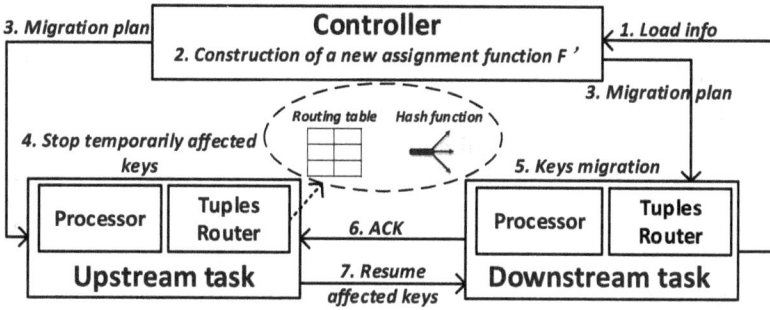

Fig. 2.4.   Overall workflow.

At the end of each time interval (e.g., 10 s as the setting in our experiments), the instances of an operator report the statistical information collected during the past interval to a *controller* module (step 1). The information from each instance d includes the computation cost $c_{i-1}(k)$ and window-based memory consumption $S_{i-1}(k, w)$ of each key assigned to it. On receiving the reporting information, the controller starts the optimization procedure (step 2). It first evaluates the degree of workload imbalance among the instances and decides whether or not to trigger the construction of a new assignment function F' to replace the existing F. If the system identifies load imbalance, it starts to execute the Mixed algorithm (Algorithm 2.2) to generate new A' and F'.

After calculating the keys in $\Delta(F, F')$ for migration, the controller broadcasts both F' and $\Delta(F, F')$, together with a Pause signal to all the instances of the upstream operator for it to update the obsolete F, and temporarily stops sending (but caching locally) data with keys in $\Delta(F, F')$ (steps 3 and 4). Meanwhile, the controller notifies the corresponding downstream instances.

Finally, there are instances of the downstream operator migrating the states of keys after the notification from the controller (step 5) and acknowledging the controller when migration is completed (step 6). As soon as the controller receives all the acknowledgments, it sends out a Resume signal to all instances of the upstream operator, ordering the tasks to start sending data with keys in $\Delta(F, F')$, since all the downstream instances are equipped with the new assignment function (step 7). It is worth noting that during the key state migration, there is no interruption of normal processing on the data with keys not covered by $\Delta(F, F')$.

2.5.1 *Compact representations of key space*

One potential problem in the workflow above is the cost of transmitting statistical information with the keys in step 1, which very often involves millions of unique keys in real application domains. The huge size of the key domain may degenerate the scalability of the algorithms on growing computational complexity and memory consumption for these metrics. To alleviate the transmission problem, we propose a compact representation for the keys with acceptable information loss for the algorithms.

The basic idea is to merge the keys with common characteristics and represent them by a single record in the statistical data structure. To accomplish this goal, we design a new six-dimensional vector structure for the statistical information $(d^n, d, d^h, v_c, v_S, \#)$, in which d^n denotes the instance to which a key will be assigned next, d is the instance with which the keys are currently associated during the reporting period (i.e., $d = F(k)$), d^h is the instance assigned by the hash function (i.e., $d^h = h(k)$), v_c denotes the value of the computation workload, v_S is the value of window-based memory consumption and $\#(> 0)$ is the number of keys satisfying these five conditions. For example, a vector $(d_1, d_2, d_1, 4, 4, 2)$ indicates that there are two keys with computation workload 4 and memory consumption 4. They are currently associated with instance d_2, and the instance suggested by hash function is d_1, indicating that the routing table A at the upstream operator must contain an entry for them. In addition, these two keys are to be assigned to d_1 shortly, meaning that the entry for them in A is to be deleted and the *move back* operation executed.

By employing this compact representation, the whole key space $\mathcal{K}$ is transformed to the six-dimensional vector space (denoted by $\mathcal{K}^c$). The upper bound on the size of the vector space is approximately $K^c = |\mathcal{K}^c| = O(N_D^3 \times |c(k)| \times |S(k, w)|)$, where N_D is the number of downstream instances, which is usually a small integer; $|c(k)|$ and $|S(k, w)|$ represent the total numbers of distinct values on computation workload and memory consumption in the current sliding window, respectively.

2.5.2 *Discretization on calculating and state workload*

As is emphasized above, the size of the six-dimensional vector space $K^c = O(N_D^3 \times |c(k)| \times |S(k, w)|)$ depends on $|c(k)|$ and $|S(k, w)|$.

In practice, the values of computation cost and memory consumption could be highly diversified, leading to large values in $|c(k)|$ and $|S(k, w)|$, and consequently huge vector space K^c. It is thus necessary to properly discretize the candidate values used in $c(k)$ and $S(k, w)$ in order to control the complexity shown by $|c(k)|$ and $|S(k, w)|$.

Value discretization can be done in a straightforward way. However, an oversimplistic approach causes huge deviations on the approximate values from the real ones. Such deviations may affect the accuracy of workload estimation and jeopardize the usefulness of the migration component. For instance, assume that there are 10 keys with computation costs $c(k_1) = 8$, $c(k_2) = 6$, $c(k_3) = 3$, $c(k_4) = c(k_5) = 2$ and $c(k_6) = \cdots = c(k_{10}) = 1$. If a simple piecewise constant function is used, i.e., $\xi(x) = 2$ when $x \in [1, 3]$, then $\xi(x) = 5$ when $x \in [4, 6]$, $\xi(x) = 8$ when $x \in [7, 9]$, and 0 otherwise. Despite a smaller $|\xi(c(k))| = 3$ (as compared to the original $|c(k)| = 5$), the total deviation, following the formula below, caused by the approximation is fairly large:

$$|\delta| = \left| \sum_{i=1}^{10} \delta_i \right| = \left| \sum_{i=1}^{10} c(k_i) - \xi(c(k_i)) \right|.$$

Figure 2.5(a) illustrates how this simple piecewise constant function fails and the deviation δ_i with respect to each value point.

To tackle the problem, we propose an improved discretization approach, denoted by $\phi(x)$, which involves two steps. In the first step, it generates a finite number of representative values. Second, instead of using the nearest representative for each value independently, our approach constructs the discretized values in a more holistic manner. Assume the input value is a series of n numbers in a non-increasing order by their values of which the smallest is at least 1 (after normalization), i.e., $x_1, x_2, \ldots, x_n$, $\forall i, i' \in [1, n]$, $i < i'$, $x_i \geq x_{i'} \geq 1$.

In the first step, a simple method (half-linear half-exponential, HLHE) with a parameter R (called the degree of discretization) is applied to determine the representative values, where we require $R = 2^r$, $r = 0, 1, 2, \ldots$. Therefore, a total number of

$$m = r + \left\lfloor \frac{\max(x_i)}{R} \right\rfloor = r + s$$

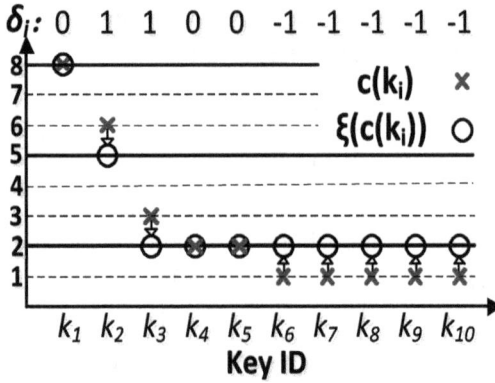

(a)

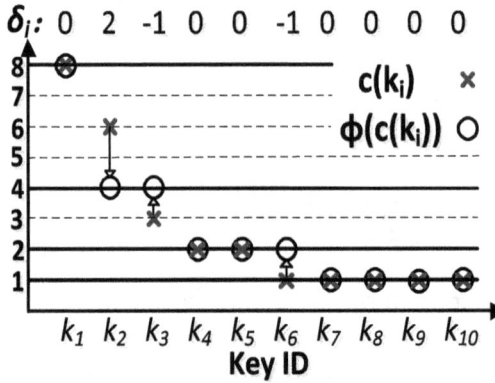

(b)

Fig. 2.5. An example of comparing the simple piecewise discretization function (a) and our proposed approach (b).

representative values are generated and reorganized as a strictly decreasing series, $y_1, y_2, \ldots, y_m$, where $y_1 = s \times R$, $y_2 = (s - 1) \times R, \ldots, y_s = R$ (the linear part), and $y_{s+1} = R/2 = 2^{r-1}$, $y_{s+2} = 2^{r-2}, \ldots, y_{m-1} = 2$, $y_m = 1$ (the exponential part).

In the second stage, a greedy method is applied to finalize the discretization by adopting an optimization framework. The basic principle is to minimize the accumulated error of all values, such that the sum over an arbitrary set of approximate values tends to be an accurate estimation of the sum over original values. Specifically, for each $x_i < y_1$, two representative values for $j \in [2, m]$ such that $y_{j-1} > x_i \geq y_j$ can be used to approximate x_i. We define such y_{j-1} and y_j as candidate representative values for x_i. For the remaining ($x_i \geq y_1$), they only have one candidate representative value, which is y_1. For each x_i, one of the candidate representative values is chosen when there are two options, denoted by $\phi(x_i)$, so that the total deviation $|\delta|$ is minimized. In particular, if the current accumulated deviation is positive, x_i is represented by the larger value y_{j-1} in order to cancel the overcounting. Otherwise, x_i chooses the representative value y_j.

In the example of Fig. 2.5(b), we let $r = 2$ and $R = 4$, thus $m = 2 + \frac{8}{4} = 4$. There are four representative values, e.g., $y_1 = 8$, $y_2 = 4$, $y_3 = 2$ and $y_4 = 1$. At the time k_3, whose $c(k_3) = 3$, is processed, the two representative values for it are $y_2 = 4$ and $y_3 = 2$. Since the accumulated deviation caused by k_1 and k_2 equals 2, we have $\phi(c(k_3)) = y_2 = 4$. This results in a reduction of the accumulated deviation by 1. When our proposed approach terminates, according to Fig. 2.5(b), the total deviation is zero, while the simple piecewise constant function generates a total deviation at $|\delta| = 3$.

As will be shown in our experimental evaluations, the above optimizations, such as compact representation of key space and improved discretization approach on both $c(k)$ and $S(k, w)$, we have made in system implementations clearly improve the system's running efficiency with relatively low estimation error on real workloads generated.

2.5.3 *Mixed algorithm over compact representations*

Apparently, the compact representation brings significant benefits by reducing both time and space complexity of the Mixed algorithm (and MinTable and MinMig as well). In this section, we briefly describe how Mixed algorithm adopts compact representation. To provide a clear description, let us revisit the Mixed algorithm and look into the steps using compact representations.

- **Phase I (Cleaning):** According to the smallest $S_{i-1}(k, w)$ first criterion, the Mixed algorithm selects n keys from A and moves them back to original instance based on the hash function. In the compact representation, the adapted Mixed algorithm does not target any individual key but the six-dimensional vectors. In conclusion, a *back move* of keys is equivalent to modifying the value of d^n to be the same as d^h of the selected vectors. The vector $(d_1, d_2, d_1, 4, 4, 2)$ mentioned above presents an example back move of a number of keys.

- **Phase II (Preparing):** When investigating the workloads of a particular instance, say d_1, the adapted Mixed algorithm calculates the weighted sum of $v_c \times$ # of all records containing $d^n = d_1$. If we have two records $(d_1, d_2, d_1, 4, 4, 2)$ and $(d_1, d_2, d_2, 8, 8, 1)$, for example, the total workload with respect to the keys is estimated as 16. Next, when the adapted Mixed algorithm needs to select keys from an overloaded instance and puts them into the candidate set $\mathcal{C}$, the algorithm again targets those vectors in compact representations and simply replaces the value of d^n with a *nil*, indicating a virtual removal of the keys linked to the vector. For example, if $(d_2, d_2, d_1, 4, 4, 2)$ is disassociated from d_2 and put into $\mathcal{C}$, the adapted Mixed algorithm finally rewrites the record as $(nil, d_2, d_1, 4, 4, 2)$. Note that when a record is added into $\mathcal{C}$, i.e., containing $d^n = nil$, it is likely that there already exists a record in $\mathcal{C}$ with exactly the same values on d, d^h, v_c and v_S. According to the definition on the uniqueness of the compact representation, these two records need to be merged by summing in the number field "#".

- **Phase III (Assigning):** The similar adaptation in Phase I and II is also applied to LLFD, with only one exception that the expected routing table A' cannot be directly derived but rather indirectly calculated. This is because the final results returned by the adapted LLFD are still in a compact form as a six-dimensional tuple. In order to derive A' and F', a series of additional actions are taken, including (i) picking up those records with $d^n \neq d$, i.e., for migration, returned by the adapted LLFD, (ii) selecting keys originally associated with instance d and computation cost at v_c, according to both the selection criteria ψ and the original complete statistical information of keys collected by the controller, and (iii) adding them to the key migration set $\Delta(F, F')$. Finally, it returns the results of F' and A' induced by combining F and $\Delta(F, F')$, and F' and $h(k)$, respectively.

2.5.4 *Extension to multi-dimensional load balance*

Load balance on multiple resources (multi-dimension) was studied in Gedik (2014) where a geometric mean was applied in evaluating the degree of imbalance on three types of resources: network, CPU and memory consumption. In Gedik (2014), the multi-dimensional balance indicator for a set of resources (denoted by $\mathcal{R}$) was defined as $b = \left(\prod_{x \in \mathcal{R}} b_x\right)^{\frac{1}{|\mathcal{R}|}}$, where for a certain resource type x, $b_x = \lambda_x / \alpha_x$, λ_x is a relative workload of x, and $\alpha_x (\geq 1)$ is a weighting factor expressing the importance of x among all the resources in $\mathcal{R}$.

In the following, we describe how our proposed approach can easily adapt to multiple bottleneck resources:

- **Phase I:** Same as that in Algorithm 2.2.

Before moving to the next phase, it is necessary for us to introduce some new definitions and notations specifically for multiple resources. In the ith interval, $c_{i,x}$ is used to denote the cost at a certain resource type x. The total cost of x on an instance d is

$$L_{i,x}(d, F) = \sum_{\{k | F(k) = d, k \in \mathcal{K}\}} c_{i,x}(k).$$

The average cost of x over all instances of downstream operator is defined as $\bar{L}_{i,x} = \frac{1}{N_D} \sum_{d \in \mathcal{D}} L_{i,x}(d, F)$. We define the composite cost of key k over all types of resources in $\mathcal{R}$ as

$$c_i'(k) = \left(\prod_{x \in \mathcal{R}} c_{i,x}'(k)\right)^{\frac{1}{|\mathcal{R}|}} = \left(\prod_{x \in \mathcal{R}} \frac{c_{i,x}(k)}{\alpha_x \cdot \bar{L}_{i,x}(F)}\right)^{\frac{1}{|\mathcal{R}|}},$$

where $\bar{L}_{i,x}(F)$ put in the denominator is for normalization among heterogeneous resources and α_x is the weighting factor consistent with the definition in Gedik (2014). Then, the composite *migration priority index* for key k is expressed as $\gamma_i'(k, w) = \frac{c_i'(k)^\beta}{S_i(k,w)}$.

- **Phase II:** During the jth iteration, $j = 1, 2, \ldots$, according to ψ', keys are selected one by one according to the priorities evaluated by $\gamma'(k, w)$, disassociated from d and put into candidate set $\mathcal{C}$. The selection procedure will not stop until $L_{i,x}(d, F) < \bar{L}_{i,x}(F) \cdot (1 + \rho)^j$ where $\forall x \in \mathcal{R}$ and $\rho \in [0, 1)$ is a parameter controlling the size of candidates in $\mathcal{C}$. After each iteration, the constraint on $L_{i,x}(d, F)$ is relaxed by a factor of $(1 + \rho)$ in order to select the minimal valid candidate key set in a greedy manner.

- **Phase III:** Keys in C, which are sorted by $c_i'(k)$ in a descending order, are sequentially assigned to the instance d, which has the smallest $L_i'(d, F)$, where $L_i'(d, F) = \left(\prod_{x \in \mathcal{R}} \frac{L_{i,x}(d,F)}{\alpha_x \cdot \bar{L}_{i,x}(F)} \right)^{\frac{1}{|\mathcal{R}|}}$. The assignment procedure requires that the total workload of any resource type in $\mathcal{R}$ on an instance is below the average, i.e.,

$$\forall x \in \mathcal{R}, L_{i,x}(d, F) + c_{i,x}(k) \leq \bar{L}_{i,x}(F).$$

Otherwise, it searches for (by brute force) an instance d to which, after assigning k, the minimum $L_i'(d, F)$ (degree of multi-dimensional imbalance) is achieved.

When the candidate set C becomes empty, the adapted Mixed algorithm evaluates whether the multi-dimensional load balance constraint is satisfied: $\forall d \in \mathcal{D}, L_i'(d, F) \leq b_{\max}$, where $b_{\max}$ is the maximal imbalance tolerance for multi-dimension. If not satisfied, it tries a larger j for the next iteration (loop back to Phase II).

2.6 Practical Verification and Study

2.6.1 *Environment setting*

In this section, we evaluate our proposals by comparing them against a handful of baseline approaches. All of these approaches are implemented and run on top of *Apache Storm* under the same task configuration N_D and routing table size $A_{\max}$. To collect the workload measurements, we add a load reporting module into the processing logics when implementing them in *Storm*'s topologies. Migration and scheduling algorithms are injected into the codes of *controllers* in *Storm* to enable automatic workload redistribution. We use the consistent hashing [Karger *et al.* (1997)] as our basic hash function and configure the parallelism of spout at 10. By controlling the latency on tuple processing, we force the distributed system to reach a saturation point of CPU resource for the N_D number of processing tasks with the requirement of absolute load balancing ($\theta_{\max} = 0$). We show that the results are averages of 5 runs. The *Storm* system (in version 0.9.3) is deployed on a 21-instance HP blade cluster with a CentOS 6.5 operating system. Each instance in the cluster is equipped with two Intel Xeon processors (E5335 at 2.00 GHz) having four cores and a 16 GB RAM. Each

Table 2.2. Parameter settings.

	Range	Description
K	$[5 \cdot 10^3, 10^4, 10^5, \mathbf{10^6}]$	Size of key domain
z	$[0, \ldots, \mathbf{0.85}, \ldots, 1.0]$	Distribution skewness
f	$[0, \ldots, \mathbf{1.0}, \ldots, 2.0]$	Fluctuation rate
θ_{max}	$[0, \ldots, \mathbf{0.08}, \ldots, 1.0]$	Tolerance on load imbalance
β	$[1, \ldots, \mathbf{1.5}, \ldots, 2.0]$	Migration selection factor
r	$[0, 1, 2, \mathbf{3}, 4, 5, 6, 7, 8]$	Level partition distance
N_D	$[1, 5, 10, \mathbf{15}, 20, \ldots, 40]$	Number of task instances
A_{max}	$[0, \ldots, \mathbf{3 \cdot 10^3}, \ldots, 5 \cdot 10^4]$	Size of the routing table
α	$[\mathbf{1}, \ldots, 4]$	Factor for multi-dimension

core is exclusively bound with a worker thread during our experiments (Table 2.2).

- **Queries and Dataset:** We experiment on three queries and three datasets (QD-1–4), namely one join operation for real workload and two aggregation operations for synthetic and real workloads (QD-1). We first use the synthetic skewed data for aggregation operation to test the load skewness phenomenon and the impact of algorithm parameters. By controlling the latency of tuple processing, we force the distributed system to reach a saturation point of CPU resource for the N_D number of processing tasks with the requirement of absolute load balancing ($\theta_{max} = 0$). Our synthetic workload generator creates snapshots of tuples for discrete time intervals from an integer key domain K. The tuples follow Zipf distributions controlled by skewness parameter z by using the popular generation tool available in Apache project. We use parameter f to control the rate of distribution fluctuation across time intervals. At the beginning of a new interval, our generator keeps swapping frequencies between keys from different task instances until the change on workload is significant enough, i.e., $\frac{|L_i(d) - L_{i-1}(d)|}{L} \geq f$ (QD-2). We do the Top-K operation on a social network to test the throughput and scalability of each approach (Figs. 2.17(a) and 2.18(a)). The *Social* data are obtained from the Chinese version of twitter (Weibo[2]) and we take the topic keywords as our distribution keys. This workload includes 5-day

---

[2]http://open.weibo.com/wiki/2/statuses/user_timeline.

feeds from a popular microblog service, in which each feed is regarded as a tuple with words as its keys. There are over 5,000,000 tuples covering 180,000 topic words as the keys and the distribution of topic keywords' frequency is unpredictable skewness. Each tuple is a piece of Weibo of approximately size 2.5 KB. We run word count topology on *Social* data, which continuously maintains current tuples in memory and updates the appearance frequency of topic words in social media feeds (QD-3). We run self-join on *Stock* data over sliding window to find potential high-frequency players with dense buying and selling behavior (Figs. 2.17(b) and 2.18(b)). This workload includes 3-day *Stock* records on buying and selling stocks, consisting of over 6,000,000 tuples with 1,036 unique and skew keys (Stock ID) for stock transactions. Each record contains 20 columns, including account ID, date, time, price and stock ID (QD-4). We use $DBGen$ to generate 1 GB TPC-H dataset. Before feeding the data to the stream system, we pre-generate and pre-process all the input datasets. We adjust the datasets with different degrees of skew on the join attributes under $Zipf$ distribution by choosing a value for skew parameter z. By default, we set $z = 0.8$. Based on the TPC-H dataset, we implement the equi-join (Fig. 2.19) E_{Q_5} [Elseidy *et al.* (2014); Lin *et al.* (2015)], which represents the most expensive operation in query Q_5 from the benchmark.

- **Baseline Approaches:** We use *Mixed* to denote our proposed algorithm, mixing two types of heuristics. We also use $Mixed_{BF}$ to denote the brute force version of the *Mixed* method, which completely rebuilds the routing table from scratch at each scheduling point. We use MinTable to denote the algorithm always trying to find a migration plan generating a minimal routing table. Finally, we also include *Readj* and PKG as baseline approaches, which are known as state-of-the-art solutions in the literature. *Readj* [Gedik (2014)] was designed to minimize the load of restoring the keys based on the hash function, implemented by rerouting over the keys with maximal workload. The migration plan of keys for load balance is generated by pairing tasks and keys. For each task–key pair, their algorithm considers all possible swaps to find the best move alleviating the workload imbalance. In *Readj*, σ is a configurable parameter, deciding which keys should take part in the action of swap and move. Given a smaller σ, *Readj* tends to track more candidate keys and thus finds better migration plans. In order to make a fair comparison, in each of the experiments, we run *Readj* with different σ's and only report the best result from all attempts. PKG [Nasir *et al.* (2015)] is a load balancing method without migration at runtime. It balances the workload of tasks by splitting keys into smaller granularity and distributing them to different tasks based on a randomly generated plan. Here, we only use the PKG approach for simple aggregation processing in the experiments because it is not appropriate for complex stateful operations such as join. Due to the unique strategy used by PKG, aggregation topologies deploying PKG must contain a special downstream operator in the topology, which is used to collect and merge partial results with respect to every key, from two independent workers in the upstream operator. Moreover, in the open source version of PKG,[3] there is a parameter p controlling the time interval between the merging of two consecutive results. After careful investigation with experiments, we find a larger p prolongs the response time of tuple processing, reduces the additional computation cost and limits the maximal number of live tuples (known as maximal pending tuples in *Storm*) under processing in the system. We finally chose p at 10 ms and set maximal pending tuples at 50, which are verified to be the best options to maximize the throughput of PKG in all settings. Note that we do not include LLFD and MinMig algorithms in the experiments because both of them cannot control the size of routing tables, thus blowing off the memory space of the tasks in some cases.

- **Evaluation Metrics:** In the experiments, we defined a group of metrics for performance evaluation purposes, as listed in Table 2.3. In the rest of the sections, we report the average values for these metrics over a complete processing procedure, as well as the minimal and maximal values when applicable, to demonstrate the stability of different balance processing algorithms.

2.6.2 *Load skewness phenomenon*

To understand the phenomenon of workload skewness with a traditional hash-based mechanism, we report the workload imbalance phenomenon

---

[3]https://github.com/gdfm/partial-key-grouping.

Table 2.3.   List of metrics used for performance evaluation.

Metrics	Description
Workload skewness	The ratio of maximal workload on individual task instance to the average workload, i.e., $\frac{\max_d L(d)}{L}$.
Migration cost	The percentage of states associated with the keys involved in migration over the states maintained by all the task instances.
Throughput	The number of tuples processed by the system in unit second.
Generation time	The amount of time spent on the generation of a migration plan by the Storm controller.
Processing latency	The amount of time take by the system to fully process an individual tuple.

on the task instances by changing the number of task instances and the size of key domain. The results of load imbalance in Fig. 2.6 are presented as the cumulative distribution of average workload among the task instances over 50 time intervals. Figure 2.6(a) implies that the skewness grows when increasing the number of task instances. When there are 40 instances (i.e., $N_D = 40$), the maximal workload at 100% is almost 2.5 times larger than the minimal workload. Figure 2.6(b) shows that the workload imbalance is also highly relevant to the size of the key domain. When there are more keys in the domain, the hash function generates more balanced workload assignment. In Fig. 2.6(b), the maximal workload for $K = 5,000$ is around 4 times larger than the minimal one and is much larger than the maximal load under a larger key domain size (e.g., $K = 1,000,000$). Therefore, workload imbalance for intra-operator parallelism is a serious problem and cannot be easily solved by randomized hash functions.

2.6.3   *Impact of algorithm parameters*

We test the algorithm parameters on synthetic datasets using two different time intervals, i.e., $w = 1$ and $w = 5$, in order to understand their impacts for short- and long-term aggregation over stream data, where the duration of a time interval is configured as 10 s. When $w = 1$ (10 s), migration decisions are made based on the current stateful and instantaneous workload. When $w = 5$ (50 s), more state information of the last five intervals is included in the decision-making procedure. Although the increase on N_D

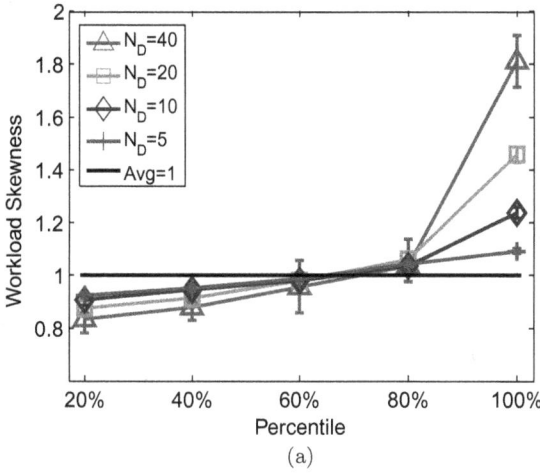

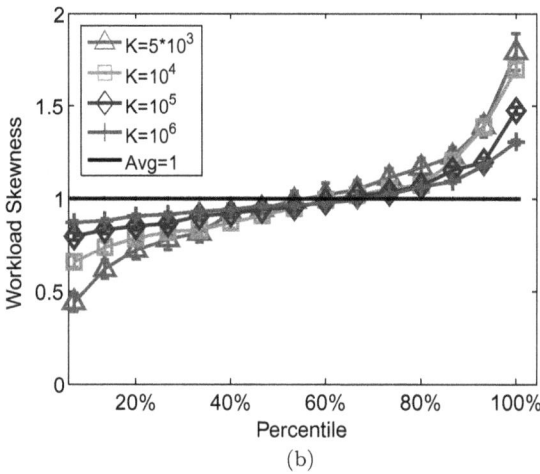

Fig. 2.6.   Cumulative distribution of workload skewness under hash-based scheme. (a) # of task instances and (b) size of key domain.

produces more workload imbalance, our migration algorithm *Mixed* performs well, by generating an excellent migration plan, as shown in Fig. 2.7. *Mixed* costs a little additional overhead as compared to the MinTable algorithm for balancing, but its migration cost is much lower than MinTable when $N_D \leq 35$ for both $w = 1$ and $w = 5$, as presented in Fig. 2.7(b). The cleaning step in the MinTable algorithm also leads to even higher skewness and migration cost in order to achieve load balancing. When $w = 5$, *Mixed*

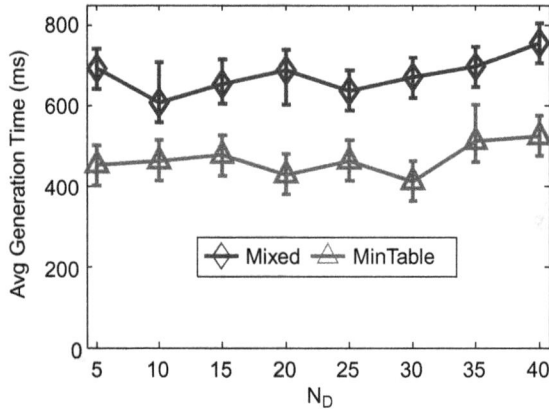

(a)

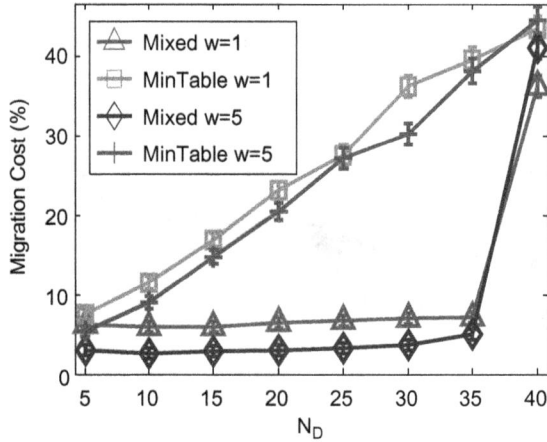

(b)

Fig. 2.7. Performance with a varying number of task instances. (a) # of instances vs. scheduling efficiency and (b) # of instances vs. migration cost.

keeps more historical tuples which can be used as the migration candidates. This makes the migration easier and less expensive, when compared to the case with $w = 1$. When $N_D > 35$, however, the migration cost of *Mixed* jumps, almost reaching the cost of MinTable when $N_D = 40$. This is because the outcome of the *Mixed* algorithm degenerates to that of the MinTable algorithm when the minimal routing table size needed for target load balancing exceeds the specified size of the table in the system.

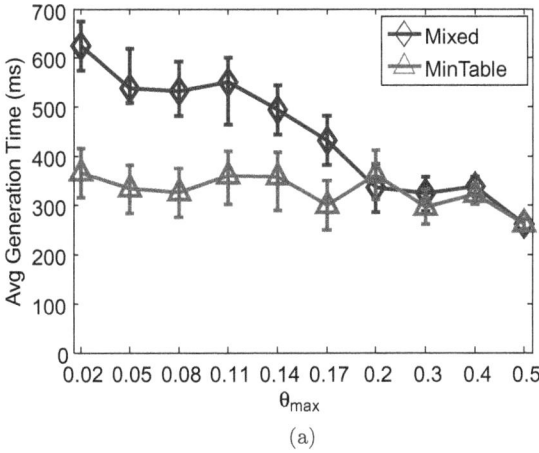

(a)

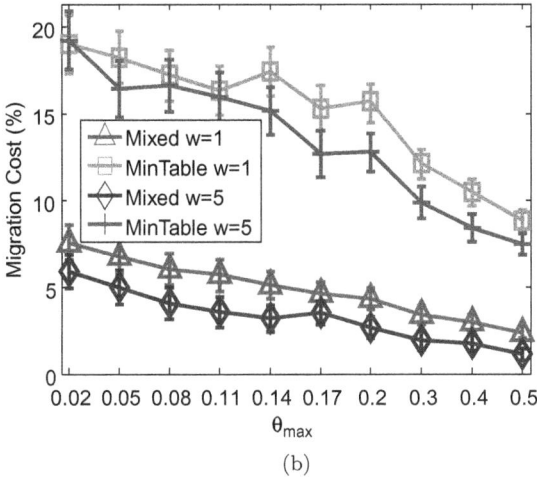

(b)

Fig. 2.8. Performance with varying θ_{max}. (a) θ_{max} vs. scheduling efficiency and (b) θ_{max} vs. migration cost.

Figure 2.8 displays the efficiency of migration plan generation and the corresponding migration cost with the varying workload imbalance tolerance parameter θ_{max}. As expected, Migration scheduling runs faster on synthetic datasets with larger θ_{max} in Fig. 2.8(a). When $\theta_{max} \geq 0.2$, the efficiency of *Mixed* catches up with that of MinTable. If stronger load balancing (i.e., smaller θ_{max}) is specified, the system pays more migration cost as shown in Fig. 2.8(b), basically due to more keys involved in migration.

But MinTable incurs three times the migration cost as *Mixed* under the same balance requirement. Even for strict $\theta_{max} = 0.02$ (almost absolutely balanced), the algorithm is capable of generating the migration plan within 1 s. Moreover, migration cost with a larger window size (i.e., $w = 5$) shrinks, as the historical states provide more appropriate candidate keys for migration plan generation.

In Fig. 2.9, we report the results on varying key domain size K. By varying K from 5,000 to 1,000,000, *Mixed* spends more computation time

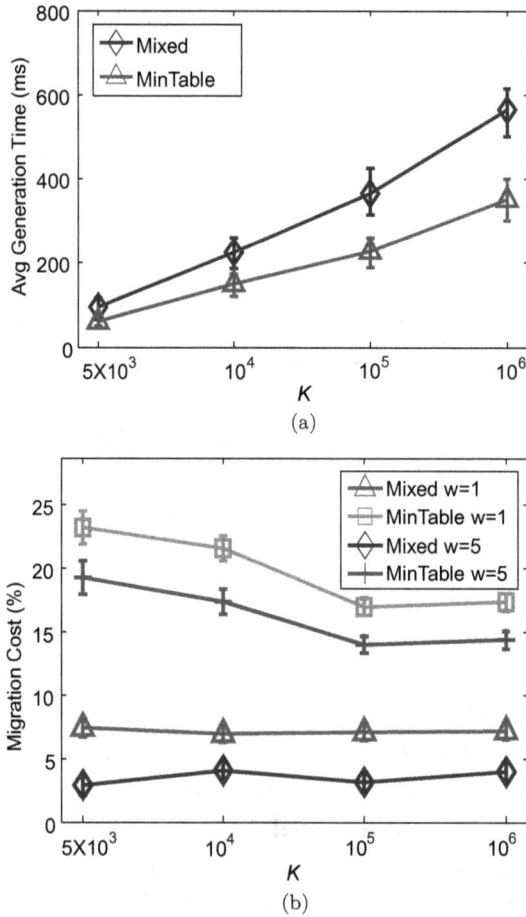

Fig. 2.9.   Scheduling efficiency in terms of average generation time and migration cost under a different key domain size, K. (a) K vs. scheduling efficiency and (b) K vs. migration cost.

on migration planning but incurs less migration cost than MinTable. As shown in Fig. 2.6(b), the smaller the key domain, the more skewed the workload distribution will be. But our proposed solution *Mixed* shows stable performance, regardless of the domain size, based on the results in Fig. 2.9(a). In particular, migration cost decreases for both MinTable and *Mixed* algorithms when the window size grows to $w = 5$.

We present the possibility of efficiency improvement by applying compact representation for key related information. In this group of experiments, we report the performance of this technique in Fig. 2.10 by varying

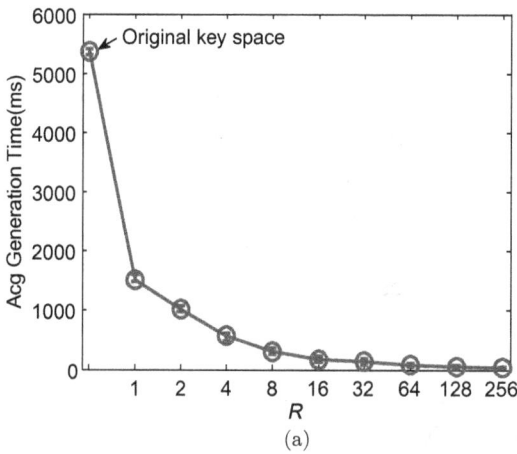

(a)

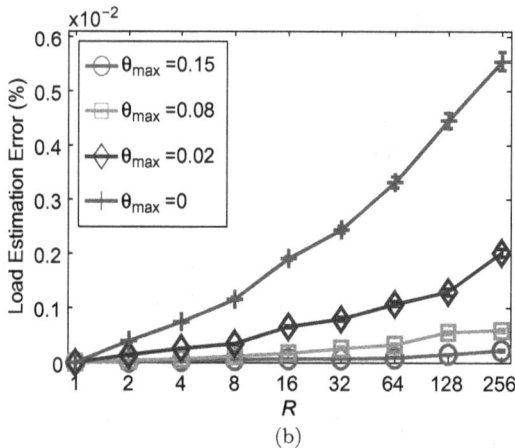

(b)

Fig. 2.10. Performance with varied degrees of discretization for partitioning granularity. (a) R vs. scheduling efficiency and (b) R vs. estimation error.

the degree of discretization (i.e., the value of R) on values of computation cost v_c and memory consumption v_S. Figure 2.10(a) shows that discretization on both v_c and v_S is an important factor in the efficiency of migration scheduling. The average generation time of the migration plan is quickly reduced when we allow the system to discretize the values at a finer granularity. Note that the point with label "Original Key Space" is the result without applying the compact representation on keys, while the point at $R = 1$ is the case of the finest degree of discretization on v_c and v_S. The efficiency is improved by an order of magnitude when $R = 8$ (i.e., 0.6 s) compared to "Original Key Space" (i.e., 6 s). Although larger R leads to smaller $|v_c|$, $|v_S|$ and smaller K^c and makes the migration plan faster, the error on load estimation grows (i.e., the percentage of divergence between actual workload of a task instance and the estimated workload based on the discretizated workload over the keys), as shown in Fig. 2.10(b), because the discretization generates inaccurate load approximation for the keys. However, such errors are no more than 1% in all cases, while the degree of discretization R varies from 1 to 256 as shown in Fig. 2.10(b).

Since *Readj* is the technique most similar to our proposal in the literature, we conduct a careful investigation on performance comparison to evaluate the effectiveness of our proposal. To optimize the performance of *Readj*, we adopt binary search to find the best δ for *Readj*. Figure 2.11 shows the performance on dynamic stream processing with imbalance tolerance $\theta_{\max} = 0.08$, by varying distribution change frequency f. When increasing f, *Readj* presents less promising efficiency when generating a migration plan since it evaluates every pair of task instances and considers all possible movements across the instances. Instead, *Mixed* makes the migration plan based on heuristic information, which outperforms *Readj* by a large margin. The results also imply that brute force search with $Mixed_{BF}$ is a poor option for migration scheduling. When variances occur more frequently (i.e., with a higher f), migration cost of *Mixed* grows slower than that of *Readj*, while $Mixed_{BF}$ performs similarly to *Mixed*.

We show the efficiency and migration cost with a different window size in Fig. 2.12. Since the computation complexity for MinTable is simpler than that of *Mixed*, it is always faster to make a migration plan as in Fig. 2.12(a), but it costs more for migration shown in Fig. 2.12(b). Furthermore, the larger window size provides more chances of finding the

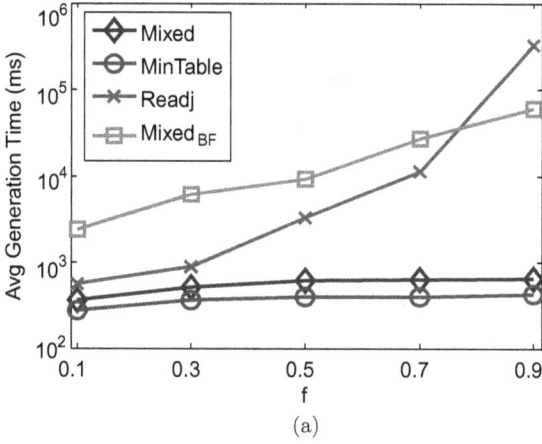

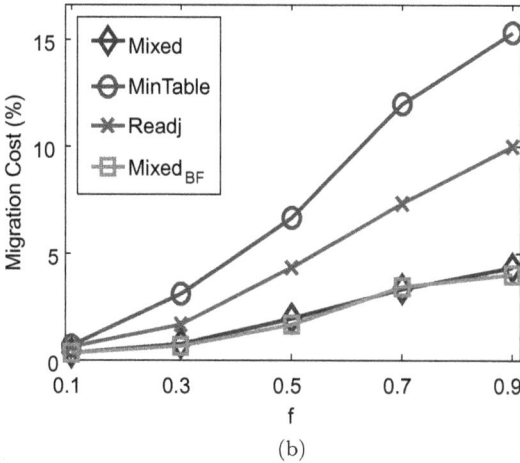

Fig. 2.11.   Scheduling efficiency and migration cost with varying distribution change frequency. (a) Stream dynamics vs. efficiency and (b) stream dynamics vs. MC.

appropriate migration keys ($\gamma_i(k, w)$), which determines that the migration cost of *Mixed* is smaller than that of MinTable.

To characterize both computation and migration costs, we propose the *migration priority index* for each key, defined as $\gamma_i(k, w) = c_i(k)^\beta S_i(k, w)^{-1}$. β is used to measure the importance of computation cost and the memory consumption which decides the *migration priority* of keys. In MinMig, a key with the larger $\gamma_i(k, w)$ has the higher priority

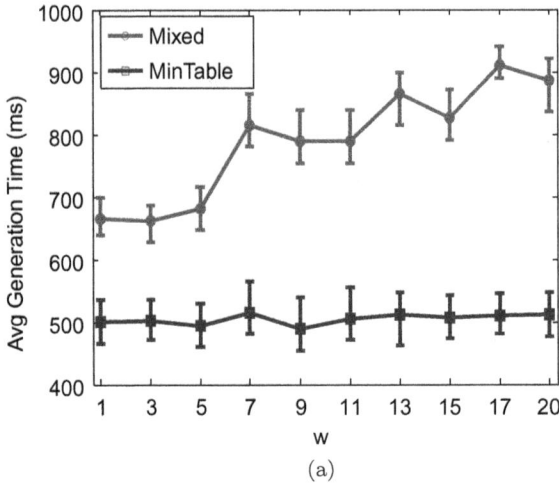

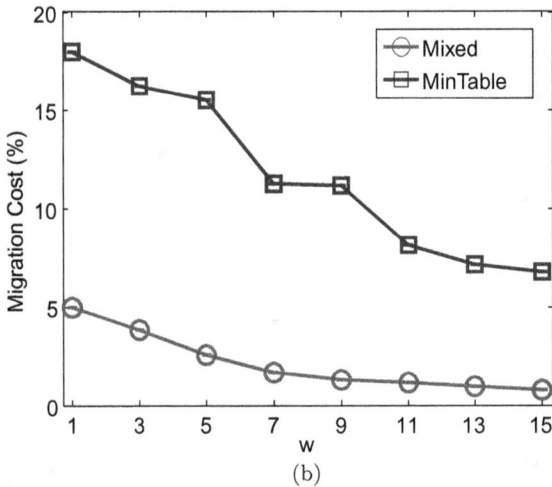

Fig. 2.12.   Window size impact testing. (a) Window size vs. efficiency and (b) window size vs. migration cost.

to be migrated. Larger β represents that the migration method concerns faster computation rather than less migration cost (memory consumption). Furthermore, larger β will produce a smaller routing table since the migration method preferentially migrates keys with a large load. Figures 2.13(a) and 2.13(b) show the change of routing table size and migration cost with different values of β. Those results are produced by the MinMig algorithm,

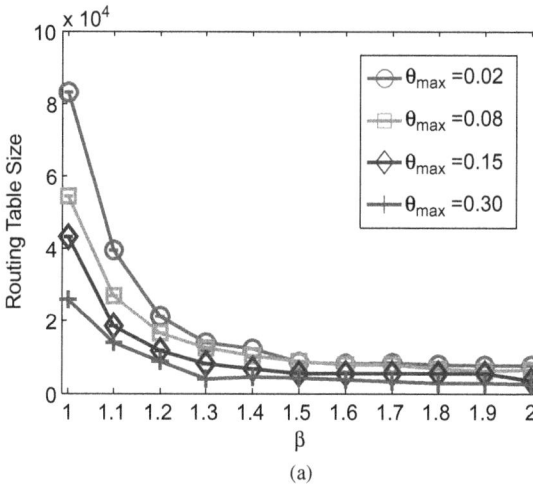

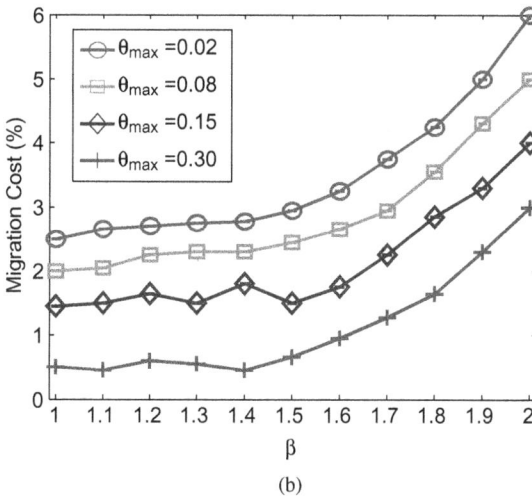

Fig. 2.13. β impact testing. (a) Routing table size in different β and (b) migration cost in different β.

and each result is an average value generated by running balance adjustments 10 times. In Fig. 2.13(a), $\beta = 1$ means the migration candidates are evaluated according to the load per unit memory consumption. In this case, keys with a smaller load would be selected and a larger routing table will be generated. As β becomes larger, the migration method gradually tends to move the bigger load keys, then the routing table size becomes smaller.

Furthermore, when $\beta \in [1.5, 2]$, the routing table size is stable because the migration candidates are almost selected only by the load of keys. The lines in Fig. 2.13(b) show results by the influence of parameter β. Based on these sets of parameter tests, we select $\beta = 1.5$ as the default value in our experiments. Figure 2.14(a) illustrates how the routing table size N_A and workload imbalance constraint θ_{max} affect the migration costs when the *Mixed* algorithm is applied. In particular, when N_A is smaller than 1,000

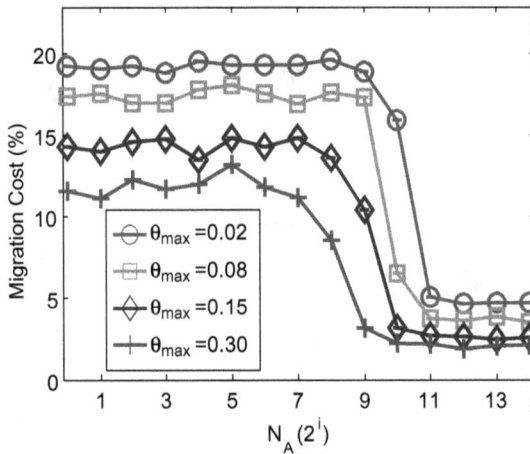

(a)

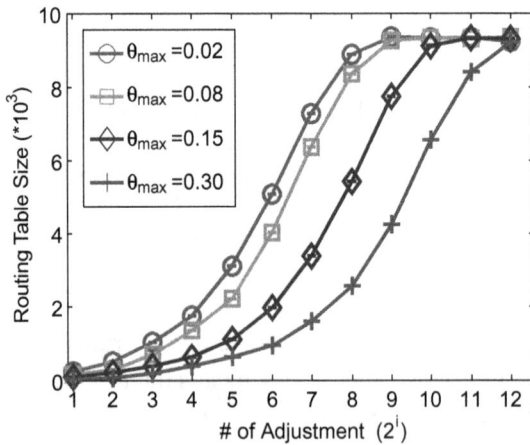

(b)

Fig. 2.14.   Routing table testing. (a) Migration cost by *Mixed* and (b) routing table changing.

(calculated by 2^i with $i \leq 10$) for $\theta_{\max} = 0.08$, our algorithm actually acts as a MinTable algorithm, thus resulting in a large amount of migration cost. When the size of N_A is relaxed to above 2,000 (i.e., $i > 11$), migration cost decreases significantly, because in this case, our algorithm acts similar to the MinMig algorithm which cares more about the cost-effectiveness of migrating key states. Furthermore, in order to fulfill a tighter load balance constraint, i.e., a smaller $\theta_{\max}$, it usually incurs higher migration costs given any particular size of routing table N_A. In addition, the marginal benefits on migration cost are decreasing as we increase the maximum size of the routing table, as shown in Fig. 2.14. It is observed that $N_A = 3,000$ is the critical point where no further gain will be obtained by increasing the upper limit of the routing table size (equivalently the memory cost), which explains the reason why we set $A_{\max} = 3,000$ as the default value in the experiments. In practice, an additional working thread can be executed for generating the curves as shown in Fig. 2.14(a) to find the most proper routing table size in the runtime.

Figure 2.14(b) shows that the number of affected entries in the routing table is increasing with the number of adjustments. Obviously, the smaller $\theta_{\max}$ accelerates the growth of affected routing entries. We also observe that all the four curves with different load balance constraints gradually converge to the same value, e.g., about 9,350. This is because MinMig achieves load balancing without considering the constraint for routing table size. In other words, a key is associated with a task randomly when the basic assignment function causes imbalance. Therefore, the probability of a key appearing in the routing table is $\frac{N_D-1}{N_D}$, and then, after a long period under load balancing, the routing table size becomes $K \cdot \frac{N_D-1}{N_D}$, where K is the key size.

2.6.4 *Multiple resources*

In reality, there may appear multiple types of bottleneck resources. In this section, we evaluate the balance status under a composite balance metric, i.e., $b = (\prod_{x \in \mathcal{R}} b_x)^{|\mathcal{R}|}$, which was introduced by Gedik (2014). It computes an overall balance indicator covering three types of resources, i.e., $\mathcal{R} = \{CPU, Memory, Network\}$. We show the efficiency and migration cost with different imbalance tolerance $b_{\max}$ in Fig. 2.15, where the weighting factor $\alpha_x = 1, \forall x \in \mathcal{R}$. For the migration plan generation time, *Mixed*

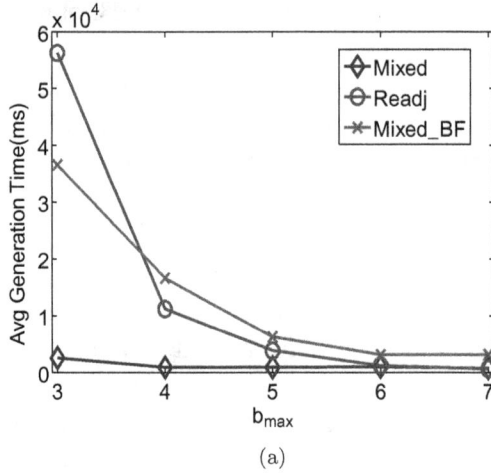

(a)

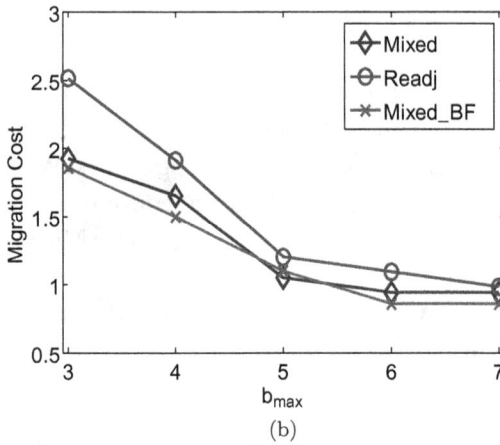

(b)

Fig. 2.15.   Load balance among multi-resources. (a) Imbalance tolerance vs. efficiency and (b) imbalance tolerance vs. MC.

performs much better than *Readj* when $b_{max} \leq 4$ as shown in Fig. 2.15(a). *Readj* shows similar efficiency as *Mixed* when the balance constraint is relaxed, i.e., $b_{max} \geq 5$. This is because the higher the imbalance tolerance, the fewer keys that will be involved in the calculation of *Readj*. In addition, as shown in Fig. 2.15(b), the migration cost generated by our *Mixed* algorithm is close to the optimal curve generated by the *Mixed$_{BF}$* algorithm which spends more time on generating migration plans.

2.6.5 Throughput and latency

Figure 2.16 shows the throughput and latency with varying distribution change frequency running on a cluster of 15 instances (Figs. 2.16(a) and 2.16(b)) and a cluster of 10 instances (Figs. 2.16(c) and 2.16(d)), respectively. In Fig. 2.16, we draw the theoretical limit of the performance with the line labeled *Ideal*, which simply shuffles the workload regardless of the keys. Obviously, *Ideal* always generates a better throughput and lower processing latency than any key-aware scheduling, but cannot be used in stateful operators for aggregations. As shown in Figs. 2.16(a) and 2.16(c), the average processing throughput of all methods degrades when using less

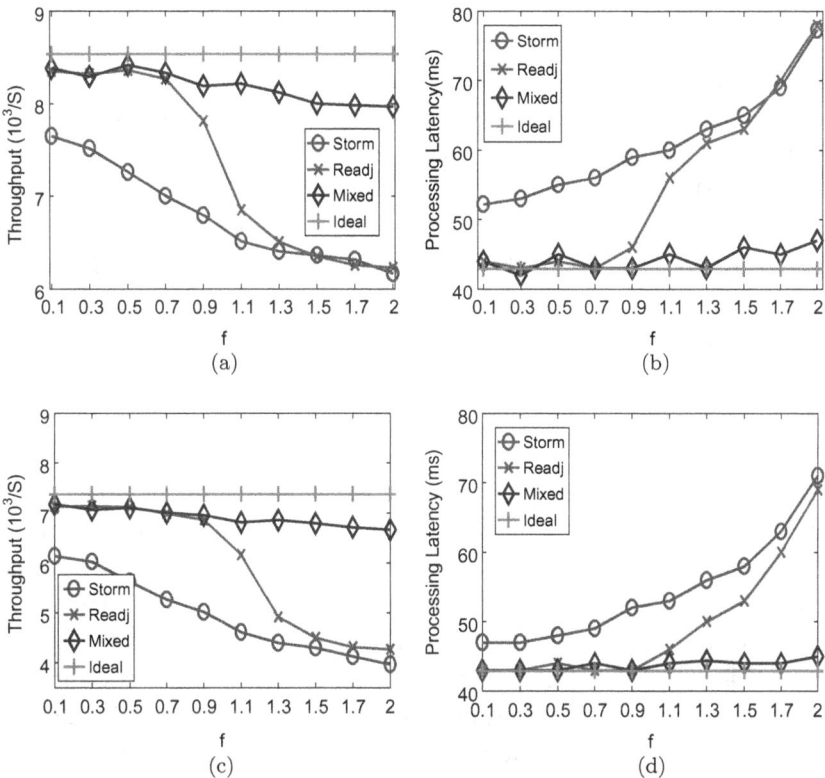

Fig. 2.16. Throughput and latency with varying distribution change frequency (a) Stream dynamics vs. throughput, (b) stream dynamics vs. latency, (c) stream dynamics vs. throughput and (d) stream dynamics vs. latency. Here, (a) and (b) run on a cluster of 15 instances, and (c) and (d) on a cluster of 10 instances.

computing resource. In the meantime, the average latency slightly drops for all methods too, as evidenced in both Figs. 2.16(b) and 2.16(d). This is because workload skewness among task instances decreases when the number of task instances is reduced, which is implied in Fig. 2.6. When varying the distribution change frequency f, both the throughput and latency of *Readj* change dramatically. In particular, *Readj* works well only in the case with less distribution variance (smaller f). On the contrary, our *Mixed* algorithm always performs well, with performance very close to the optimal bound set by *Ideal*.

On *Social* data, we implement a simple word count topology on Storm, with upstream instances distributing tuples to downstream instances for store and aggregation on keywords. On *Stock* data, a self-join on the data over sliding window is implemented, which maintains the recent tuples based on the size of the window over intervals. The resulting throughputs are presented in Fig. 2.17. The most important observation is that the best throughput, on both of the workloads, is achieved by running *Mixed* with $\theta_{max} = 0.02$, implying that strict load balancing is beneficial to system performance. *Mixed* also presents a huge performance advantage over the other two approaches, with throughput about 2 times better than *Storm* and *Readj* at smaller θ_{max} in Fig. 2.17(b). The performance of *Readj* improves by relaxing the load balancing condition, catching up with the throughput of *Mixed* at $\theta_{max} = 0.3$ (or $\theta_{max} = 0.15$) on *Social* (or *Stock*). This is because *Readj* works only when the system allows fair imbalance among the computation tasks, for example $\theta_{max} = 0.3$. MinTable does not care about migration cost and then it incurs larger migration volume, which reduces the throughput of the system during the process of adjustment. PKG splits keys into smaller granularity and distributes them to different tasks selectively. Therefore, throughput of PKG is independent of the choice of θ_{max}, validated by the results in Fig. 2.17(a). The throughput of PKG is worse than *Mixed*, because its processing involves coordination between two operators. Despite its excellent performance on load balancing, the overhead of partial result merging leads to response time increase and overall processing throughput reduction. Overall, as shown in Fig. 2.17(a), when $\theta_{max} = 0.02$, our method outperforms PKG on throughput by 10% and on response latency by 40%. Moreover, we emphasize that PKG cannot

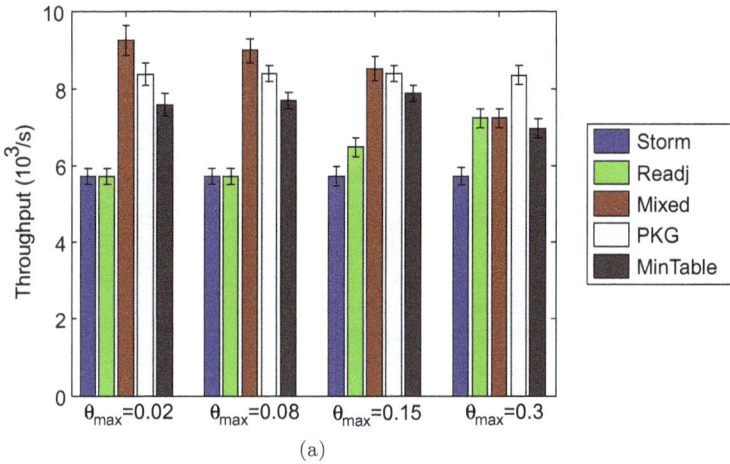

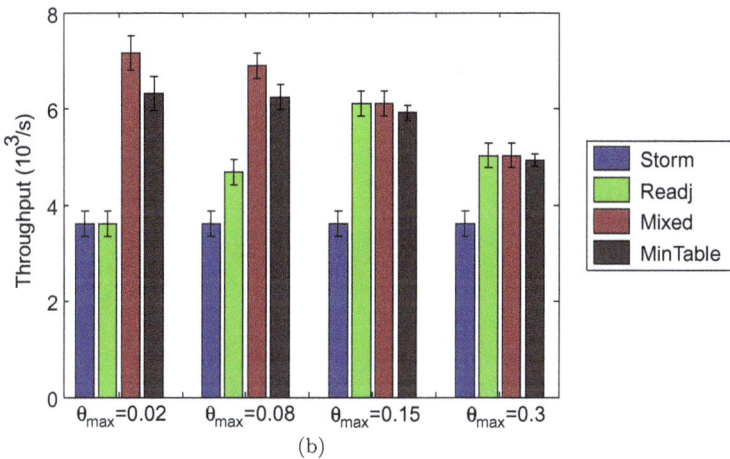

Fig. 2.17. Throughput on real data. (a) *Social* data and (b) *stock* data.

be used for complex processing logics, such as join, and therefore is not universally applicable to all stream processing jobs.

2.6.6 *Scalability*

To better understand the performance of the approaches in action, we present the dynamics of the throughput over time on two real workloads,

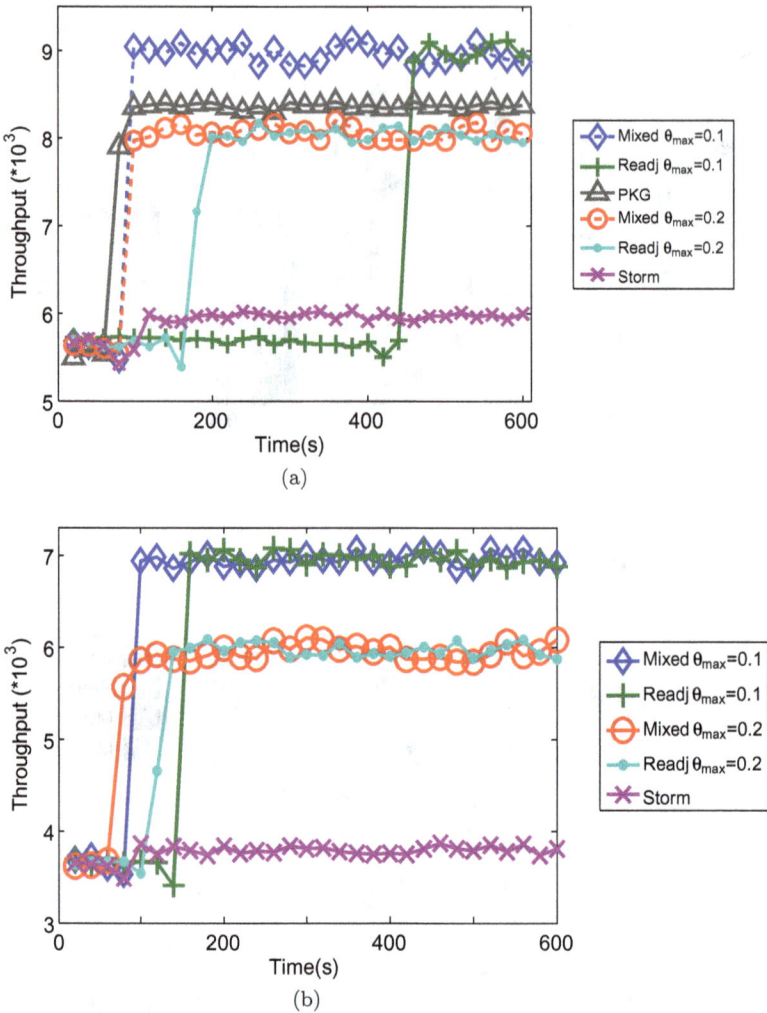

Fig. 2.18. Performance during system scale out. (a) *Social* data and (b) *stock* data.

especially when the system scales out the resource by adding a new computation resource to the operator. The results are available in Fig. 2.18. In order to test this kind of scale out ability of different algorithms, we run the stream system to a balance status, and then add one more working thread (instance) to the system starting the balance processing algorithms. The results show that our method *Mixed* perfectly rebalances the system within a much shorter response time than that of *Readj*. Though PKG is θ_{max} insensitive, it produces a lower throughput than *Mixed* while $\theta_{max} = 0.1$. Following the explanation shown in Fig. 2.17(a), PKG needs to keep track of all the derived data from a spout until it receives ack response and this action exacerbates its processing latency. On *Social* data with $\theta_{max} = 0.10$, *Readj* takes at least 5 min to generate the migration plan for the new thread added to the system. Such a delay leads to huge resource waste, which is definitely undesirable in cloud-based streaming processing applications. Similar results are also observed in *Stock*. The quick response of *Mixed* makes it a much better option for real systems.

2.6.7 *Dynamicity*

We run E_{Q_5} on the generated dataset for 1 h and set window size as 5 min since the join operations in E_{Q_5} are implemented by different processing operators. The data imbalance slows down the previous join operator (upstream instances) and suspends the processing on downstream join operators. This bad consequence of such suspension may be amplified with the growing number of task instances. In particular, we test the effects by triggering the distribution change every 15 min with $f = 1$. The results are shown in Fig. 2.19. Without any balancing strategy, *Storm* presents poor throughputs. *Mixed* is capable of balancing the workload in an efficient manner and achieving the best throughput under any balancing tolerance.

The basic idea of *Readj* is trying to move back the keys to the destinations indicated by hash function during each round of balancing, which results in migration schedules on keys with relatively larger workload. In addition, the computation complexity of the *Readj* algorithm, which is based on brute force searching, is higher than our proposed algorithm. This is why *Readj* leads to lower throughput and higher latency than ours when key distribution changing frequency f becomes large, as shown in Fig. 2.16, or under general dynamic scenarios, as illustrated in Figs. 2.17–2.19.

In practice, how to set θ_{max} is a non-trivial problem, because there are obvious operational trade-offs. For example, a smaller value of θ_{max} helps to increase the resource usage, overall throughput and processing efficiency, (shown in Figs. 2.17–2.19), but also increases the computation cost of the proposed key reassignment algorithm, and the migration costs when the key distribution changes frequently (as shown in Fig. 2.8). Additionally, θ_{max}

(a)

(b)

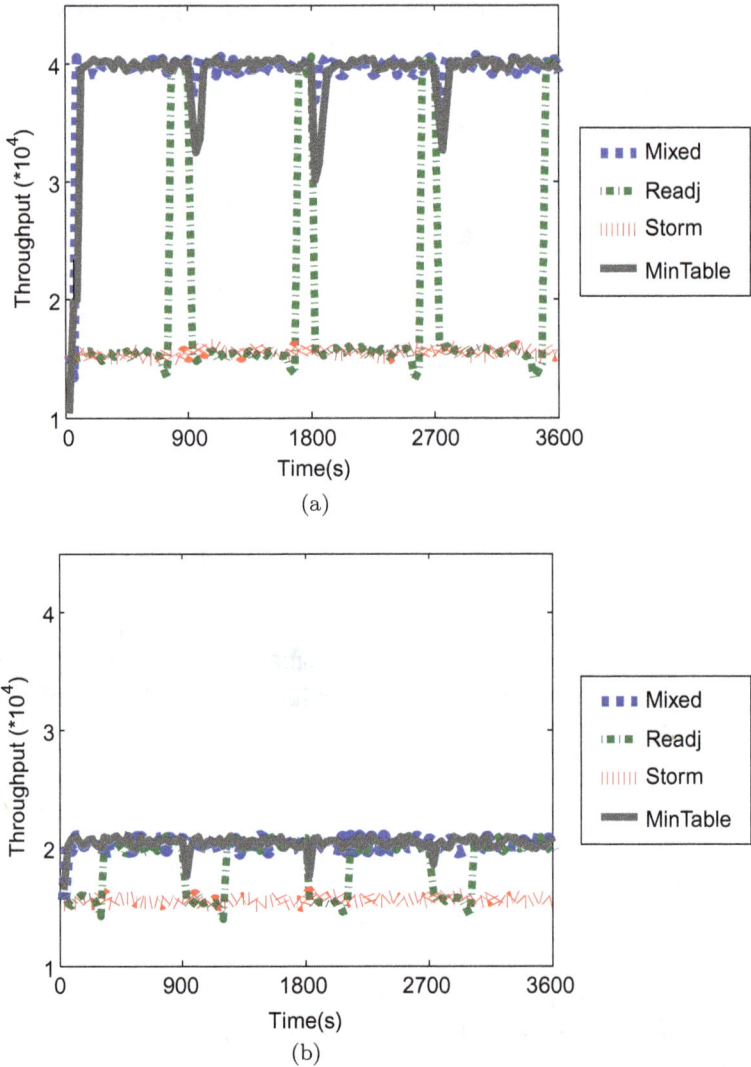

Fig. 2.19.   Dynamic adjustment on TPC-H data for E_{Q_5}. (a) $\theta_{max} = 0.1$ and (b) $\theta_{max} = 0.2$.

is relative to the average load level configured for each task instance, too. For example, a larger θ_{max} with higher probability leads to task instance overloading when the average CPU usage is above 90%. In practice, the administrator can adjust the value of θ_{max} whenever the requirements on the system performance specified by the users are not fulfilled.

2.7 Summary

This chapter presents a new dynamic workload distribution mechanism for intra-operator load balancing in distributed stream processing engines. Our mixed distribution strategy is capable of assigning the workload evenly over task workers of an operator under short-term workload fluctuations. New optimization techniques are introduced to improve the efficiency of the approach to enable practical implementation over mainstream stream processing engines. Our tests on the Apache Storm platform show excellent performance improvement with a variety of workloads from real applications, also presenting a huge advantage over existing solutions on both system throughput and response latency.

Chapter 3

Workload Balance by Key Splitting

3.1 Motivation and Basic Idea

3.1.1 *Basic idea*

Online and real-time analysis on stream data is essential for an increasing number of applications, such as stock trading aggregating, hot topic detection and network information monitoring. For example, it is necessary for Twitter to capture and analyze user comments on hot topics in time, which is of great benefit to learn public opinion, suppress rumors and put in advertisements. With the development of communication technology and hardware services, the explosive growth of data poses great challenges to traditional centralized processing architecture. Generally, there are two kinds of load balancing strategies, namely operator-based and data-based load adjustment. Operator-based strategy is specially designed for the early stream processing systems where the basic load distribution unit is the operator. Due to the disparity of runtime and complexity among different operations, some execution plan may result in a single node processing multiple complex operations, which directly leads to load imbalance. Data-based strategy, intuitively, is designed for stream processing systems which use initial data as a basic load distribution unit. According to distribution granularity, existing solutions can be divided into the following two types:

(1) **Key as Granularity:** During load balancing adjustment, it needs to transfer all the status related to a key while maintaining the semantics of key-based operation. *Readj* is a typical representative.

(2) **Tuple as Granularity:** In this domain, parallel processing tasks are mainly organized in the form of customized structures, and tuples are randomly distributed to each processing task. Random distribution has fundamentally solved load imbalance problems caused by data skew. However, it may lead to some operational limitations. For example, the matrix model organizes the processing tasks as a matrix, which supports θ-join and promises excellent load balancing, but consumes large memory space and network bandwidth. Lin *et al.* (2015) adopted a complete bipartite graph to organize processing tasks, which is memory efficient but supports equi-join and only a small range of θ-join.

In summary, data-based strategies face the following challenges: (1) Key as granularity can maintain key-based semantics to the utmost, but usually does not perform well for system equilibrium since the skewed key distribution of workload may break the balancing status among the parallel processing tasks. (2) Tuple as granularity is in favor of system equilibrium, but it pays an extra cost for maintaining the correctness of key-based semantics. For example, aggregation always adds one more layer in processing topology to merge the final results. Furthermore, the join operation will inevitably incur more cost such as redundant data duplication and distribution path tracing.

Furthermore, the data are time-sensitive in many areas, which means the "freshness" of the data becomes the deterministic factor affecting their value. The DSPE has been playing an essential role in the real-time applications, such as online detection of the instrument malfunction in the telecommunication station controller, quick detection of fraudulence in financial markets and real-time integration of multi-source personal data. To preserve the "freshness" of the input data, such a stream processing system has to be highly efficient in data processing and invulnerable to system faults. However, due to the inherent weaknesses of the distributed system on workload balancing and system faults, the current research on workload balancing and fault tolerance in DSPEs has already become an indispensable part in the development of stream processing systems.

Nevertheless, achieving both high efficiency and high availability is a challenging task. Hitherto, the existing optimizations could only take either workload balancing or fault tolerance as the single optimization objective. Specifically, the main ideas of those solutions are categorized as follows:

- **Workload balancing:** Workload skewness and variance are common phenomena in distributed stream processing engines. When massive stream data flood into a distributed system, even a slight distribution change in the incoming data stream may affect the system performance significantly. Traditional load balancing approaches attempt to balance the workload of the system by evenly assigning a variety of heterogeneous tasks to distributed nodes [Ahmad and Cetintemel (2004); Abadi *et al.* (2005); Xing *et al.* (2005, 2006); Khandekar *et al.* (2009)]. The existing strategies consist of two classes, namely the operator-based and the data-based strategies. The operator-based strategies [Xing *et al.* (2005, 2006); Khandekar *et al.* (2009)] assume the basic computation units are operators, while data-based strategies [Lin *et al.* (2015); Elseidy *et al.* (2014); Nasir *et al.* (2015)] allow the system to repartition the workload according to the keys of the tuples in the stream.
- **Fault tolerance:** High availability is a key requirement of the stream processing systems [Cherniack *et al.* (2003)] since they process the live data which are continuous, dynamic and unpredictable. In particular, data stream usually does not allow the system to redo a process because the volume of those incoming data may be boundless and the state information cannot be stored in extenso. Furthermore, since a topology in a DSPE is usually distributed over a set of machines for high performance and scalability, the possibility of a node failure increases simultaneously. Two studies [Vishwanath and Nagappan (2010); Heinze *et al.* (2015)] estimated that the failure probability for an individual cloud host is 4% or 8%, respectively, which means it is very likely to experience failures during runtime. Existing fault-tolerant techniques can be classified into two major classes [Hwang *et al.* (2005)]: active replication and upstream backup. The active replication [Ghanbari *et al.* (2011); Balazinska *et al.* (2008); Hwang *et al.* (2008)] deploys two or more identical instances of the same operator on different hosts, while upstream backup [Castro Fernandez *et al.* (2013); Hwang *et al.* (2007); Qian *et al.* (2013)] restores the operator in case of any error based on a checkpoint of the current operator state and the output queue.

To achieve both high performance and high availability in one solution, it is straightforward to just combine the workload balancing and fault-tolerant strategies mentioned above. However, such a simple solution works at the expense of huge resource consumption since the parallel processing tasks in both active and duplication operators have to handle the workload imbalance caused by input data independently. Meanwhile, the current trend of research on both workload balancing and fault tolerance starts to focus on a finer granularity. Specifically, in terms of the workload balancing, the current key-based methods are more resource sensitive and flexible in responding to the dynamic data flows compared with operator-based strategies. In the work of fault tolerance, the backup granularity from big to small can be divided into cluster based [Heath *et al.* (2002); Schroeder and Gibson (2010)], logical operator based [Salama *et al.* (2015); Upadhyaya *et al.* (2011)] and execution thread based [Su and Zhou (2016); Jacques-Silva *et al.* (2011)], and it is no doubt that a finer backup granularity makes the system more adaptive to the duplicate contents it wants. Therefore, based on our previous investigations, we propose a solution that integrates the workload balancing and fault-tolerant mechanisms which balance the workload in the key granularity and backup the process through active replications. The advantages of such a combination are as follows:

(1) **Cheaper workload balancing cost:** In the distributed stream processing system, the degree of the workload imbalance is determined by multiple factors, such as the key cardinality, the degree of data skewness and the number of parallel processing instances, as discussed in our previous work in Fang *et al.* (2017). In particular, the degree of workload imbalance is in proportion to the instance number and skewness degree of the incoming data while inversely proportional to the key cardinality. Therefore, the existence of the duplication can be deemed to be a way to enlarge the key cardinality, which in turn relieves the data skewness in parallel instances and therefore reduces the frequency of migration action.

(2) **More flexible fault-tolerant model:** Note that the backup granularity determines the flexibility of the fault-tolerant strategy. For instance, the node-based backup strategy guarantees that the backup contents

of a node are located in another node for the sake of the stability and availability of recourse [Schneider (1990)], and the task-based backup strategy provides a finer fault-tolerant granularity which enables the system to back up the contents based on a specific operation [Su and Zhou (2016)]. The task-based backup strategy, in contrast, is a more flexible way to ensure system fault tolerance while providing more room for utilizing available resources and a lower recovery latency. In this chapter, we propose a data-based backup strategy which is the finest granularity enabling system backup according to the specific content to provide the most flexible fault-tolerant solution.

Although a finer granularity of fault-tolerant mechanism can provide the aforementioned advantages, it raises new challenges for the distributed system regarding solutions to handle the dynamic of data stream while maintaining a high resource utilization rate at any time. In our solution, to accomplish the integration of the fault-tolerant mechanism on a data level, we have to tackle the following questions:

(Q1) How to distribute the active and backup data to ensure the system correctness during the processing stage or after the task failure occurs.

(Q2) When the workload among parallel processing task instances is imbalanced, how to generate a lightweight computing model to repartition states among parallel tasks to rebalance the workload.

(Q3) How to create migration plans for a set of involved tasks as quickly as possible especially for computationally heavy tasks with limited migration capacity.

In this chapter, we focus on load imbalance caused by data skew in DSPEs and propose a flexible and adaptive load balancing adjustment strategy. To rebalance the system, we develop a novel partitioning method that is effective during the changing of workloads where the domain of partitioning key may be large and data distribution may be very skewed and dynamic. Furthermore, we propose a fine-grained fault-tolerant strategy for economical resource utilization on the premise of efficient data recovery. By considering both workload balancing and fault tolerance, our proposed method can achieve low recovery latency with efficient balance processing. Overall, the technical contributions of this chapter include the following:

(1) We adopt a hybrid routing policy composed of an implicit hash function and an explicit routing table for data distribution, and always choose tasks with minimal load to maintain good balance. (2) We propose two simple balancing algorithms and a hybrid one which is based on the idea of "Split keys on demand and merge keys as far as possible" and is resilient to skewed workload distribution. The choice for the kind of strategy is decided by users. We provide an accurate analysis on the cost and effectiveness of our proposed algorithms. (3) We design a fault-tolerant framework that combines workload balancing at the same time, which leads the workload balancing and fault-tolerant mechanisms to a "mutually beneficial and win–win" situation with each other, and conducive to the generation of rebalancing strategies, reduction of migration costs and more flexible backup strategies. (4) We propose a rebalance approach that takes into account the fault-tolerant mechanism. In the premise of workload balance, we select the primary and secondary data storage locations in a location-sensitive manner and selectively activate the backup data for fault tolerance to reduce the migration cost. (5) We present a concise data structure for identifying activities and backup actions, and design a data routing solution to ensure the correctness of the system's operations, while making the system scalable, effective and efficient. (6) We implement our algorithms on Storm and compare our proposed techniques with existing methods by extensive experiments on abundant synthetic and real datasets.

The rest of this chapter is organized as follows: We first introduce the motivations of this work. Section 3.2 reviews a wide spectrum of related studies on stream join and workload balancing in distributed systems. In Section 3.3, we introduce the background knowledge and concepts used throughout the rest of chapter. Section 3.4 discusses the cost of our model. Section 3.5 presents our load balancing algorithms. Section 3.6 presents integrating workload balancing with fault tolerance. Section 3.7 presents practical verification and study. Section 3.8 finally concludes the chapter.

3.1.2 *Motivation*

In our previous work [Fang *et al.* (2017)], we presented a detailed theoretical analysis of the relation between imbalance degree and key/task workload granularity. Based on those theories, we summarize the motivations of introducing workload balancing in solving the fault-tolerant problem as follows.

- **Motivation 1: Easier workload balancing.** It is easier to apply workload balancing strategies on the data containing multiple replications. Considering our workload balancing solution proposed in Abadi *et al.* (2005), the advantages lie in two aspects: (1) the balancing plan can be calculated in a much easier manner; (2) the data migration cost can be reduced. In terms of the balancing plan, Fig. 3.1 shows the workloads of six different tasks under various levels of fault tolerance. Specifically, six different keys(k_{1-6}), whose loads are 7, 5, 4, 2, 1, 1, respectively, are sent to d_1 and d_2. The average load is 10 for each task, and the tasks are required to be *absolute balanced* ($\theta_{max} = 0$), which means both tasks should have the same workload, equivalent to the average $\bar{L} = 10$. Figure 3.1(a) demonstrates the idea of the task-level fault-tolerant method. In order to satisfy

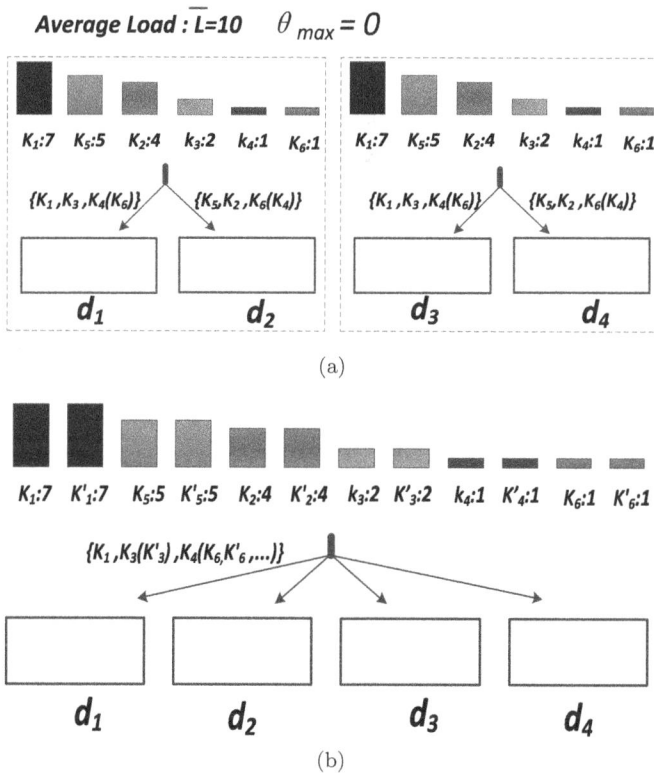

(a)

(b)

Fig. 3.1. Workload balance under different fault-tolerant methods. (a) Task-based fault tolerance and (b) data-based fault tolerance.

the fault-tolerant property, it first introduces two more tasks d_3 and d_4 to save the replicated data. In the task-level fault-tolerant method, d_3 and d_4 store the exact copy of d_1 and d_2, respectively. In particular, according to the *absolute balanced* requirement, one possible solution is to send $\{k_1, k_3, k_4(k_6)\}$ to $d_1(d_3])$ and send $\{k_5, k_2, k_6(k_4)\}$ to $d_2(d_4)$. However, Fig. 3.1(b) demonstrates the idea of the data-level fault-tolerant method. In this method, d_{1-4} play the same role and we make a copy of k_{1-5} into k'_{1-5}. Then, we apply our load balancing method among 10 keys and four tasks. In this case, the number of possible solutions increases significantly since more keys and tasks help to make a viable plan more easily. The data migration cost can also be reduced due to the fact that some of the data migration, like moving the data from a task that has active data to a task containing replicas, can be avoided by switching the active/inactive state between the data and the replicas.

- **Motivation 2: More flexible replication strategy.** A finer granularity of fault-tolerant strategy enables the sensitivity of data features. It is obvious that data replication increases the system workload; however, since the importance of the data varies in different applications, replication is compulsory in many scenarios, and the number of replicas varies with its importance as well. In other words, although processed through the same procedure, different data sources can produce different values. For instance, services that provide multiple purchase options care more about the users who spend more, which means data that potentially bring more profit (generated by VIP users) are more valuable to the service providers. Moreover, the online video websites make money by adding real-time ads, and the website income is determined by the difference between the profit gained by user clicks and costs paid to the video provider. For higher profit, the video websites must determine the priority between recommending videos or ads by monitoring the click rates of related videos and ads in real time. However, since different videos and ads vary in price, a fault-tolerant system is required that deals with them differently, which means the system tends to ensure more safety to the video and ad information with higher profit potential. Hence, decreasing the fault-tolerant granularity to data level can help generate more flexible data-based replication strategies. Therefore, the data can be copied more selectively so as to achieve low latency recovery while maintaining a low system cost.

- **Motivation 3: Lower recovery latency.** Data-level recovery is more efficient due to two reasons: (1) less data to recover and (2) parallel recovery process. As shown in Fig. 3.1, assuming the task d_1 fails and we start the recovery process, the task-based fault-tolerant method, shown in Fig. 3.1(a), has to activate the backup task d_3 and replace the failed task d_1. Meanwhile, to ensure the correctness, the system must update the data in d_3 to the same state in d_1 before its failure. Specifically, the system should update the state of key $\{k_5, k_2, k_6(k_4)\}$. Figure 3.1(b) shows the idea of data-level fault tolerance, since task d_1 contains both active keys and backup keys; after the failure of it, the recovery process only focuses on the state of those active data which contribute to the results. Therefore, the total amount of data to recover is just part of the task capacity. In Fig. 3.1(b), the recovery process of failed task d_1 is to send the state of all its active data to the corresponding backups and activate them. Since the backup data are located in different tasks, this step can be done in parallel, which significantly reduces the time spent in synchronization.

Based on the above discussion, the data-level fault tolerance can not only simplify the workload balancing process between parallel tasks, which increases the system throughput, but can also reduce the overhead of system recovery by partially replicating data and recovering data state. However, the data-level fault-tolerant method still faces a few challenges: (1) the consistency of the recovered data state, (2) the routing mechanism between the active and backup data, and (3) making a reasonable load balancing plan. Hence, this chapter focuses on proposing the data-level fault-tolerant solution. We aim to design a workload balanced fault-tolerant method which guarantees the system correctness. By locating the main/backup data properly and activating the backup wisely, our system aims to reduce the migration cost during the workload balancing process after the system failure.

3.2 Related Work and Literature

Different from distributed batch processing database systems, due to data skew and inherent stream features such as dynamics and unpredictability, load imbalance happens and puts great pressure on distributed stream processing systems. In the past few decades, much effort has been devoted to designing algorithms to cope with the rapid growth of stream data. There have been two types of data-based strategies, namely tuple-based and key-based data distribution.

Since the increasing of stream data, a processing task can easily run out of computation resources. Distributed stream processing over the shared-nothing architecture has been a scalable processing candidate. However, if we do not have the global task processing cost information or data skew information, workload distribution will meet with imbalance. It will bring down the whole processing ability, e.g., low throughput or high latency. Dynamic load balancing technology is essential for promising system usability. Existing work usually splits high performance and high availability in real-time processing systems into two parts:

- **Workload balance:** Generally, there are two kinds of balancing mechanisms: *operator-level* and *data-level*. The operator-level balancing migrates the whole operator from one task to another, with the assumption that each operator can be assigned to one machine. In contrast, the data-level balancing groups the data into migration units and processes them separately during the runtime. (1) In terms of the operator-level balancing, the basic System S [Wolf *et al.* (2008)] performs the scheduling during the job submission. It then migrates the jobs or sub-jobs to machines with less load during runtime according to the task workload, operator workload and the priority of the applications. Khandekar *et al.* (2009) combined multiple operators to reduce communication. In order to improve the balance property of storm, Aniello *et al.* (2013) presented a more flexible method which included online and offline ways to minimize the network traffic. (2) Regarding the data-level balancing, Lin *et al.* (2015) and Elseidy *et al.* (2014) both primarily focused on designing a distributed scalable stream join processing model. Elseidy *et al.* (2014) designed an adaptive balancing strategy on the square matrix, each side of which corresponded to the partitions of one relation. To avoid high usage of memory and network, Lin *et al.* (2015) proposed a join-biclique model that takes a large cluster as a complete bipartite graph for joining big data streams. For key grouping, Nasir *et al.* (2015, 2016) introduced a new stream partitioning scheme for balanced key grouping, namely Partial Key Grouping (PKG). This solution applies the power of the *two-choices approach* to provide better load balancing. Gedik (2014) introduced a partitioning function which consists of a basic consistent hash function and an explicit hash to solve the stateful load balance problem. Katsipoulakis *et al.* (2017) book both tuple imbalance and aggregation cost into account to partition an incoming stream. Rupprecht *et al.* (2017) conducted lazy partitioning to deal with transient network skew among clusters adaptively to avoid the straggling workers prolonging the join completion time.

- **Fault tolerance:** In DSPEs, traditional fault-tolerant methods, including active backup, passive backup or upstream backup, usually apply to all operations in the application in order to gain low latency recovery performance. LAAR [Bellavista *et al.* (2014)] provides *a priori* guarantees about the achievable levels of fault tolerance, expressed by an internal completeness metric that captures the maximum amount of information that can be lost in case of failures. Su and Zhou (2016, 2017) proposed a new fault-tolerant framework, which is Passive and Partially Active (PPA). In a PPA scheme, the passive approach is applied to all tasks while only a selected set of tasks will be actively replicated. The number of actively replicated tasks depends on the capacity of available resources. If tasks without active replicas fail, tentative outputs will be generated before the completion of the recovery process. Noghabi *et al.* (2017) used the *Host Affinity* mechanism to reduce the overheads of the rebuilding state for a restarted task. This mechanism can reduce the restart time to a constant value, rather than linearly growing with the state size. Salama *et al.* (2015) selected a subset of intermediates to be materialized such that the total query runtime is minimized under mid-query failures. FTOpt [Upadhyaya *et al.* (2011)] is a cost-based fault-tolerant optimizer. It automatically selects the best strategy for each operator in a query plan in a manner that minimizes the expected processing time with failures for the entire query. Similar to the upstream backup, the TimeStream [Qian *et al.* (2013)] uses a recovery mechanism that tracks which upstream data each operator depends on and replays them serially through a new copy of the operator. In contrast, D-Streams [Zaharia *et al.* (2013)] uses stateless transformations and explicitly put state in data structures (RDDs) which forgo conventional streaming wisdom by batching data into small timesteps.

3.3 Preliminaries

This section describes the basic knowledge of key grouping, outlines a hybrid routing policy, defines the terms and notations used in the rest of this chapter, and illustrates resource utilization during load balancing.

3.3.1 *Key grouping*

Stream is an unbounded sequence of data items (tuples) in the form $\langle k, v, t \rangle$ ordered by the timestamp t, where k is the tuple's key and v is the value. To improve the effectiveness of stream processing, it tends to partition a stream into disjoint sub-streams and assign them to parallel task instances for concurrent processing. Key Grouping (KG) has gained much attention and in most cases it maps a key domain to task instances using a global hash function. Analogous to MapReduce, KG can ensure that tuples with the same key are assigned to the same task, so that there is no need to space extra cost for tracing distribution paths of keys.

If we have uniform workload distribution among tasks, KG works well. However, when workloads are skewed on keys, KG may result in high-load imbalance among parallel processing tasks. In Fig. 3.2, we give an example to illustrate the potential problem of such a partitioning method. Tuples from data source are distributed by a *Routing Operator* to *Joining Operator* using hash function $F(key)$, and join results are collected in *Merging Operator*. Due to high frequency of some keys, the first task instance in *Joining Operator* is delegated workload twice more than the others and gets overloaded. As a result, *Merging Operator* is suspended to wait for task completion in *Joining Operator*, slowing all the processing down.

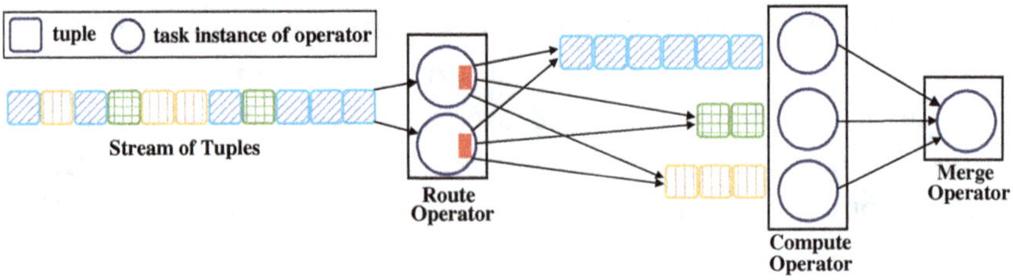

Fig. 3.2.   A skewed key distribution leads to load imbalance when partitioning the workload by key grouping. Tuples of same color have the same key.

3.3.2 *Hybrid routing policy*

When load imbalance happens, it is an intuitive way to migrate a certain quantity of workload from overloaded tasks to underloaded ones. As illustrated in Fig. 3.3, we unload two tuples from the first task in *Joining Operator* and migrate them to the second and third tasks. In order to ensure the computation correctness, it is necessary to keep track of keys that have been migrated during load balancing adjustment.

In this section, we adopt a hybrid policy that combines a basic hash function and an explicit routing table. The basic hash function takes the key as input and returns a corresponding task ID. It can be uniform hashing, consistent hashing and so on. The routing table is used for keys that have been migrated and each task instance which is responsible for data distribution should maintain a routing table in memory.

Our routing table has more direction information. Specifically, we define a routing item in the table as $\langle k, \{d\} \rangle$ where k is a key and $\{d\}$ is a set of tasks which stores the key. Keys in the routing table will not be routed by the basic hashing function. There are two cases when a key shall be added to the routing table: (1) If tuples with key k are migrated wholly to a certain task d and $d \neq F(k)$, k and d need to be added. (2) If tuples with key k are split and separately stored in several tasks, then k and all the tasks containing k need to be added. Figure 3.3 shows the overall operator structure. There are three classes of operators: a routing operator is responsible for distributing tuples, a joining operator is in charge of actual computation, while a merging operator merges and reports final results.

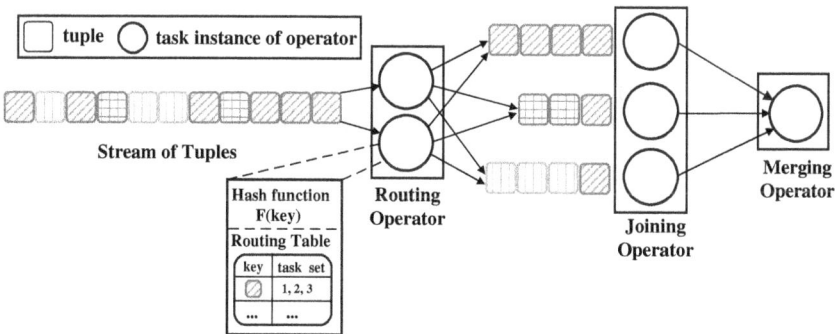

Fig. 3.3. Hybrid routing policy.

Before the *Routing Operator* distributes a tuple, it first checks whether the key of the tuple exists in the routing table. If it exists, the task with minimal load among the set $\{d\}$ will store that key; otherwise, basic hash function is applied to get the destination task.

3.3.3 *Definition of related terms*

If key k does not exist in the routing table and it is routed to task $d = F(k)$ by the basic hashing function, then task d is called *basic task* of key k. To facilitate the description of load balancing adjustment strategies in the rest of the chapter, several operations are defined as follows:

- **Migrate back:** This operation migrates a key which is not stored in its basic task back to its basic task.
- **Migrate to:** This operation migrates a key from one task to another. Neither of these two tasks is its basic task.
- **Migrate out:** This operation migrates a key from its basic task to some other task.

Among the three operations above, *Migrate Back* can reduce the number of mapping entries in the routing table, whereas *Migrate Out* adds new entries to the routing table and increases table size. *Migrate To* has no influence on routing table size.

During load balancing adjustment, the impacts of these operations on the key status can be classified into three types as follows:

- **Split:** The operation only migrates a certain quantity of tuples with key k to other tasks.
- **Merge:** The operation assembles tuples with the same key that are separately stored in different tasks into one task.
- **Whole Move:** Contrary to Split, the operation migrates entire tuples with a key from one task to the other.

3.4 Cost Model Analysis

Once load imbalance happens, load adjustment will be an inevitable action to improve system performance. A highly efficient migration strategy needs to minimize system cost while guaranteeing load balancing.

3.4.1 *Basic principle*

3.4.1.1 *System resource usage for load balance*

System resource generally includes CPU, memory and network. It is discovered that routing table size($routingtable$), migration volume($migration$) and broadcast volume($broadcast$) have great impacts on resource utilization. Here we use notation C_δ^τ to represent resource usage uniformly, where $\tau \in$ {routing table, migration,broadcast} and $\delta \in$ {CPU, Memory, Network}.

- **CPU and Memory Cost:** To ensure the correctness of processing, each task of the routing operator must maintain the same routing table in memory; for each tuple distributing to the processing operator, the routing operator checks if there exists an entry related to the key of tuple. Obviously, the larger routing table will require more memory and cost more look-up time. The CPU cost C_{cpu}^r is defined as $C_{\text{cpu}}^r = T \cdot |RT|$, where $|RT|$ is routing table size and equals $\sum_{k \in RT} |list_k|$, i.e.,$|list_k|$ is the size of all entries for key k. The memory consumption C_{mem}^r of the routing table is defined as $C_{\text{mem}}^r = N_r \cdot s \cdot |RT|$, where s represents the size of each entry in $list_k$. Then we get that $C_{\text{cpu}}^r \propto C_{\text{mem}}^r$.

- **Broadcast Cost:** The broadcast cost is produced by two phases during system running, namely (1) *subsequent input tuples* while the process is going on and (2) *migration states* when load adjustment occurs. Let us take join processing for example to show the impact from input tuples. For each key k separately stored in different tasks, incoming tuples with k must be broadcast to all these tasks to ensure result completeness. Hence, the broadcast operation puts pressure on the network. Then network cost C_{net}^b for broadcasting can be defined as $C_{\text{net}}^b = \sum_{k \in RT} D_k \cdot G_k$. Without loss of generality, during load adjustment, we only unload a certain quantity of keys out of overloaded tasks and migrate them to underloaded ones, not involving move-out operations on underloaded tasks. Hence, once load imbalance happens, no matter which key is chosen for migration, the total migration volume is the same (based on the key split method) and can be calculated as $C_{\text{net}}^m = \sum_{d \in UD}(L(d) - \frac{\sum_{d' \in D} L(d')}{N_d})$.

3.4.1.2 *Solution approach*

Our primarily goal is to improve system performance under workload imbalance, but minimize resource usage. As described above, we can draw a conclusion that routing table size and subsequent broadcast volume are two predominant factors affecting system resource usage. Without loss of generality, we use throughput to measure the influence of these two factors on system performance.

To achieve our goal, we propose to estimate the influence of these two factors on throughput first, which can be achieved by conducting massive experiments on varying routing table size and broadcast volume. Then we draw mapping relationships between them and throughput. Based on these two mapping relationships, we expect to get a fitting function considering both routing table size and broadcast volume, guiding to select keys to migrate under the current system environment.

3.5 Balance Algorithms with Key Splitting

In this section, we first introduce the overall load balancing adjustment framework. Then we apply a novel decision-making algorithm to select a strategy to achieve our goal. Finally, we present two types of adjustment strategies.

3.5.1 *Algorithm framework*

The algorithm of overall load balancing adjustment is described in Algorithm 3.1. First, average workload BL and maximized non-balance workload UL of downstream tasks are calculated in line 1. The parameter τ is the maximized imbalance degree of workload defined as $\frac{|L(d)-BL|}{BL}$. Once the workload of one task is more than UL, it is identified to be overloaded and needs to unload extra workload to underloaded tasks as in lines 4 and 7. Then, as described in line 2, a decision-making algorithm is applied Finally, the corresponding adjustment strategy will be executed.

Broadcast volume and routing table size are two main factors influencing system performance. Therefore, decision-making algorithm combines both factors. It takes a combine function which represents a mapping relationship between broadcast volume and routing table size. The function takes the accumulated broadcast volume since the last adjustment as input

---

Algorithm 3.1 Overall Load Balancing Adjustment Framework

---

input: processing tasks D, broadcast volume $\sum_{u \in U} broadcast$, routing table size RTS

output: Migration plan MP and routing table RT

1: $BL \leftarrow \frac{\sum_{d \in D} L(d)}{N_d}$; $UL \leftarrow BL \cdot (1 + \tau_{max})$
2: **if** splitOrWhole($\sum_{u \in U} broadcast, RTS$) equals to *Split* **then**
3:     **foreach** each task d in D **do**
4:         **if** $L(d) > UL$ **then** splitAtFirstAdjustment(d)
5: **else**
6:     **foreach** each task d in D **do**
7:         **if** $L(d) > UL$ **then** wholeAtFirstAdjustment(d)
8: **return** MP and RT

---

and returns a corresponding routing table size. If the returned value is bigger than the current routing table size, it applies *split-keys-at-first* strategy; otherwise, it applies *whole-move-keys-at-first* strategy.

3.5.2 Split-keys-at-first load balancing strategy

A migration plan defines how to migrate data among tasks when load imbalance happens, which is formalized as $MP = \langle k, d_{\text{from}}, d_{\text{to}}, qty \rangle$. It migrates tuples with key k from task d_{from} to d_{to} with the quantity of qty. Usually the adjustment procedure can be decomposed into two steps, as shown in Algorithm 3.2:

- **Step-1 — Data unload:** It first unloads partial data to a temporary storage buffer C until the load of overloaded task d is lower than average workload BL as in lines 3–10 in Algorithm 3.2. The keys on overloaded tasks are arranged in decreasing order based on their loads in line 1. When starting the unloading, if the load of key k is lower than the difference between task load $L(d)$ and average load BL, the entire tuple with k will be buffered in C and deleted from task d. Besides, if $\langle k, (d, \#) \rangle$ entry exists in the routing table, it must be deleted as in line 5, or else partial tuples with k will be buffered and will update the load of k in task d. Similarly, if $\langle k, (d, \#) \rangle$ entry exists in the routing table, it must be updated; otherwise, a new entry will be added as in line 9.

Algorithm 3.2 splitAtFirstAdjustment()

---

input: The key load set $KL = \{(key, load)\}$ of overloaded task d

output: Migration Plan MP and routing table RT

1: Arrange KL in decreasing order on key load; $C \leftarrow \emptyset$

2: **foreach** each key load entry $(k, l) \in KL$ **do**

3:     **if** $L(d) - BL > l$ **then** Add (k, l) to C; Delete (k, l) from KL

4:         **if** $< k, (d, \#) >$ exists in RT **then** // # is the proportion of data for k

5:             Delete $< k, (d, \#) >$ from RT

6:     **else**

7:         $\delta \leftarrow L(d) - BL$; Add (k, δ) to C; Replace (k, l) as $(k, l - \delta)$ in set KL

8:         **if** $< k, (d, \#) >$ exists in RT **then** Replace $< k, (d, l - \delta) >$ in RT

9:         **else** Add $< k, (d, l - \delta) >$ to RT

10:         **break**

11: **foreach** each temporary storage entry $(k, l) \in C$ **do**

12:     Choose a task d' which is underloaded

13:     **if** $BL - L(d') > l$ **then** $\delta \leftarrow l$; Delete (k, l) from C

14:     **else** $\delta \leftarrow BL - L(d')$; Replace (k, l) as $(k, l - \delta)$ in set C

15:     **if** key k exists in task d' **then** $\delta \leftarrow \delta + l'$ // l' is the load of k in d'

16:     Add $< k, d, d', \delta >$ to MP; Add $< k, (d', \delta) >$ to RT

17: **return** MP and RT

- **Step-2 — Data load:** After unloading operation, it loads the data in C to each underloaded task instance as in lines 11–16. If load of key k in temporary storage C is lower than the difference between load of an underloaded task $L(d')$ and average load BL, then it will be *whole moved* to task d' and deleted from C as in line 14; otherwise, it still needs to split k and move partial tuples with k in line 16.

3.5.3 *Whole-move-keys-at-first load balancing strategy*

Frequent key splitting may lead to massive subsequent network cost (e.g., for join). In this section, we present a whole-move-keys-at-first strategy

---

Algorithm 3.3 wholeAtFirstAdjustment()

---

input: The key load set $KL = \{(key, load)\}$ of overloaded task d

output: Migration Plan MP and routing table RT

1: Differentiate the key load set $KIT = \{(key, load)\}$ in which keys exist in the routing table

2: **foreach** each key load entry $(k, l) \in KIT$ **do**

3:     **if** $< k, (F(k), \#) >$ exists in RT **and** $L(F(k)) < BL$ **then**   Add $< k, d, F(k), l >$ to MP;Delete $< k, (d, \#) >$ from RT; Update $< k, (F(k), \#) >$ in RT

4:     **else if** $|list_k| > 1$ **then** //more than one entry in the list of key k in RT

5:         Choose a underloaded task d' that contains k

6:         Add $< k, d, d', l >$ to MP; Delete (k, l) from KIT

7:         Add $< k, (d', l + l') >$ to RT // l' is the load of k in d'

8:     **else**

9:         Choose a underloaded task d' that does not contain k

10:         Add $< k, d, d', l >$ to MP; Add $< k, (d', l) >$ to RT; Delete (k, l) from KIT

11: **foreach** each underloaded task d' **do**

12:     Arrange $KL - KIT$ in decreasing order on key load

13:     Choose a subset $SubKeys$ from $KL - KIT$ that $\sum_{k \in SubKeys} load_k \approx BL - L(d')$

14:     **foreach** each key load entry $(k, l) \in SubKeys$ **do**

15:         Add $< k, d, d', l >$ to MP; Add $< k, (d', \delta) >$ to RT; Delete (k, l) from $KL - KIT$

16: **if** $L(d) > BL$ **then**

17:     call splitAtFirstAdjustment() in Alg.3.2

18: **return** MP and RT

---

which tries to migrate entire tuples for a key of small granularity. The algorithm of this strategy is described in Algorithm 3.3 and can be divided into three steps as follows:

- **Step-1 — Whole move keys in routing table:** As shown in lines 2–10, it first assigns priorities to keys existing in the routing table. If the basic task $F(k)$ of key k exists in the list $list_k$ in the routing table, and the basic task $F(k)$ still has enough storage, then the *Migrate Back* operation is executed as in line 3. Besides, for current overloaded task d, the routing entry $(d, \#)$ is deleted from $list_k$. If the routing table does not contain entry for k, it invokes *Migrate Out* operation. If k is stored in more than one task, it prefers to merge tuples to one task containing k with enough free space; otherwise, it will be migrated to one task not containing k.

- **Step-2 — Whole move keys not in routing table:** If task d is still overloaded by step-1, it then copes with keys that are not in routing tables as in lines 14–15. For each underloaded task d', it selects a subset of keys and the total tuples of these keys are equal to the free storage of d'. The goal is to minimize the number of keys in such a subset. We take the approximate solutions for this problem. Before the selecting operation, we arrange keys that do not exist in the routing table in decreasing order on key loads. Then we use greedy algorithm to find out such a subset. Once a subset is returned, it needs to add or update the corresponding entries in the routing table and generate migration plans.
- **Step-3 — Split the remaining keys:** If necessary, the split operation will be executed as in line 17.

The whole-move-keys-at-first adjustment strategy focuses on migrating tuples with the same key as a whole. Though the routing table size may grow rapidly with more keys of smaller granularity to be migrated, we take the moving back or merging operations to control the rapid growth of the routing table size to a certain extent.

3.6 Integrating Workload Balancing with Fault Tolerance

3.6.1 *Fault-tolerant mechanism*

In this section, we first introduce how the data-level fault-tolerant method guarantees system correctness. Then we discuss the consistency issue in failure recovery and demonstrate our detailed fault-tolerant process.

3.6.1.1 *Synchronization protocols*

The system availability is determined by two factors: the synchronization process between the active and backup operations, and the recovery process after task failure. Note that the fault-tolerant strategy may differ according to the requirements from different operations and applications. For example, the *filter* and *map* operations usually deal with single data primitive, so the process of those operations is not affected by other procedures, while operations like *aggregation, join* and *union* are usually applied on multiple data sources, which require the timestamps of different data sources to follow the same sequence. To further understand the challenges of our solution, we now discuss the potential consequences of task failure on the system availability and consistency. Our discussion starts with both operation and data aspects. In terms of the time dependency of system output, the current operations can be categorized into two types: time-dependent and time-independent operations.

Definition 3.1. In data stream processing, an operation is called *time-dependent* operation if the process of the operation relies on the timestamps of the input data.

Definition 3.2. In data stream processing, an operation is called *time-independent* operation if the process of the operation does not rely on the timestamps of the input data.

The different time dependency feature requires a different synchronization level between active/backup data: If the operation is time dependent, the output result is strongly related to the time feature. On the contrary, if the operation is time independent, the system only needs to ensure that the calculation is correct and the data order is the same for both the main and backup tasks. Based on this, we define three synchronization protocols which can ensure the correctness of different operations.

The timestamp feature is indispensable in every stream data tuple. For some operators, if the data come in a muddled order, the processing result of the data sequence may vary from the actual result when the data come successively. For instance, in the *join* operation, if the disorder happens in either of the data sources, the join results may lose some of the records [Ji *et al.* (2016)]. Hence, we define the *data order synchronization* based on the data features.

Definition 3.3. For the data stream input, regardless of whether it is single sourced or multi sourced, if the tuples are increasingly input into an active/backup task according to their timestamps, such a stream sequence is termed as *data order guaranteed.*

If the active task fails, the system should activate its replica to ensure the output correctness. However, the synchronization between active and backup data usually determines the system availability and consistency [Balazinska *et al.* (2008); Upadhyaya *et al.* (2011)], i.e., strong synchronization reduces the system availability, while high availability will challenge the synchronization strategy. The following definitions describe the synchronization relationship between active and backup data during different processing stages:

Definition 3.4. In the stream data processing system, if the speed of the data input flows to active and backup operations is strongly synchronized, we call the main and backup data input *input synchronization.*

Definition 3.5. In the stream data processing system, if the operating progress between active and backup operations is strongly synchronized, we call the main and backup processing task *process synchronization.*

It is the prerequisite of process synchronization that the active/backup data are sent to processing tasks simultaneously. Meanwhile, the process synchronization is also the precondition of the downstream input synchronization. As for the aforementioned definitions, the time-dependent/independent types are used to categorize the operations, the data order guaranteed is to regulate the data input, while the input/process synchronization is to formalize the consistency issue during the active/backup data processing. In simple terms, as shown in Fig. 3.4, time-dependent applications require all the criteria of input/process synchronization and data

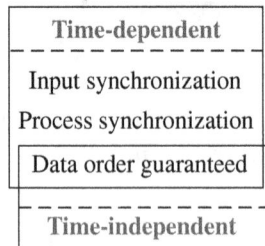

Fig. 3.4. The critical factors for fault-tolerant methods under different applications.

order guaranteed, while time-independent applications only need tuples in active and duplication has the same order to produce the correct results. Based on this, in the rest of this chapter, we describe our strategies including how to ensure input/process synchronization in Section 3.6.1.2 and data order in Section 3.6.1.3.

3.6.1.2 *Input/process synchronization*

The output results of the time-dependent operation are strongly related to the time feature (like real-time hot topics); in other words, the result will become invalid if it is processed later than the given time. Hence, making sure data flow rate and processing speed are all synchronized is the only way to ensure that the active/backup data can be switched with no delay. However, it is unrealistic to make sure the active and duplication states of each tuple are strongly synchronized both in input and processing procedure, which will incur significant synchronization cost for massive stream processing.

To avoid the significant synchronization cost caused by the continuous synchronization process, as shown in Fig. 3.5, we introduce a reconstruction mechanism for each computation state. This is similar to TimeStream [Qian *et al.* (2013)], which tracks the state and output dependencies for each vertex during the stream computation. In our computational state reconstruction mechanism, we take each tuple as the state reconstruction granularity and the dependency duplication tuples are maintained according to

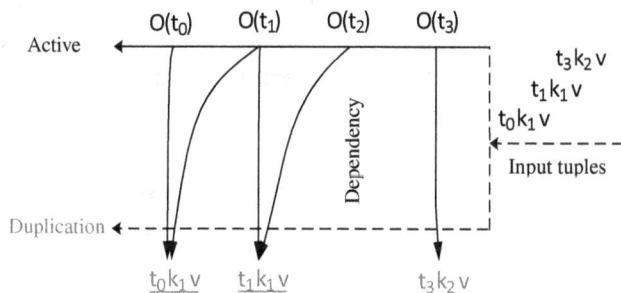

Fig. 3.5. Example of dependency relationship between active and duplication data streams with $w = 2$.

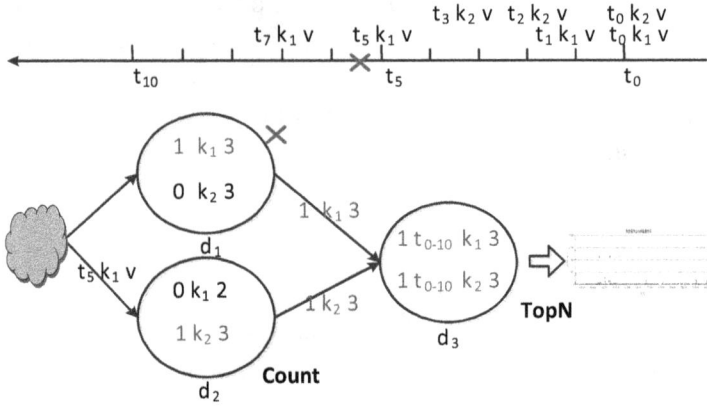

Fig. 3.6.   Example of recovery based on dependencies.

the real application. For instance, in Fig. 3.5, the output result O_{t_i} depends on a tuple with timestamp t_i and t_{i-1} when the window size is 2.

The example in Fig. 3.6 shows the recovery flow based on dependencies. Specifically, (t_x, k_y, V) represents a tuple that carries key k_y at time x, and V represents the rest of the information. In Fig. 3.6, the order of the data input is as follows: tuples carrying k_1 and k_2 are input at time t_0, a tuple with k_1 comes at t_1, t_2 has a tuple with k_2, a tuple k_2 comes at t_3, a tuple k_1 comes at t_5 .... The topology demonstrates two operations: the counting (Count) and the aggregation (TopN). The parallel degree of the counting operation is 2; hence, the k_1 is at an active state in d_1 and at a duplication state in d_2. On the contrary, k_2 is at an active state in d_2 and at a backup state in d_1. Assuming that the physical server containing task d_1 fails between t_5 and t_6, at that moment, the counting of k_1 in d_1 has been processed till t_5, and the counting result has been sent to the downstream task d_3 for aggregation. Meanwhile, due to the network latency, the backup state has not yet processed the tuple (t_5, k_1, V), meaning that the counting result only contains two tuples. Corresponding to the above analysis, if the TopN result is output in real time (i.e., the result of every operation is strictly time dependent), either input disordered, input delay or processing delay will cause the results from the main and backup data to be useless. However, if the data in Fig. 3.6 are time independent, i.e., the result is not necessarily synchronized with the timestamps (such as log data analysis), the data

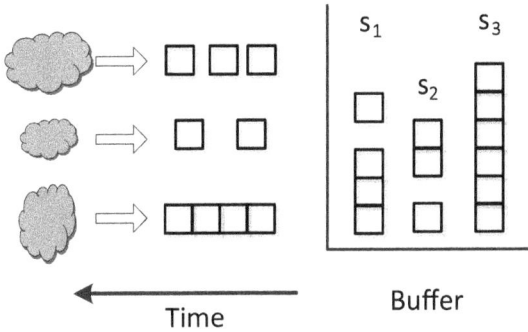

Fig. 3.7. Example of data stream inputting.

stream only needs to ensure that its data are monotonically increasing by the timestamps, and the synchronization of input and processing is not necessary. Figure 3.6 shows the case where the backup data arrive later than the active ones, which can be solved by simply preserving the state of the downstream operation(d_3). If the active data arrive later, we replace the state of downstream operation with the backup data state.

3.6.1.3 *Data order guarantee*

To solve the inputting tuples' synchronization issue as shown in Fig. 3.4, in this section, we introduce the operation-level data state synchronization solution, which is to ensure synchronization happens before each operation. As per the fault-tolerant method proposed in Balazinska *et al.* (2008), since each copy can provide service individually, the synchronization between copies should be strictly processed to ensure consistency. Different from the method in Balazinska *et al.* (2008), to ensure consistency between the main and backup data in terms of the input order, flow rate and processing speed, our data-level fault-tolerant method only sends active keys to the downstream tasks before the data are input into the system. We use a fix-sized cache to store and sort the input data sequence to negate its uncertainty. Figure 3.7 shows three different stream data inputs which are incrementally sorted by time in the cache. The cache size is determined by the quality of the data source. A larger cache will reduce the efficiency of the data process, while a smaller cache cannot handle an extremely disordered data source.

The buffer strategy shown in Fig. 3.7 guarantees the data order defined in Definition 3.3 and, meanwhile, ensures the recovery speed after the failure of a processing task. The detailed solution is to set up a buffer for each operation; as denoted by Fig. 3.7, each data source (S_{1-3}) in the buffer is sent from one upstream operation. Based on this buffer strategy, the system can be recovered by simply continuing the process or replacing the fault states, when the input or process inconsistency happens between the main and backup tasks. Specifically, if the backup task is slower than the active task in terms of the processing state, the recovery starts from the current state of the downstream task and continues updating it. If the backup task is faster, the recovery can be done by replacing the state in the active task with the state in the backup task. Now we are ready to discuss the recovery process after the task failure.

3.6.1.4   *Fault recovery*

As mentioned above, the data stream is a sequence of tuples formatted as $(t, k, v_1, v_2, \ldots)$ [Abadi *et al.* (2003)], t and k are the timestamps and key, respectively, while $v \in V$ represents the attributes carried by the tuple. For better understanding, we define a few additional symbols to better represent the state of a tuple, denoted as

$$(t, P_k, v_v, RN, AC, V^-).$$

In this representation, t is still the timestamps. P_k is the identifier used for tuple distribution, for example, P_k is the hashing result if the tuples are distributed by a hash function. v_v is the value indicator representing how valuable this tuple is, which is specified according to the user's description. Replica Number (RN) indicates that the number of replicas this tuple should have, which is determined by its value v_v. AC is a boolean value indicating its state, $AC = 1$ means this tuple is at an active state and its processing results should be sent to two downstream tasks as active and backup data and $AC = 0$ indicates that it is backup data which need no output action after being processed. Lastly, V^- is the actual information of this tuple.

Figure 3.8 shows the process of the main and backup data. For simplicity, we use the key itself to represent the tuples in Fig. 3.8. The keys in red or green are tuples with $AC = 1$, while the black ones are keys carrying $AC = 0$. All six different keys have one replica ($RN = 2$), and both the

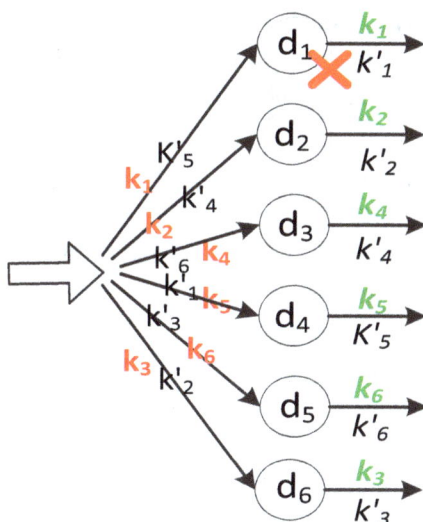

Fig. 3.8. Data-level fault-tolerant workflow.

active and backup one are sent to corresponding tasks by the same hash function. In accordance with the aforementioned representation, the tuple k_1 in Fig. 3.8 is represented as $(t, P_{k_1}, v_v, 2, 1, V^-)$ and k'_1 is represented as $(t, P_{k'_1}, v_v, 2, 0, V^-)$. The identifiers P_{k_1} and $P_{k'_1}$ will lead the tuples to different tasks. In the result output stage, only the red tuples are output to the downstream tasks, the output results include active (marked as green italic) and backup (marked as black italic) data. The routing and backup strategies are the same in the downstream tasks.

When the task failure happens, the data-level fault-tolerant method can recover the data through the following three steps:

- **Step-1 — Recovery process triggered:** When the task failure happens, the system first finds all the active keys located on the failed task. And then, it sends such failed information to the tasks containing such keys' backup and triggers the recovery process on those tasks.
- **Step-2 — State confirmation:** Since the task failure happens randomly, when the task fails, we cannot get the states of the keys directly from the failed task. Hence, this step ensures that we can obtain the keys' last states through the state of the downstream operations in order to recover the lost data accordingly.

- **Step-3 — Recovery action:** With the help of the buffered data of each operation and the state of the lost data obtained from downstream tasks (mentioned in step-2), we now can restore the active data from the backup one.

Continuing with Fig. 3.8 as an example, if the task d_1 fails, the system first decides which active key is affected according to the key distribution function, then it sends the *recover* command to the tasks that contain the backup of those lost active keys, i.e., sending recover command to d_4 which contains the backup of k_1. Lastly, the system obtains the downstream operation state of k_1 and the buffer data of the operation in d_4, which can be used to reproduce the state of k_1 when d_1 fails using the state of k_1' in d_4.

Overall, this chapter introduces the procedure of the data-level fault-tolerant method: the system correctness is guaranteed by the strong processing order and the active/backup synchronization which happens in the time-dependent operations. The fault-tolerant method ensures the input order by sorting the input in the buffers. In terms of the data distribution, this method only sends the active data to the downstream main and backup tasks so as to localize the synchronization process. However, due to the occurrence of the replicas, the data routing rule and workload balancing plan have to consider both the active and backup data. Different from the key-based workload balancing method mentioned in Chapter 2, this chapter focuses on combining both the fault tolerance and the load balancing. No matter how data are distributed or migrated, the active and backup data are not allowed to be sent to the same processing task. We will introduce the data routing and balancing problem in Section 3.6.2.

3.6.2 *Tuple routing strategy*

Regarding the goal of our chapter, $(\theta_i(d, F) \leq \theta_{\max})$ implies that the constraint of workload balancing is a variance of the well-known bin packing problem, i.e., objects (keys) must be packed into a fixed number of bins in such a way that load imbalance is minimized, which is known to be an NP-hard problem. In this section, we first introduce the routing strategy for the incoming tuples while ensuring the active and duplication state correctness. Then we propose an approximate algorithm based on the least-load first principle. Finally, the analysis of the algorithms is presented to illustrate the theoretical properties of our approaches.

A tuple τ can be formatted as (k, v), while k is used to determine the destination(s) for τ. According to our mixed routing strategy in Eq. (2.1), incoming tuples are assigned to the processing tasks based on a routing table and a mapping function. Furthermore, for the duplication state of tuples, a Service Level Agreement (SAL) is used to determine how many copies should be generated for different keys. Specifically, SAL is a document containing a set of keys and their importance level. The pseudo code of tuple routing in our mixed architecture is listed in Algorithm 3.4. It produces the routing plan for the incoming tuple set, which assigns the incoming tuples to one of the instances of the downstream operator and ensures the correctness of the stream processing.

Algorithm 3.4 first extracts the key form incoming tuple as shown in line 1. Then, it determines the number of replicas for the tuple according to SLA. Finally, it directs the incoming tuple according to the mixed routing strategy in Eq. (2.1). Specifically, if the incoming tuple is to be routed by a routing table, which means its key has been migrated, it will be set as an active state and routed according to the active destination column in the routing table (lines 4–5). At the same time, the replicated tuple(s) will be

---

Algorithm 3.4 Pseudo Code of Tuple Routing

---

input: Input tuple: τ, Service-level agreements: SLA

output: Active task ID: d, Duplication task ID(set): d'

1: $k \leftarrow \mathcal{N}(\tau)$ ⊲ extract the key of incoming tuple τ
2: $\tau' \leftarrow SLA(\tau)$ ⊲ determine the duplication tuple(s) τ' according to SLA
3: **if** $k \in \mathcal{R}$ **then**
4: $\quad \tau \leftarrow Set(\tau_{ac=1})$ ⊲ set this tuple as active state
5: $\quad d \leftarrow A.d;$ ⊲ determine routing for τ according to Eq. (2.1)
6: $\quad \tau' \leftarrow Set(\tau'_{ac=0})$ ⊲ set this tuple(s) as duplication state
7: $\quad d' \leftarrow \{B.d\};$ determine routing for τ according to Eq. (2.1)
8: **else**
9: $\quad \tau \leftarrow Set(\tau_{ac=1})$
10: $\quad d \leftarrow h(k)$
11: $\quad \tau' \leftarrow Set(\tau'_{ac=0})$
12: $\quad d' \leftarrow \{f(h(k))\}$
13: **return** d, d'

---

marked as a duplication state and sent to task(s) according to the duplication destination column of the routing table (lines 6–7). In contrast, the tuple routed by mapping function has a similar procedure except that the routing strategy in lines 10 and 12 is determined by the mapping function.

3.6.3   *Load balance adjustment plan*

In this section, we first briefly introduce a basic and heuristic assignment procedure proposed by us, namely *least-load fit decreasing* (LLFD), which is also used in Chapter 2. It is inspired by the classic First Fit Decreasing (FFD) designed for the bin packing problem [Coffman Jr *et al.* (1984)]. Then, we propose the FTLB (Fault Tolerance and Load Balancing) algorithm in this chapter to make the system achieve workload balancing and fault tolerance at the same time.

3.6.3.1   *Least-load fit decreasing (LLFD)*

As described in Section 2.4.1, LLFD produces the key assignment plan from an input candidate key set to one of the instances of the downstream operator for the purpose of achieving load balance. Assuming if at the beginning of each interval we apply LLFD with all the keys as its input (the candidate key set), this may result in a huge explicit assignment table that contains entries for almost every key. Despite the fact that it is not practical in that it only deals with the load balancing constraints, disregarding either the limitation on assignment table size or the migration cost, it is the basis of other practical approaches we will introduce later. Also, we give a proof that the degree of load imbalance among downstream instances produced by the LLFD approach is upper bounded, under several types of heavy-tail distributions on key frequencies, e.g., Zipf.

The following theorem shows the robustness and soundness of LLFD on basic load balancing problem.

Theorem 3.1. *If there exists a solution for perfect load balancing, i.e.,* $L(d) = \bar{L}, \forall d \in \mathcal{D}, LLFD$ *is capable of finding a solution resulting in balancing indicator* $\theta(d, F)$ *no worse than* $\frac{1}{3}(1 - \frac{1}{N_D})$ *for any task instance d.*

Furthermore, the number of keys is more than the number of instances ($|\mathcal{C}| \gg |\mathcal{D}|$) and the accumulative load for the tails in skew data distribution is significant. Therefore, we believe that LLFD can produce a well-balanced adjustment.

3.6.3.2 *Fault tolerance and load balance algorithm*

The LLFD reshuffles all the keys according to their workload information. However, the reshuffle operation will cost an incredible amount of network transmission and generate a huge assignment table. We have to avoid the reshuffle operation while still preserving the load balancing with our pre-defined imbalance tolerance under a limited assignment table. Here, we propose an improved method based on LLFD, named FTLB.

The key difference from FTLB to LLFD is that for the ith interval, only a subset of keys is chosen as the candidates for migration instead of the whole key set used by LLFD. The balancing procedure consists of two parts: selecting candidate keys from instances and putting candidates to instances.

In the first phase, we define evaluation metric $M(k)$ to evaluate the importance of key k for migration purposes and order the keys by their importance. The value of metric $M(k)$ can be obtained according to two factors: the granularity, memory consumption and the duplication distribution of keys. Different to the *migration priority index* defined in Chapter 2, $M(k)$ takes the duplication information into account. Specifically, the candidate move keys are sorted in an ascending order of the *migration priority index*, which is our evaluation metric $M(k)$ defined by $\gamma_i(k, w) = \frac{S_i(k,w)}{c_i(k)^\beta}$. The physical meaning of the index $\gamma_i(k, w)$ is intuitive, i.e., the key with smaller state size (equivalently migration cost) or larger workload has the higher priority to be migrated, and the parameter β is used for tuning the weights between the two factors. The *migration priority index* here can be defined as $M(k) = \frac{S_i(k,w)}{c_i(k)^\beta} \cdot dn_i(k)^\gamma$ where $dn_i(k)$ is the number of the duplication for k in time interval i^{th} and $dn_i(k) \in (|B.d|, |f(h(k))|)$ as shown in Eq. (2.1). Furthermore, the parameters β and γ can be obtained from SLA, which measures the importance of routing table and correctness, respectively. FTLB gets out the keys one by one along the order until the overloaded tasks disappear (lines 3–9). $M(k)$ is the function to order keys and get the best migration candidate (line 5). The selected candidates are inserted into the candidate set C. This step will not stop until no instances are overloaded.

In the second phase, we distribute the loads in $\mathcal{C}$ to our instances. First, we take the same process as LLFD (lines 12–14). The load being loaded to instance d may cause the overload of d (line 15). In such a case, we have to remove some loads to unload d. In order to improve the process efficiency, we define *cursor* for each instance to guide the selection of loads on instance d (lines 16–17). Those cursors monitor the maximum workload that could be migrated out of the instance d which shall be less than *cursor*$[d]$. If instance d is still overloaded (line 20) in Algorithm 3.5, $FTLB$ will cancel this insertion of k to instance d (line 21). Then select the second least loaded instance and redo from line 14 in Algorithm 3.5. In this way, $FTLB$ will be able to find a suitable instance for $c(k)$.

After the new workload assignment plan has been generated by Algorithm 3.5, we do the actual migration action as the procedure shown in Algorithm 3.6. To generate the migration key set $\mathcal{K}_i$, Algorithm 3.6 first generates the routing function F_i for workload in time interval ith according to Eq. (2.1) (line 1). Then, *KSM* finds the different items between F_i and F_{i-1} (line 2) to generate the candidate migration key set $\mathcal{K}_i$. Finally, keys belonging to $\mathcal{K}_i$ will be migrated (line 3).

3.6.3.3 *Implementation and cost analysis*

Generally, workload adjustment among tasks takes the following steps:

B1. **Load reporting:** Each task reports current workload to Controller, and Controller checks overall system balance status;

B2. **Detailed information asking:** If unbalanced, Controller requires all instances to report detailed information;

B3. **Detailed information collecting:** Instances report their detailed load information to Controller, including key ID, located task ID, migration cost and workload information;

B4. **Migration plan generation:** Controller makes balancing plan. Keys which will be migrated should be buffered and all $\mathcal{R}_i$ in upstream instances should be updated;

B5. **Migrating:** System runs migrate action among tasks;

B6. **Re-launching:** System starts all Paused jobs again.

According to the balancing framework, we give a detailed cost analysis in the following content.

Algorithm 3.5 Pseudo Code of $FTLB$

input: instance set $\mathcal{D}$, hash $h(k)$, Upbound upb, metric $M(k)$

output: explicit assignment table $\mathcal{R}$

1: Initialize: $\mathcal{C} = \emptyset$, $cursor[] = \infty$
2: /*1st: select loads into $\mathcal{C}$ from tasks*/
3: **for** each $d \in \mathcal{D}_i$ **do**
4:    **while** $L_i(d) > upb$ **do**
5:       get k with the best $M(k)$ from set $\{k | F_{i-1}(k) = d\}$
6:       add k to $\mathcal{C}$
7:       $L_i(d) = L_i(d) - c_i(k)$
   /*2st: re-distribute loads in $\mathcal{C}$ to tasks*/
8: **while** $\mathcal{C} \neq \emptyset$ **do**
9:    $c(k) \leftarrow$ get k with largest computation cost
10:   $L(d) \leftarrow$ get d with least load of all instances in $\mathcal{D}$
11:   $L(d) = L(d) + c(k)$
12: **if** $L(d) > upb$ **then**
13:    $cursor[d] \leftarrow c(k)$
14:    $\mathcal{C} \leftarrow$ get k with best $M(k)$ and $c(k) < cursor[d]$
15:    update $L(d)$
16: **if** $L(d) > upb$ **then**
17:    undo Line 14–19
18:    get the next least loaded instance d
19:    redo from Line 14
20: **if** $h(k) \neq d$ **then**
21:    add (k, d) to $\mathcal{R}$
22: remove k from $\mathcal{C}$
23: Return $\mathcal{R}_i$

- **Preparation Phase:** B1–B3 compose the cost for this phase with B3 introducing the main cost. For example, assuming each item reported to the controller is 8 Byte, when K is larger such as 10^8, the network transmission cost is about 800 MB, which is considerable quantity.
- **Plan Construction Phase:** As described in Section 3.6.3.2, FTLB utilizes a two-step strategy for load balance with the predefined routing table size. Balance migration plan generation B4 includes two functions:

Algorithm 3.6 Pseudo Code of key state migration (KSM)

---

input: $F_{i-1}, \mathcal{R}_i$ and implicit hash $h_i(k)$
output: Balance state
1: $F_i \leftarrow \mathcal{R}_i \bigcup h_i$
2: $\mathcal{K}_i \leftarrow F_i \bigoplus F_{i-1}$
3: Migrate states of keys in $\mathcal{K}_i$

---

generating moving candidates (GMC) and pairing load–instance. The computation complexity for GMC is $O(\log_2 \frac{K}{|\mathcal{D}|})$. Moreover, in order to balance the overloaded instances, the overall computation complexity is $O(\log_2 \frac{K}{|\mathcal{D}|} * K * \log_2 N)$. For $K \gg |\mathcal{D}|$, then the computation complexity is $O(K \log_2 K)$.

- **Migration Phase:** $B4–B6$ generate cost in this phase. If processes are paused when generating a migration schedule on upstream instances, it may lead to job ceasing in downstream instances. So a tidy and small routing table is required to shorten migration time and improve processing efficiency.

When unbalance occurs in the stream system, it is expected to complete balancing quickly and correctly. A lightweight computing model is required. In this chapter, though we expect to design algorithms to achieve load balance with small migration cost and limited routing table, our balancing framework shows that either computational complexity or transfer cost is decided by the size of K, which is usually huge.

3.7   Practical Verification and Study

3.7.1   *Environment setting*

In this section, we evaluate our proposals by comparing against a handful of baseline approaches. All of these approaches are implemented and run on top of *Apache Storm* under the same task configuration and routing table size. The *Storm* system (in version 0.9.3) is deployed on a 21-node HP blade cluster with a CentOS 6.5 operating system. Each node is equipped with two Intel Xeon processors (E5335 at 2.00 GHz) containing four cores and a 16 GB RAM in total. Each core is exclusively bounded to a worker thread during the experiments.

We use the consistent hashing [Karger *et al.* (1997)] as our basic hash function. On the contrary, to simulate the computation cost for both simple and complicated tasks, we manipulate the *CPU* processing time for each key by adding a constant delay to the processing (e.g., 1 ms per tuple) so as to get the maximum computation capacity of each node. We also set the *setMaxSpoutPending(50)* to control the speed of the input tuple flow. We run experiments on both synthetic and real data.

- **Datasets & Workload:** We conduct experiments using TPC-H generator *dbgen* to generate data. We adjust parameter z for different skewness, with default value as 0.8. We run equi-join query E_{Q_5} from TPC-H benchmark as our workload.

For fault-tolerant testing, we perform the TopK query on two datasets: a synthetic dataset and a real-world dataset. In terms of the synthetic one, we use a data generator which can generate skewed datasets and generate a test dataset satisfying Zipf distribution. The overall data skewness is controlled by factor z, and the data distribution in each task is dynamically changed with time, which is configured by the factor f. Such a continuously changing input flow requires the system to balance the workload consistently in order to reduce the unbalance rate down to the bearing threshold θ_{max}. We also test our performance on a real-world dataset *Social* obtained from social network *Weibo*. The *Social* dataset contains 10 days of Weibo posts, which is about 20 GB and contains roughly 2×10^6 tuples after the text processing. The experiments on *Social* dataset are to analyze the hottest topic. Therefore, the topology of this query consists of three stages: topic extraction, topic count and aggregation. The first operation is a mapping operation, while the latter two are aggregation operations.

- **Baseline Approaches:** We compare our method *SAM* with *Dynamic* [Elseidy *et al.* (2014)], *MFM* [Fang *et al.* (2016)], B_i [Lin *et al.* (2015)] and *Readj* [Gedik (2014)]. *Readj* runs full pairing of load task. *Dynamic* and *MFM* are based on the join-matrix model but *MFM* supports the irregular shape of the matrix and eliminates the restriction on task number. B_i organizes tasks as a complete bipartite graph, inside of which it is still a matrix model.

Furthermore, we separate the baseline method into two parts: workload balancing and fault tolerance. The baseline of the workload balancing method was mentioned in Fang *et al.* (2017) in which it is called *Mixed* method; we also use MinTable algorithm (MRT) in the meantime. The experiment results in Fang *et al.* (2017) showed that the MinTable algorithm tries to generate a migration plan that minimizes the size of the routing table, and makes the migration procedure as simple as possible. Hence, this method performs well in terms of the efficiency, and we aim to compare our efficiency with it. Meanwhile, we also use *Readj* as our baseline method. The *Readj* method pairs the task instance with the key and creates a workload balance plan. For each pair, this method considers all possible combinations so as to find the best migration plan which reduces the load unbalance. In terms of the fault-tolerant solutions, since we are the first to propose data-level fault tolerance, we compare our method to the task-level backup method TaskB (Copy Whole Task) regarding the resource utilization rate and efficiency.

- **Evaluation Metrics:** *Throughput* is the average number of tuples processed per second in a system; *Task Number* is the total number of tasks used in *Processing Operator* and each task is equipped with a constant quota of memory V; *Migration Volume* is the total number of tuples migrated to other tasks during system scaling out; *Adjustment Plan Time* is the average time spent on generating a new migration plan and routing table during load adjustment; and *Load Imbalance Degree* is the maximal load imbalance degree among all the tasks of *Processing Operator*. The *Average Generation Time* is the average time spent on making a migration plan; the *Recovery Latency* is the average delay of the tuples being recovered. The following section will report the average value of the above metrics based on the complete workflow so as to evaluate the advantages of different methods.

3.7.2 *Load balancing capability*

To estimate the influence of broadcast volume on throughput, we continuously load all the 10^7 tuples with 10^4 unique keys into our system while executing query E_{Q_5}. Once load imbalance happens, the decision-making method takes the accumulated broadcast volume since last adjustment as input and returns an intermediate routing table size irs. Then we compare irs with the current routing table size since last adjustment. If irs is larger, we choose the *whole-move-keys-at-first* strategy for the next adjustment; otherwise, we choose the *split-keys-at-first* strategy. According to the experimental results of Figs. 3.9(a) and 3.9(b), we then generate a polynomial relation between broadcast volume bv and routing table size $func(bv)$ as shown in Fig. 3.9(c). In our implementation, we set *func()* as follows:

$$func(bv) = 2e - 10 \cdot bv^2 + 1.7e - 3 \cdot bv + 18331. \qquad (3.1)$$

LBC measured by the degree of system imbalance is defined as $\tau = \frac{L(d) - BL}{BL}$. For balanced statuses, each task has a load lower than $UL = (1 + \tau_{max}) \cdot BL$ with the maximum imbalance tolerance τ_{max}. For this experiment, we set $\tau_{max} = 0.01$.

As shown in Fig. 3.10(a), when using 50 task instances, system imbalance of *Readj* increases dramatically when the degree of skewness is higher than 0.5. As skewness becomes more severe, the load of some key may become so large that it even exceeds the average workload of tasks. No matter how *Readj* migrates keys across tasks, it can never get balanced in that *Readj* does not support a splitting operation. On the contrary, our proposed Alg. *SAM* can migrate extra data from overloaded tasks via splitting keys on demand; hence, it can always meet load balancing. *MFM, Bi* and *Dynamic* take random distribution as routing policy regardless of the change in skewness. However those two methods may meet with high broadcasting cost for some specific operations, such as join in Figs. 3.10(c) and 3.10(d). In Fig. 3.10(b), we expand the task parallelism to 100. Moreover, *Readj* leads to much higher system imbalance, which is worse.

3.7.3 *Scalability*

We continue to load 12 GB data into the Storm system and perform full-history join on E_{Q_5}. Figures 3.10(c) and 3.10(d) demonstrate the task consumption and migration volume during system scaling out. The maximum input rate is set by calling the method *setSpoutPending()* in Storm to consume all the computing power of each task.

Figure 3.10(c) illustrates the changes of task requirements when we increase the stream volume. As data are loaded in, *Dynamic* meets a sharp increase in task number because it has a strict requirement that the number

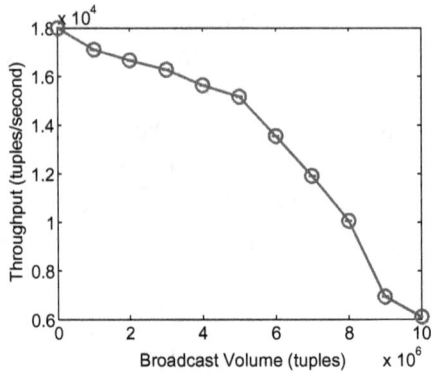

(a)

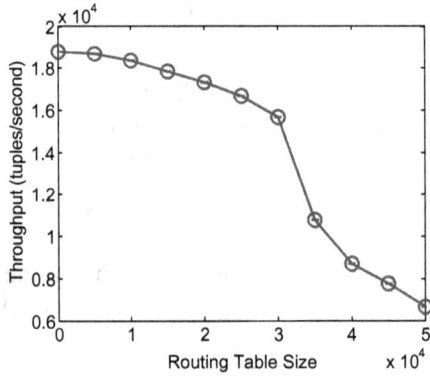

(b)

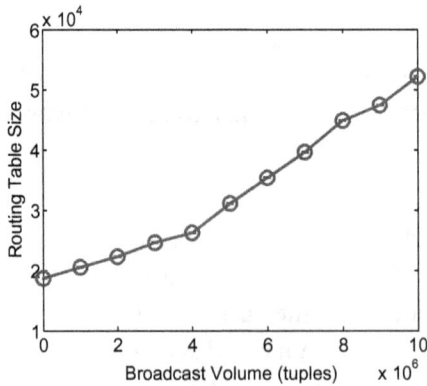

(c)

Fig. 3.9. Effects of broadcast volume, routing table size on throughput. (a) Broadcast volume, (b) routing table size and (c) fitting function.

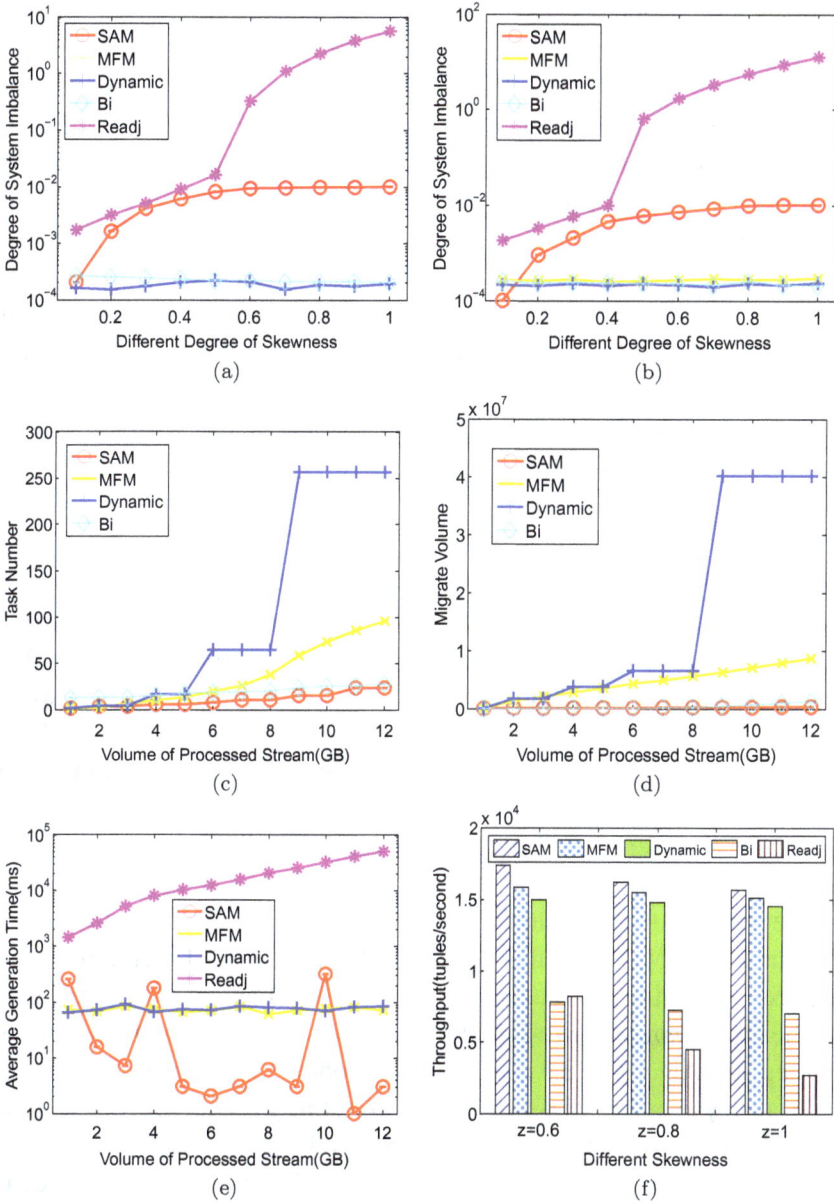

Fig. 3.10. The balance capability, scalability and adaptivity of different methods. (a) LBC of 50 tasks, (b) LBC of 100 tasks, (c) task number, (d) migration volume, (e) adjustment plan time and (f) average throughput.

of tasks must be a power of two and leads to high resource waste. Though *MFM* eliminates the limit on the task number, it is based on the join-matrix and consumes more tasks. Since B_i is designed especially for memory optimization, it is obvious that B_i uses less quantity of tasks. Contrarily, our algorithms perform best among all the methods. They apply for resource on real demand and especially support to join tasks one by one. Figure 3.10(d) illustrates the changes of migration cost during scheme scaling out. Due to the massive data replication to maintain matrix structure, *Dynamic* leads to the highest migration volume as compared to all other methods. *MFM* has less migration volume as it involves fewer tasks than *Dynamic*. *SAM* yields low migration volume in that it adopts consistent hashing to do task deployment. Once a new task is added, only a small quantity of data needs to be migrated owing to the inherit characteristics of consistent hashing.

3.7.4 *Dynamics*

In order to verify the dynamics and adaptivity of algorithms under different degrees of workload skewness, we conduct query E_{Q_5} execution using the window-based model with window size as 3 minutes. The average input rate is about $1.2 \cdot 10^4$ tuples per second to make full use of the CPU resource. We examine the latency of adjustment plan generation and throughput as shown in Figs. 3.10(e) and 3.10(f). *Readj* meets much higher latency than other algorithms because of its full mapping processing as shown in Fig. 3.10(e). Both *Dynamic* and *MFM* take random distribution as the routing policy, and there is no need to balance scheduling calculation. The migration plan generation latency of *SAM* varies a lot according to the choice of adjustment strategy. The higher generation latency corresponds to the *whole-move-keys-at-first* strategy in that the selection of key subsets in step-2 of Algorithm 3.3 is an NP-hard problem, while the lower generation latency represents the *split-keys-at-first* strategy because it split keys of large granularity at first, without complicated key selection. Figure 3.10(f) draws the throughput of each algorithm under different skewness. Throughput of *Readj* decreases as the skewness becomes more severe, because it spends more time generating a migration plan. B_i represents decreasing throughput as well due to data broadcasting among groups. On the contrary, *SAM* has the highest throughput as it controls the growth of broadcast volume and routing table size, and uses a decision-making strategy to build a checks-and-balance relationship between these two factors. Owing to the random distribution policy, throughputs of *MFM* and *Dynamic* change slightly under different skewness.

3.7.5 *Workload balance performance*

Figure 3.11 shows the time spent on making a migration plan and the migration cost using different methods when changing the unbalance bearing threshold θ_{max}. As per the aforementioned definition of unbalance bearing threshold, the greater the θ_{max}, the more unbalance the system can afford. In other words, a higher θ_{max} makes the system much easier to be balanced, and the migration process runs much faster on a synthetic dataset. Hence, the overall time cost is reduced as shown in Fig. 3.11(a). When the $\theta_{max} < 0.2$, since the *Mixed* algorithm has to call the heuristic method iteratively to generate a better migration plan, the overall cost is relatively higher. When the $\theta_{max} \geq 0.2$, the system is much easier to be balanced. Therefore, the effectiveness of *Mixed* is equivalent to the MRT (MinTable algorithm). However, although the FTLB uses the same heuristic method to generate a better migration plan, its time spent on making plans is still shorter due to more available keys (keys from backup data) participating in the balancing process. Figure 3.11(b) shows the migrated data sizes using different migration planners. The smaller θ_{max} usually means the system has to move more data in order to achieve the balance and therefore leads to higher migration cost. The trend in Fig. 3.11(b) proves such an analysis. Since different migration planners focus on different principles, the MRT spends a higher migration cost than the *Mixed* algorithm when in the same configuration. Meanwhile, since the FTLB considers moving backup data instead of moving active data, it can achieve even lower migration cost. Overall, Fig. 3.11 shows that our method outperforms other baselines in terms of both the time cost in generating a migration plan and the cost of data migration. Even when $\theta_{max} = 0.02$, which is close to absolute balance, our FTLB algorithm can still generate the plan within one second. Moreover, since our method utilizes the backup copies, we can find more possible solutions to the load balancing problem and the role switching between active and backup data helps reduce the migration cost significantly.

The number of distinct keys in the dataset affects the skewness of the tasks. Figure 3.12 shows the influence on migration planning time and migration cost under different cardinalities of keys K. We test the cases

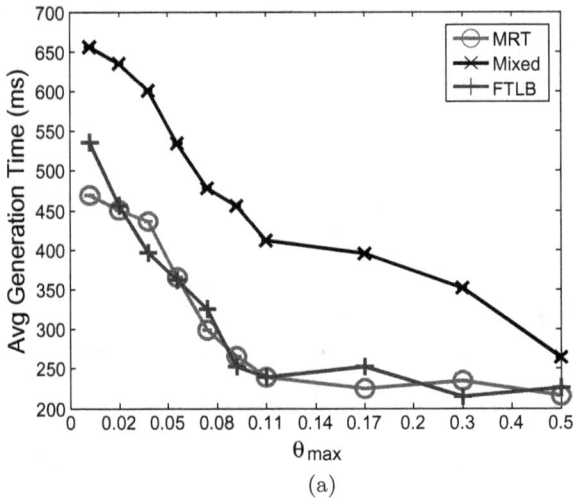

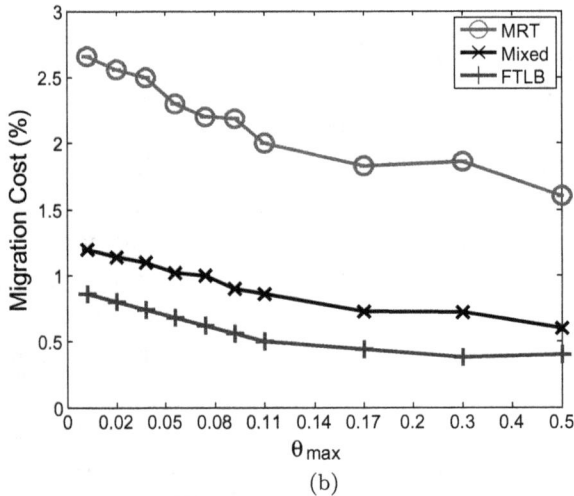

Fig. 3.11. Performance under different θ_{max}. (a) θ_{max} vs. scheduling efficiency and (b) θ_{max} vs. migration cost.

wherein when $K \in [5{,}000, 1{,}000{,}000]$, the data skewness is $z = 0.8$. Figure 3.12(a) shows the change of migration planning cost when changing K. As the number of keys increases, the cost of all methods increases as well. It is because with more keys available, the planner will consider moving more keys to achieve a better balancing performance. Among all solutions,

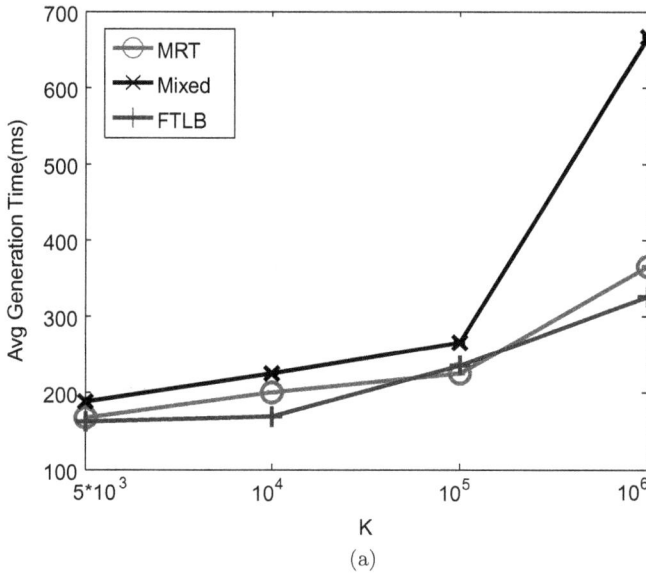

(a)

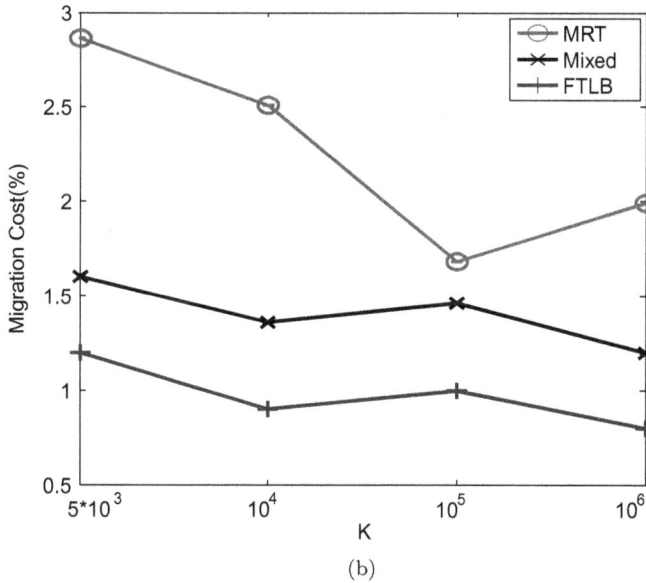

(b)

Fig. 3.12. Performance under different key numbers. (a) K vs. scheduling efficiency and (b) K vs. migration cost.

the *Mixed* method shows a relative high migration planning cost since it uses a heuristic method to find a better migration plan through iteration as shown in Fig. 3.11. Meanwhile, although the FTLB method finds the migration plan in a similar way as Mixed, its time cost is much closer to the MRT algorithm, shown in Fig. 3.11(a), due to its considerably larger number of viable balancing solutions. On the contrary, Fig. 3.12(b) shows that with the help of replications, our FTLB algorithm achieves an overall lower migration cost under the different cardinality of K.

Figure 3.13(a) denotes the throughput of different methods when no task failure is happening. The *Ideal* represents the optimal throughput, which can be achieved when the workload is shuffled randomly. However, a random distribution of tuples does not preserve the semantic meaning of the key-based operations. Hence, although having an optimal throughput, the *Ideal* method does not fit state-based aggregation operations. Therefore, we regard its throughput as the ideal scenario and compare the other methods with it. The performance of those methods, except FTLB, when changing the distribution fluctuation frequency f has a similar trend as performance degradation. Note that the throughput of FTLB is slightly lower than the *Mixed* method in Fig. 3.13(a) as the extra cost of maintaining the state of replications increases the latency of processing the tuples, and thus affects the overall throughput. However, since the *Mixed* method sacrifices the fault-tolerant feature, its throughput is overwhelmed by our method once the failure happens, which will be discussed in Section 3.7.6.

3.7.6 *Fault-tolerant performance*

In Fig. 3.13(b), the throughput of each method is compared when the task failure happens. We configure the *message.timeout.secs* and *acker* settings in the Storm configuration file to ensure every record is processed, and we obstruct the output of tuples in one of the parallel tasks to simulate a task failure scenario. If the obstructed tuple has a replica, we stop the resend of the replicated tuple by changing the value of its *acker*. The *Ideal* in Fig. 3.13(b) represents the optimal throughput when no task failure happens, and the workload is absolutely balanced. Compared to the case in Fig. 3.13(a) where no task failure happens, the performance of *Mixed*, *Readj* and *Storm* decreases significantly when a task fails. This is because

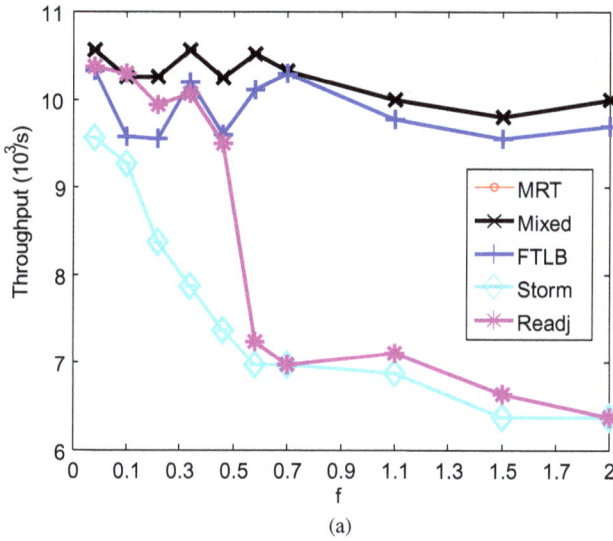

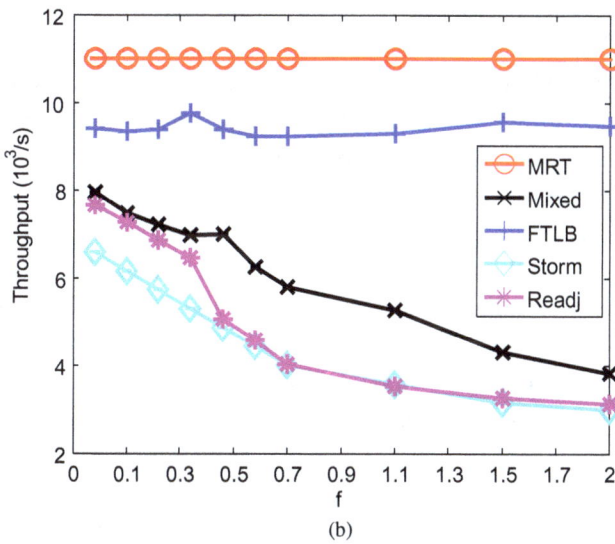

Fig. 3.13. Throughput performance. (a) Throughput without fault task and (b) throughput with fault task.

the fault-tolerant mechanisms of those methods purely rely on the inbuilt fault tolerance of Storm, which is achieved by redistributing the time-out tuples. The Storm system keeps monitoring the data output port and decides whether to resend a tuple or not according to the preset maximum time limit. If the system does not receive a "processed successfully" message from a processing tuple within the given time, it will mark this tuple as lost and resend it. Since such a method of fault tolerance is guaranteed by resending the failed data, it can significantly increase the latency. Moreover, the severity of the latency is determined by the topological position of the failed task and the active duration of the failed data. For instance, if the failed task is located at the last step of the topology, the recovery usually requires more recalculation. Similarly, if the failed data are correlated to many other data, the recovery also incurs a huge cost as all the relevant data have to be recalculated. Overall, our proposed method FTLB achieves the best throughput in Fig. 3.13(b), and it did not lose much throughput with varying workload fluctuation frequency despite a few errors sent as shown in Fig. 3.13(a).

Figure 3.14 shows the recovery latency and throughput of various methods when task failure happens. The recovery method in *TaskB* focuses on task-level fault tolerance. When the failure happens, it activates the backup task to continue the data process. The x-axis in the figure represents the size of the data state in the operation buffer when the system is running, which is controlled by varying the size of the data buffer time windows from 0.5 min to 1 h. Figure 3.14(a) compares the recovery latency between the data-level fault-tolerant method FTLB and the task-level method *TaskB*. As shown in the figure, the *TaskB* has an overall higher latency than FTLB since the FTLB sends the backup data to all the tasks that contain failed data simultaneously so as to do the recover locally and continue the data process. Moreover, compared with task-level backup method *TaskB*, the FTLB recovers less data. Figure 3.14(b) shows a similar trend as Fig. 3.14(a) in terms of the average throughput under various buffer sizes when dealing with a fixed size dataset. In general, the experiments indicate that the data-level fault-tolerant methods outperform the task-level solution in throughput.

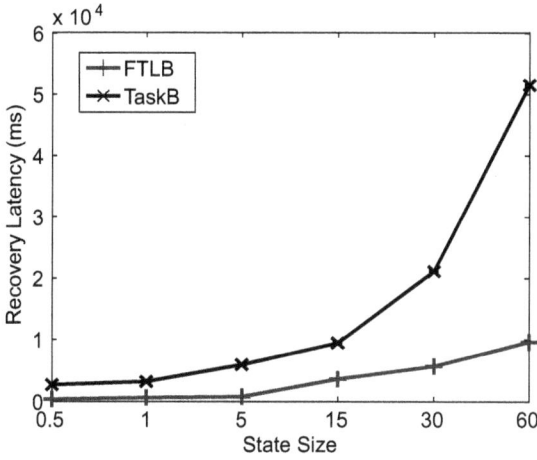

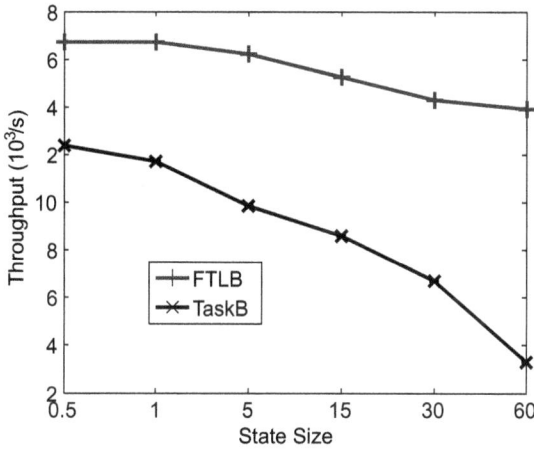

Fig. 3.14. Fault-tolerant performance. (a) Recovery latency in different state size and (b) throughput in different state size.

3.8 Summary

In this chapter, we focus on designing an adaptive and cost-effective partitioning methods to handle load imbalance problems in distributed stream systems. Inspired by the idea of "Split keys on demand and Merge keys as far as possible", we propose a novel cost model to guide designing of balance schedules. Based on this cost model, our load balancing adjustment algorithms include two types of adjustment strategies, with the aim to have high throughput and low latency while using less resource. In the future, we will continue seeking a more comprehensive cost model and more flexible and adaptive load adjustment strategies to improve system performance.

In this chapter, we focused on solving the fault tolerance and workload balancing issues in distributed stream processing systems. Different from the previous works that solved these two problems separately, we aimed to generate a solution that achieves both goals in one shot. Despite the inherent characteristics of data streams, such as persistence, dynamism, and unpredictability, we proposed a new dynamic workload distribution mechanism for intra-operator load balancing and fault tolerance which achieved a lower resource consumption compared to the previous methods. To achieve the fault tolerance and ensure the result correctness, we defined synchronization protocols and classified the current popular operations into different categories according to their time dependency. Furthermore, we proposed a rebalanced approach that takes into account the fault-tolerant mechanism. Through extensive experimental verification, it is proved that our algorithm helps the system achieve efficient load balancing and fault tolerance with low computation resource requirement.

Chapter 4

Workload Balance for
Multi-stream θ-Join

4.1 Motivation and Basic Idea

With the development of communication technology and hardware equipment, especially the widespread use of small wireless sensors, data show the scale of explosive growth in many fields, such as online financial analysis, environment monitoring, and mobile and network information management systems. It poses challenges to such applications to provide efficient online stream processing in real time. Efficient streams are employed in processing with arbitrary predicates, which are essential and critical to data stream systems. Data skew is a common phenomenon in those scenarios and leads to lingering processing in a parallel shared-nothing environment. In this context, load balancing [Liu *et al.* (2005); Xing *et al.* (2006); Xu *et al.* (2008); Gufler *et al.* (2012); Kwon *et al.* (2012)] is crucial for improving throughputs by vanishing those lingering tasks that are overloaded. Measures have been taken to solve the imbalance problem among tasks for different operations, such as Summarization [Cormode and Muthukrishnan (2005)], Aggregation [Nasir *et al.* (2015, 2016)] and Join Xu *et al.* (2008); Bruno *et al.* (2014); Vitorovic *et al.* (2016), which may group data by keys for processing. One of the most challenging tasks is to support θ-joins [Elseidy *et al.* (2014); Lin *et al.* (2015); Okcan and Riedewald (2011)] in a flexible, efficient and scalable manner under workload skewness.

There has been great interest in designing stream join algorithms. On the one hand, existing centralized algorithms [Wilschut and Apers (1993); Urhan and Franklin (2000); Ives *et al.* (1999); Tao *et al.* (2005); Dittrich *et al.* (2002a)] are mainly tailored for a single server, and hence, they cannot scale out and deal with massive datasets; on the other hand, existing distributed and parallel join algorithms are mostly suitable for equi-join processing and present poor performance when handling θ-join operators.

In processing θ-joins on streams with skew data distribution, there are two kinds of popular processing models, namely join-biclique [Lin *et al.* (2015)] and join-matrix [Okcan and Riedewald (2011); Elseidy *et al.* (2014)]. Lin *et al.* proposed a join-biclique model [Lin *et al.* (2015)] that organizes all the processing units as a complete bipartite graph where each side corresponds to one stream. Given $m + n$ units (tasks), m units from one side of the bipartite graph are used for managing/storing tuples in one stream while flowing tuples from the other stream among those m units; n units are for the other one. The join-matrix model supports distributed join processing with arbitrary join predicates perfectly. It was studied a decade ago and has been revisited in both MapReduce-like system [Okcan and Riedewald (2011)] and stream applications [Elseidy *et al.* (2014)]. Apparently, it models a join operation between two streams as a matrix, where each side is on behalf of one stream. Based on this model, [Okcan and Riedewald (2011)] introduce two partitioning schemes in a MapReduce job, namely 1-Bucket and M-Bucket. It performs well only when the input or the output dominates processing cost and it requires to get the input statistics before the execution of optimization. *Dynamic*, a join operator designed in Elseidy *et al.* (2014), adopts a grid-layout partitioning scheme on the matrix. Although it is resilient to data skew as taking a random distribution as routing policy for input tuples and it can perfectly handle any join predicates for it ensures that each tuple of one stream meets any tuple in the other stream. However, it suffers from inflexibility and huge a amount of tuple duplication while scaling out or down. For example, *Dynamic* assumes the number of tasks in a matrix must be a power of two and scales out by splitting the states of every task to four tasks for a task storing a number of tuples exceeding the specified storage capacity or processing capacity, and vice versa.

The matrix model seems to be the most suitable one for θ-join with correctness guarantee and balance load distribution, but it still has the following two inherent disadvantages:

(1) The number of tasks is strictly decided by the number of cells in the matrix, which is calculated by multiplying the number of rows and columns of the matrix;
(2) In the case of stream change, that is, stream volume increasing or shrinking, adding or removing processing tasks must be consistent with matrix cells.

Since the allocation of tasks is decided by the number of cells of the matrix, it greatly limits the flexibility of processing with the dynamics of stream and may cause resource waste by generating more tasks than needed.

According to the preceding discussion, the join-matrix model exposes two challenges: (1) how to generate an appropriate matrix scheme to achieve maximum utilization of resources; (2) when the scheme is changed, how to repartition states among tasks to minimize the migration cost.

In this chapter, we propose a flexible and adaptive model for distributed and parallel stream join processing. It inherits the characteristics of the traditional matrix model and allows irregular shaping of the matrix to allocate resource in demand, promising the efficient resource utilization.

Furthermore, over the last decade, the ubiquitous of GPS-embedded devices generate a large scale of trajectory data, which enable a variety of LBS applications, e.g., car pooling [Trasarti *et al.* (2011); Zheng *et al.* (2013a)], navigation and tourist tour planning [Li *et al.* (2018); Shang *et al.* (2014, 2016)]. As it represents the moving trace of an object, the trajectory has been commonly used as a basic ingredient for the calculation of location-based commercial and public services [Su *et al.* (2013, 2015); Sun *et al.* (2018)]. Among those applications, the distance measure between trajectories is a fundamental and necessary operation for calculating the similarity of entities' behaviors [Shang *et al.* (2017, 2018); Xie *et al.* (2017)]. Moreover, since most of the LBS applications require interactive responses to the users and the similarities are usually performed on the ongoing trajectories, it is necessary to handle the large-scale trajectory similarity in an online scenario.

The DSPE, which is designated for massive stream data processing with low latency, offers an effective solution for such a workload. However, the traditional solutions for Real-Time Trajectory Similarity (RTTS) cannot be directly extended to DSPE systems due to two main reasons: First, a two-tier state information including trajectories and their adjacency should be maintained in DSPE, which should be designed differently to the standalone solution. Second, workload skewness and variance are common phenomena in DSPE, which are not considered in a standalone system.

In this chapter, we also take both the computational requirements and workload dynamic characteristic of RTTS into account and propose a flexible and adaptive model, named as Adaptive Framework for Real-time Trajectory Similarity (ART), for trajectory similarity join query in a distributed and parallel manner. To handle the dynamic of incoming trajectories, we design an easy-to-use data partition scheme which only adopts some simple mapping function, e.g., random, range and broadcast. For the computational requirements, a compact representation structure for distance information is introduced, which greatly reduces the memory requirement and hence improves the system capacity to efficiently support in-memory real-time analytics. Overall, the major contributions of this work are summarized as follows: (1) We design a general strategy to generate the processing scheme for θ-join operator under dynamic stream changes at runtime, which achieves scalability, effectiveness and efficiency by a single shot. (2) We propose a lightweight computation model to generate a migration plan, which brings in minimal data transmission overhead. We present a detailed theoretical analysis for the proposed model to prove the usability and correctness. (3) We propose the ART framework to handle real-time trajectory similarity calculation. The framework guarantees the completeness of join results with optimized computation resource utilization. (4) We design a new computing model for RTTS and a series of data partition functions designated for ART, which ensure a high throughput and a low processing latency under workload variance. (5) We empirically evaluate our model against the state-of-the-art solutions on both standard benchmarks and real-world stream data workloads with detailed explanations on experimental results.

The remainder of this chapter is organized as follows. Section 4.2 reviews the existing studies on trajectory similarity processing and workload balancing in distributed systems. Section 4.3 introduces the preliminaries. Section 4.4 shows how the matrix model used for multi-stream θ-join. Section 4.5 describes how to generate the processing scheme. Section 4.6 explains the detailed implementation of our proposed method. Section 4.7 shows the experimental results. Section 4.8 finally concludes the chapter.

4.2 Related Work and Literatures

In the past decades, there have been much effort put into designing distributed join algorithms to deal with the rapid growth of data. Blanas *et al.* (2011) proposed a direct parallel variant of the canonical hash join for modern multi-core processors. Balkesen *et al.* (2012) designed hardware-conscious join algorithms. Graefe (1993) gave an overview of parallel join algorithms. However, all these algorithms were mainly proposed for non-streaming scenarios and cannot be directly deployed in streaming processing environments. For non-stream join processing, there also has been numerous research. To name a few, the symmetric hash join (SHJ) [Wilschut and Apers (1993)] extends the traditional hash join algorithms and highly supports pipelined processing in parallel database systems. However, it requires that the entire hash tables should be kept in the main memory. Both XJoin [Urhan and Franklin (2000)] and DPHJ [Ives *et al.* (1999)] are based on SHJ and allow parts of the hash tables to be spilled out to disk for later processing, enhancing the applicability of the algorithm. Similarly, RPJ [Tao *et al.* (2005)] takes a statistics-based flushing strategy and tries to keep tuples that are more likely to join in memory. Dittrich *et al.* (2002a) developed the sorted-based but non-blocking progressive merge join algorithm (PMJ). However, all these algorithms delegated the processing work to a centralized entity and were not easy to scale when handling the massive data stream workload.

In recent years, great interest has developed in designing stream join algorithms in a distributed environment. Photon [Ananthanarayanan *et al.* (2013)] is a prototype system designed by Google to join data streams such as web search queries and user clicks on the advertisements. It relies on a central coordinator to support fault tolerance and scale-out join. It processes incoming tuples through key-value matching in real time in a non-blocking way, but cannot support θ-join well. D-Streams [Zaharia *et al.* (2013)]

is a data stream operating object defined in Spark Streaming. It adopts mini-batch on data streams in a blocking way. Though it supports θ-join well, some tuples may miss each other due to the constraint of window size. As a result, it can only give approximate join results. TimeStream [Qian *et al.* (2013)] exploits the resilient substitution and dependency tracking to ensure the dependability of stream computing. It provides MapReduce-like batch processing and non-blocking tuple processing, but encounters high communication cost due to the maintenance of join states. Join-biclique [Lin *et al.* (2015)] is based on a bipartite-graph model and supports both full-history and window-based stream joins.

Joining on streams is generally modeled as a matrix, each side of which corresponds to one stream. Stamos and Young (1993) adopted the idea of replicating input tuples, extended the fragment and replicate (FR) algorithm [Epstein *et al.* (1978)] and proposed a symmetric fragment and replicate algorithm. Okcan and Riedewald (2011) employed the join-matrix for processing θ-joins in MapReduce and designed two partitioning schemes, namely 1-Bucket and M-Bucket. The former scheme is content-insensitive and performs load balancing well by assigning equal cells to each region but suffers from too much replication, while the latter scheme is content-sensitive because it maps a tuple to a region according to its join key. Due to the nature of MapReduce, the algorithms are offline and require that all input statistics must be available beforehand, which incurs blocking behaviors. Consequently, it is more favorable for batch computing rather than stream computing. In data stream scenario, Elseidy *et al.* (2014) present a (n, m)-*mapping scheme* dividing the matrix into $J(J = n \times m)$ regions of equal area and introduce the DYNAMIC operator which adjusts the state partitioning scheme adaptively according to data characteristics continuously. However, all the approaches are based on the hypothesis that the number of partitions J is restricted to powers of two and predefined without intermediate change and that the ratio of $|R|$ and $|S|$ (the number of arrived tuples of two data streams, respectively) falls in between $\frac{1}{J}$ and J. Moreover, the flexibility of the matrix structure is deteriorated when the matrix needs to scale out (down).

Other works related to this chapter can be summarized into two categories: trajectory similarity processing strategies and real-time processing techniques.

Thanks to the major advances in sensor technology, location-based services are now greatly facilitating people's lives and more in-depth applications are currently generated and managed in many domains. In those applications, trajectory similarity search is a fundamental operator which is non-trivial to process [Xie *et al.* (2017); Wang *et al.* (2013); Shang *et al.* (2017)]. With the demand of more diverse applications, in the past decades, a great deal of effort has been put into the study of different distance measures such as Dynamic Time Warping (DTW) [Ying *et al.* (2016)] and Longest Common Sub-Sequence (LCSS) [Vlachos *et al.* (2002)], Hausdorff, Frechet distance [Xie *et al.* (2017)]. In addition to proposing new distance measures, recent studies also focus on the indexing and pruning strategies which boost the similarity search queries on specific distance measures. Chen *et al.* (2005a) introduced a novel distance function, Edit Distance on Real (EDR) sequence, to measure the similarity between two trajectories. EDR is based on edit distance on strings and removes the noise effects by quantizing the distance between a pair of elements to two values. Frentzos *et al.* (2007) addressed the issue of trajectory similarity by defining a similarity metric, proposing an efficient approximation method to reduce its calculation cost. Moreover, it proposes a best-first query processing algorithm to perform the k-MST search on R-tree-like structures. Yanagisawa *et al.* (2003) proposed an efficient indexing method to retrieve similar trajectories for a query by combining a spatial indexing technique (R^+-tree) and a dimension reduction technique. However, most existing similarity join algorithms cannot achieve high performance for really large datasets [Jiang *et al.* (2014)], and thus, it needs a cluster of machines for storage and processing in a parallel manner. This naturally brings challenges in designing efficient distributed query processing algorithms and frameworks for the large-scale trajectory data. Shang *et al.* (2017) introduced a temporal-first matching and two-phase algorithm to process the TS-join efficiently on very large trajectory datasets. Furthermore, Xie *et al.* (2017) designed a distributed framework that leverages segment-based partitioning and indexing to answer similarity search queries over large trajectory data.

A distributed stream processing engine provides an effective solution which facilitates processing of a massive data stream with a low latency. However, as a common phenomena in DSPEs, the workload skewness and variance are the main challenges that hinder the existing centralized solutions to perform well in a distributed environment. When massive stream data flood into a distributed system, even slight distribution change on the incoming data stream may significantly affect the system performance. Meanwhile, the trajectory similarity processing is an intricate stateful operator, which means the system is supposed to maintain historical information of the operator. To handle stateful operators under workload variance, Gedik (2014) introduced a similar tuple distribution function, consisting of a basic hash function and an explicit hash table. Shah *et al.* (2003) designed a widely adopted load balancing strategy for traditional distributed streaming processing systems. It simply measures the workload of the tasks and attempts to migrate workload from overloaded nodes to underloaded nodes. Lin *et al.* (2015) proposed a joinbiclique model that organizes the clusters as a complete bipartite graph for joining big data streams. Other authors [Elseidy *et al.* (2014); Nasir *et al.* (2015, 2016)] designed a series of randomized routing algorithms to balance the workload of stream processing operators. However, those approaches only perform well for stateless operators in streaming processing. The proposal in this work targets at the problem of processing trajectory similarity under workload variance and proposes a lightweight computation model to make such operations achieve scalability, effectiveness and efficiency in a single shot.

4.3 Preliminaries

4.3.1 *Matrix model*

In this chapter, we give a detailed introduction to the related matrix model, and then we present our optimization goal on the matrix model.

4.3.1.1 *Parallel processing tasks arrangement*

In order to make it easy for explanation, all notations used in the rest of this chapter are summarized in Table 4.1. A partitioning scheme on the matrix model splits $R \bowtie S$ into a number of smaller parallel join processing units which are the cells in the matrix decided by rows and columns. Each cell holds a partial subset of data from each stream, which is represented as a range $[b, e]$ to denote the begin b and end e points along the stream

Table 4.1. Notations for multi-stream join.

Notations	Description
$M/M_o/M_n$	Matrix/old matrix/new matrix
R, S	R, S stream
α, β	Number of rows and columns of M
i/j	ith row, jth column in old scheme
k/l	kth row, lth column in new scheme
m_{ij}	Element of ith row and jth column
r_i/s_j	Stream in ith row or jth column
mp	The migration plan
h_{ij}^R/h_{ij}^S	The sub-range of stream R/S that has been stored in m_{ij}
s_{kl}^R/s_{kl}^S	The sub-range of stream R/S that should be stored in m_{kl}
$V(V_h)$	Memory size of each task (half size $V_h = \frac{V}{2}$)
npi	The mapping of tasks between old and now schemes
$\|o\|$	The volume of set o
NP/MP	The set of npi/mp
P/Q	Trajectory P/Q
p_i/q_i	The ith point of trajectory P/Q
$\mathcal{D}/D/d$	The task set/size of $\mathcal{D}$/task
G/g_i	Sub-group set/the ith sub-group of G
$d(p_i, q_j)$	The distance of points p_i and q_j
M/M_{PQ}	Bitmap/bitmap formed by P and Q
c_{ij}	Cell located at the ith row, jth column in M
c_{i*}/c_{*j}	The ith row/jth column of M
$\|o\|$	The volume of set o

window. In Fig. 4.1(a), a join operation between two data streams R and S can be modeled as a matrix, each side of which corresponds to one stream. The calculation area can be represented by a rectangle with width $|R|$ and length $|S|$. A partitioning scheme splits the area into cells $m_{ij} = (r_i, s_j)$ $(0 \le i \le \alpha - 1, 0 \le j \le \beta - 1)$ of equal size representing stream volume as shown in Fig. 4.1(b).

4.3.1.2 *Characteristics*

Specifically, any process scheme M has the following characteristics when we use it to perform the operation of $R \bowtie S$.

(1) $\forall j, j' \in [0, \beta - 1], \forall i \in [0, \alpha - 1]$, then $h_{ij}^R = h_{ij'}^R$ and $\forall i, i' \in [0, \alpha - 1], \forall j \in [0, \beta - 1]$, then $h_{ij}^S = h_{i'j}^S$;

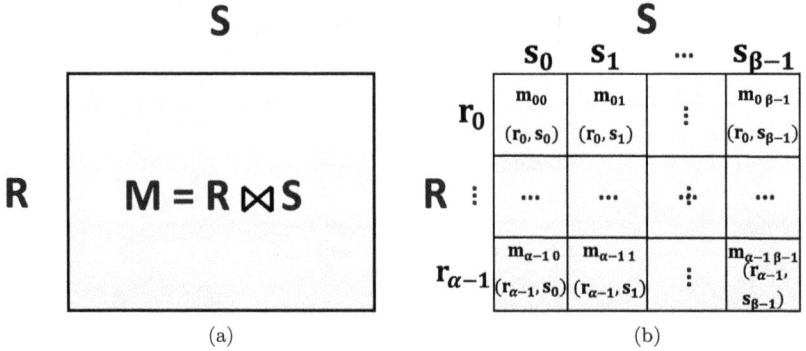

Fig. 4.1.   Example of partition scheme. (a) Calculation area and (b) partition scheme.

(2) $\forall j \in [0, \beta - 1], \forall i, i' \in [0, \alpha - 1], i \neq i'$, then $h_{ij}^R \cap h_{i'j}^R = \emptyset$ and
$\forall i \in [0, \alpha - 1], \forall j, j' \in [0, \beta - 1], j \neq j'$, then $h_{ij}^S \cap h_{ij'}^S = \emptyset$;

(3) $\forall j \in [0, \beta - 1]$, $\bigcup_{i \in [0, \alpha - 1]} h_{ij}^R = R$ and $\forall i \in [0, \alpha - 1]$, $\bigcup_{j \in [0, \beta - 1]} h_{ij}^S = S$.

For those characteristics in matrix model, points (2) and (3) enable this model to support arbitrary join calculation by the tuples in one stream that can meet all the tuples in the other stream. Furthermore, points (2) and (3) also ensure the correctness of $R \bowtie S$. Specifically, point (2) guarantees that reduplicated results do not exist and point (3) ensures that there will be no missing results. In this context, points (2) and (3) act as our principles in designing the scheme generation algorithm.

4.3.1.3 *Optimization goal*

Our optimization goal is to figure out the proper values for α and β to achieve the optimal resource usages. Supposing the maximum memory size for each task is V, we formulate our goal as an optimization problem defined as Eq. (4.1):

$$\min \quad \alpha \cdot \beta,$$
$$\text{s.t.} \quad |R| \cdot \beta + |S| \cdot \alpha \leq \alpha \cdot \beta \cdot V \qquad (4.1)$$
$$\alpha \geq 1, \ \beta \geq 1.$$

In Eq. (4.1), we can find the minimal number of tasks for a regular matrix scheme. In other words, our purpose is to find the proper values for α and β in Eq. (4.1). However, it is still too strict to generate tasks according to the regular matrix scheme. Then our optimization goal is changed to find an irregular matrix while guaranteeing correctness.

4.3.2 *Adaptive model*

A data stream is an unbounded sequence of tuples with its intrinsic characteristics including continuity, dynamicity, and unpredictability. To maximize the throughput and improve the utilization rate of the computation resource, streams are usually processed in a parallel or distributed fashion. Therefore, a global execution plan is required so that the whole process can be divided into sub-tasks which are assigned to various workers. Such a plan is usually described by a directed graphical model (e.g., Storm [Toshniwal *et al.* (2014)], Heron [Kulkarni *et al.* (2015)] and Spark Streaming [Zaharia *et al.* (2013)]), in which a vertex denotes a computation operator and an edge denotes the data flow from one operator to another. Meanwhile, the workload of each computation operator is partitioned and concurrently processed by a number of threads, known as *tasks*, each of which processes the incoming tuples independently (see Fig. 4.2).

Besides, since each operator is performed by multiple task instances concurrently, the input tuples should also be distributed to the tasks evenly to ensure optimal throughput. Likewise, after a tuple is processed and emitted by one of the upstream task instance, the receiving downstream

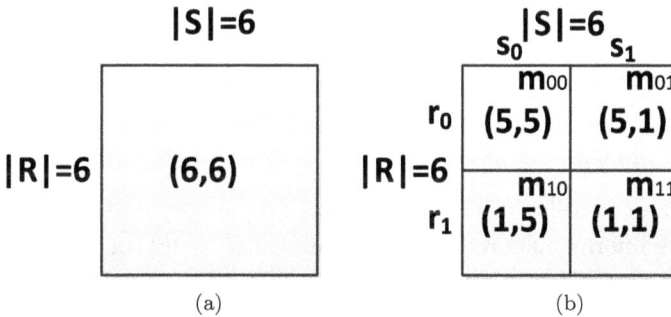

Fig. 4.2.   A toy example of calculation partition. (a) Calculation area of $|R| = 6$, $|S| = 6$ and (b) calculation area partition of $|R| = 6$, $|S| = 6$.

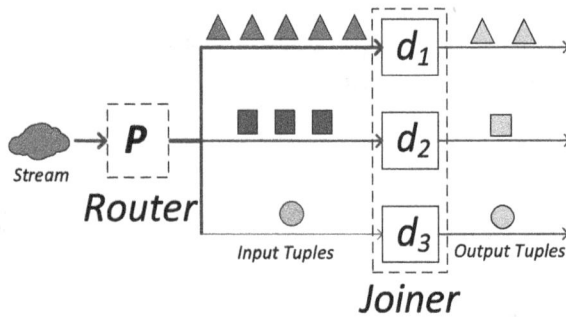

Fig. 4.3. The potential problem of workload imbalance within tasks in DSPE. P is the partition function in Router, tuples marked by different shapes indicate that they are assigned to different tasks.

task instance should also be chosen wisely, which is achieved by a tuple-to-instance assignment function implemented as a mapping from the key domain of tuples to the task instance in the succeeding operator, such as *Fields Grouping* in Storm. However, such strategy may not perform as expected in distributed stream processing systems due to the lack of balancing on the homogeneous tasks within the same abstract operator. Fig. 4.3 shows an example illustrating the potential problem with such strategy. In this example, there are three task instances running in a join operator, denoted by rectangles. Because of the distribution skewness on the input tuples, the number of tuples assigned to the first task instance is five times of that to the third task instance. Hence, regardless of how well the system allocates the tasks to the available nodes for optimal computation resource utilization, the higher latency in the first task instance still dominates the total processing time of this operation, which slows down the whole process significantly.

4.3.2.1 *Stateful operation*

An operator is called a stateful operator if a memory buffer is required to cache the intermediate results, which are called states, of the keys appear that in the latest tuples. Basically, each state is associated with an active key in the corresponding task in a stateful operator. It, for example, can be used to record the counts of the words or recent tuples in the sliding window.

Functions such as *random* or *round-robin* are naturally load balanced among all the instances. However, this is at the price of other additional compensation operations to maintain the stateful information. For example, [Nasir *et al.* (2015, 2016)] designed a series of randomized routing algorithms to balance the workload of stream processing operators. Their strategy is based on the theoretical model and its variant of *power-of-two*, which evaluates two or more randomly chosen candidate destinations for each tuple and chooses the one with the smaller workload estimation. Their approach performs well for stateless operators in streaming processing, and a wide class of stateful operators, like counting, by introducing an aggregator to combine the results of tuples sent to different working threads. For some stateful operators, e.g., join and median, the partial result is insufficient for simple aggregation, almost all original tuples have to be forwarded to the aggregator for further processing.

It is no doubt that the join operation in RTTS is stateful. Its processing flow using random routing strategy can be reflected by the example of Fig. 4.4. Given two data streams $S_1 = \{\tau_1, \tau_2, \tau_3, \tau_4\}$ and $S_2 = \{\tau_5, \tau_6\}$, each tuple τ_i in both streams has exactly the same join key. Therefore, the join result $S_1 \bowtie S_2$ contains eight pairs of tuples. By applying partial key grouping, $\{\tau_1, \tau_3\}$ and $\{\tau_2, \tau_4\}$ are sent to two processing instances d_1 and d_2, respectively. Similarly, τ_2 and τ_4 are processed by d_1 and d_2, respectively. These two instances d_1 and d_2 can only generate four pairs of join results based on the received tuples. They have to forward all these tuples to the merge operator in order to generate complete join results. Therefore, the communication cost of partial key grouping is doubled, while the merge operator has exactly the same workload as d_1 and d_2 have.

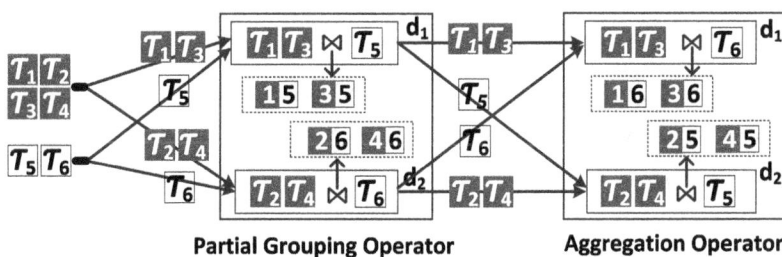

Fig. 4.4.   Example of partial key grouping used in join operator.

The problems mentioned in both Figs. 4.3 and 4.4 imply that the most difficult problem of the partition function in RTTS is how to ensure workload balance among tasks with state maintenance.

4.3.2.2 *Problem statement*

A trajectory P consists of a sequence of spatial-temporal points: $P = \{p_1, p_2, \ldots, p_i, \ldots\}$, each of which is a 4D vector expressed as (*trajectory-id, timestamp, longitude, latitude*). Here, a spatial-temporal point can be seen as an independent inflowing item. Therefore, each point of ART is a tuple in DSPE. Due to the continuity feature of the data stream, queries on the unbounded streams are usually performed over sliding windows, which are finite snapshots of the incoming streams. Given that the time domain is usually discretized and represented by integer timestamps and each time window holds the data within its time range, we state that all the trajectories mentioned in the following content refer to the data in the current window.

Then, the problem to be solved in this chapter can be defined as follows.

Definition 4.1. Given a set of trajectories $\mathbb{P} = \{P_1, P_2, \ldots, P_M\}$, a trajectory similarity measure criteria $\mathcal{H}$, and a distance threshold ϑ, the *real-time trajectory similarity* query is defined as $\Gamma(\mathbb{P}, \mathcal{H}, \vartheta)$, meaning the trajectories are set for each $P \in \mathbb{P}$ with distance measured using criteria $\mathcal{H}$ and lower than ϑ.

The query result is a nested set $\mathbb{B}$, where $\mathbb{B} = \{B_i\}$ and B_i is the selected trajectories set of P_i, expressed as

$$\text{s.t. } B_i \subseteq \mathbb{P}, \tag{4.2}$$

$$\forall P_j \in B_i, H(P_i, P_j) \leq \vartheta. \tag{4.3}$$

In the above expression, H is the specific distance metric. In this chapter, we take Hausdorff distance as our distance metric. Overall, the goal of this chapter is to design and implement an advanced processing scheme for trajectory similarity, which is capable of (a) supporting the stateful operators (RTTS) in a cost-effective way and guaranteeing the computation correctness; and (b) achieving load balance by handling highly skewed and/or dynamically changing key distributions.

4.4 Model Design for Multi-stream θ-Join

4.4.1 *Basic principle for matrix model*

We first introduce two theorems to explain the guild for generating the optimal matrix scheme. Then, we describe the adaptive process of generating a matrix scheme based on these two theorems according to the real workload.

Since those subsets may be replicated along rows or columns, the values of α and β decide the memory consumption that is proportional to the subarea's semi-perimeter valued as $|r_i| + |s_j|$ as in Elseidy *et al.* (2014). Given the area or the perimeter, we introduce the following two well-known theories:

Theorem 4.1. *Given the area with a constant value, the square has the smallest perimeter among all the rectangles.*

Theorem 4.2. *Given the perimeter with a constant value, the square has the biggest area among all the rectangles.*

Based on these two theories, we have the following corollary on partitioning scheme.

Corollary 4.1. *If there exist α and β which can make $\frac{|R|}{\alpha} = \frac{|S|}{\beta} = V_h$, the consumption of processing resource for $R \bowtie S$ is minimal.*

Proof. Supposing CPU resource is a constant value in each task, in order to ensure any tuple meets the others, the computation complexity for stream join is $|R| \cdot |S|$. However the memory usage will be minimized if $\frac{|R|}{\alpha} = \frac{|S|}{\beta} = V_h$ according to Theorem 4.1. Supposing the memory resource of each task is constant, the number of tasks used for the calculation (total area) is smallest when $\frac{|R|}{\alpha} = \frac{|S|}{\beta} = V_h$ according to Theorem 4.1. The network communication cost is relevant to the memory for the volume of tuples stored equal to the transmission volume. Based on the preceding discussion, we can draw a conclusion that Corollary 4.1 is established. □

According to Corollary 4.1, if the volumes of two streams $|R|$ and $|S|$ can both be divisible by V_h, receiving tuples with quantity of V_h from both streams is a prefect solution to generate a matrix scheme M with minimal resource usages. However, stream volumes may not always be divisible by V_h. Given that the number of rows (columns) in matrix M must be an integer, we get the row number $\alpha = \lceil \frac{|R|}{V_h} \rceil$ and the column number $\beta = \lceil \frac{|S|}{V_h} \rceil$. Then the number of tasks N used in matrix M can be expressed as

$$N = \left\lceil \frac{|R|}{V_h} \right\rceil \cdot \left\lceil \frac{|S|}{V_h} \right\rceil. \tag{4.4}$$

In those N cells, we primarily load the first $\alpha - 1$ rows or $\beta - 1$ columns of cells. When the stream volume cannot be evenly divided by V_h, it generates fragment data for the tasks (called fragment tasks) in the last row or the last column in matrix M.

For example, given task memory $V = 10\,\text{GB}$, R stream volume $|R| = 6\,\text{GB}$ and S stream volume $|S| = 6\,\text{GB}$, its calculation area is shown in Fig. 4.2(a). Processing $R \bowtie S$ will take up four tasks for its matrix M with two rows and two columns shown as in Fig. 4.2(b). In M, $m_{00} = (5\,\text{GB}, 5\,\text{GB})$, $m_{01} = (5\,\text{GB}, 1\,\text{GB})$, $m_{10} = (1\,\text{GB}, 5\,\text{GB})$ and $m_{11} = (1\,\text{GB}, 1\,\text{GB})$. Then m_{01}, m_{10}, m_{11} are fragment tasks in that the sum memory consumption of $|r_{ij}|$ and $|s_{ij}|$ in these tasks is smaller than V.

4.4.2 *Generation processing scheme*

To find an optimal processing scheme, we differentiate the two streams as a primary stream P and a secondary stream D. Supposing we split P into P_γ subsets assigned to each task, we first ensure the memory usage for those subsets from P. The remaining memory $V - \frac{P}{P_\gamma}$ in each task is used for the subset of data from D. The number of tasks D_γ required for D can be calculated as

$$D_\gamma = \left\lceil \frac{D}{V - \frac{P}{P_\gamma}} \right\rceil. \tag{4.5}$$

We use N_c to represent the number of tasks and it can be calculated as Eq. (4.6)

$$N_c = P_\gamma \cdot D_\gamma = P_\gamma \cdot \left\lceil \frac{D}{V - \frac{P}{P_\gamma}} \right\rceil. \tag{4.6}$$

As declared in Corollary 4.1, the number of tasks is minimized when $\frac{|R|}{\alpha} = \frac{|S|}{\beta} = V_h$, but we cannot promise to find such α and β. According to

Theorem 4.3, we can select P_γ from $\{\lceil \frac{|R|}{V_h} \rceil, \lfloor \frac{|R|}{V_h} \rfloor, \lceil \frac{|S|}{V_h} \rceil, \lfloor \frac{|S|}{V_h} \rfloor\}$, and there exists one P_γ to generate the minimal number of tasks N_c calculated as in Eq. (4.6).

Theorem 4.3. *Given stream volumes $|R|$, $|S|$ and memory size V of task, using the matrix model for $R \bowtie S$, the number of tasks generated by $P_\gamma * D_\gamma$ as Eq. (4.6) by selecting P_γ from $\{\lceil \frac{|R|}{V_h} \rceil, \lfloor \frac{|R|}{V_h} \rfloor, \lceil \frac{|S|}{V_h} \rceil, \lfloor \frac{|S|}{V_h} \rfloor\}$ is the minimal.*

Proof. We assume that there exists a matrix M' with row number α' and column number β' which can be used for $R \bowtie S$ and the number of tasks N' is smaller than N_c. In other words, there is a number P'_γ: $P'_\gamma \notin \{\lceil \frac{|R|}{V_h} \rceil, \lfloor \frac{|R|}{V_h} \rfloor, \lceil \frac{|S|}{V_h} \rceil, \lfloor \frac{|S|}{V_h} \rfloor\}$ and $N' < N_c$. According to Corollary 4.1, square has the largest area. Then $\frac{|R|}{\alpha'}$ is closer to V_h than $\frac{|R|}{\alpha}$, and $\frac{|S|}{\beta'}$ is also closer to V_h than $\frac{|S|}{\beta}$. However, it is impossible for $\frac{|R|}{\alpha'}$ and $\frac{|S|}{\beta'}$ to get closer to V_h simultaneously. Moreover, P_γ occupies all possible values that make $\frac{P}{P_\gamma}$ nearest to V_h. Hence, smaller N' does not exist. □

The algorithm of finding an optimal partition scheme is described in Algorithm 4.1. First, the minimal number of tasks is determined in line 1 according to Eq. (4.6); then in lines 5–8, the number of rows α and columns β can be calculated according to values of P and P_γ. If $P_\gamma \in \{\lceil \frac{|R|}{V_h} \rceil, \lfloor \frac{|R|}{V_h} \rfloor\}$, R is the primary stream, or else S is the primary one. After we select the P

Algorithm 4.1 Scheme Generation

input: Stream R, Stream S, Memory size V
output: Row number α, Column number β
1: **foreach** $P^i_\gamma \in \{\lceil \frac{|R|}{V_h} \rceil, \lfloor \frac{|R|}{V_h} \rfloor, \lceil \frac{|S|}{V_h} \rceil, \lfloor \frac{|S|}{V_h} \rfloor\}$ **do**
2:      $D^i_\gamma \leftarrow \lceil \frac{D}{V - \frac{P}{P_\gamma}} \rceil$
3:      **if** $P_\gamma \cdot D_\gamma > P^i_\gamma \cdot D^i_\gamma$ **then**
4:          $P_\gamma \leftarrow P^i_\gamma$ and $D_\gamma \leftarrow D^i_\gamma$
5: **if** $P_\gamma \in \{\lceil \frac{|R|}{V_h} \rceil, \lfloor \frac{|R|}{V_h} \rfloor\}$ **then**
6:      $\alpha \leftarrow P_\gamma, \beta \leftarrow D_\gamma$
7: **else**
8:      $\alpha \leftarrow D_\gamma, \beta \leftarrow P_\gamma$
9: **return** α, β

---

stream, each task will first be fed with data from P with memory $\frac{|P|}{P_\gamma}$ and the remaining memory $V - \frac{|P|}{P_\gamma}$ is used for the D stream.

Theorem 4.4. *Algorithm* 4.1 *will consume the minimal number of tasks and ensure the correctness of operation when using the matrix model for* $R \bowtie S$ *with the memory size of each task* V.

Proof. Assuming that there exists another matrix M' with the number of rows α' and columns β'. It could be used for $R \bowtie S$ and the number of tasks N' used in M' is smaller than N_c. To find the smaller N_c, Algorithm 4.1 tries all possible values that make $\frac{|P|}{P_\gamma}$ nearest to V_h in line (1–4). In other words, it is impossible for $\frac{|R|}{\alpha'}$ and $\frac{|S|}{\beta'}$ to get more closer to V_h than $\frac{|R|}{\alpha}$ and $\frac{|S|}{\beta}$. According to Theorem 4.1, squared cells consume minimal resources. Then, the assumption of the existing regular matrix M' does not hold. For ensuring the correctness of join, it is obvious that Algorithm 4.1 can ensure join correctness when it generates a regular matrix scheme according to the characteristics of the matrix model in Section 4.3.1.2.   □

4.4.3 *Processing framework of adaptive model*

In this section, we introduce our processing model and assumptions made in this chapter, and give an overview of our framework. Specifically, we first introduce the framework for RTTS. Then, a similarity search algorithm is proposed to illustrate the routing strategies of ART, with the constraint of workload balance.

4.4.3.1 *Processing model*

We assume that the total workload of the underlying area is L and the ideal workload of each parallel task is $\overline{L}$, then $\lceil \frac{L}{\overline{L}} \rceil$ tasks are needed for the RTTS operation. Figure 4.5 shows an example of partitioning the area with a size of 40×40 into multiple sub-areas, each of which is executed by a task instance. Assuming that the area in Fig. 4.5 will be processed by ($\lceil \frac{L}{\overline{L}} \rceil = 16$) tasks. Intuitively, it can be easily divided into 16 sub-areas evenly using a range partition strategy, shown as the red grid in Fig. 4.5. Despite the advantages of range function on partition process and routing cost, such schemes cannot handle the workload variance and key skewness.

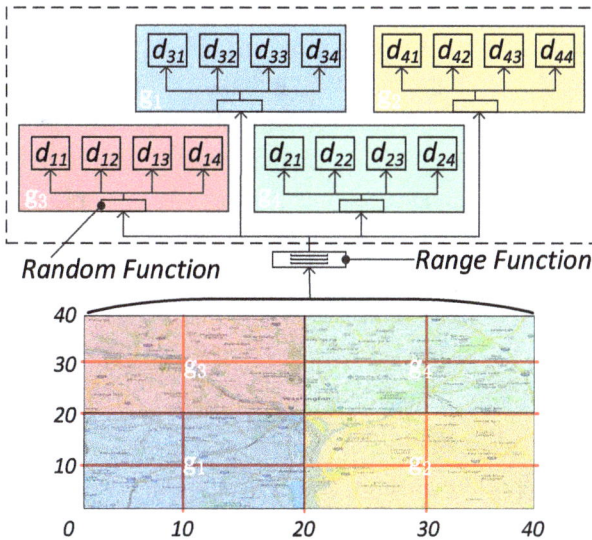

Fig. 4.5.   The partition strategy of ART.

For the parallel processing tasks in a share-nothing infrastructure, the data transmission cost is minimum when each task only communicates with its upstream/downstream to receive/transmit tuples and no data transmission occurs between tasks within the same operation. To this end, the partition strategy of our ART contains a two-layer global mapping function to assign the incoming tuples. First, ART divides the entire mission into several big sub-areas according to a basic range function. Since each sub-area will be processed by a group of tasks eventually, we then apply a random function in each group to generate the destination for each point that comes from the corresponding sub-area. As shown in Fig. 4.5, ART uses a range function to partition the target area into four sub-areas, and each sub-area corresponds to one group of tasks ($\{d_{11\sim14}\} \sim \{d_{41\sim44}\}$). The range of each sub-area is a rectangle, denoted by $[l_{(i,j)}, l_{(i',j')}]$, where $l_{(i,j)}$ and $l_{(i',j')}$ represent the lower left and top right corner of the rectangle, respectively. Based on this, the out layer mapping function can be expressed as $[(0,0), (20,20)) \mapsto g_1$, $[(20,0), (40,20)) \mapsto g_2$, $[(0,20), (20,40)] \mapsto g_3$, and $[(20,20), (40,40)] \mapsto g_4$. Then, the routing strategy in each task group is random.

Similarly, the anti-imbalance process of ART also consists of two phases: P_{range} and P_{random}. In P_{range}, ART splits the whole workload according to a content-sensitive routing rule. Note that although the P_{range} uses key-based routing strategy, each group is usually processed by multiple tasks which can smooth the workload imbalance. In other words, P_{range} in ART always acts as a cushioning layer to relieve the workload imbalance. This *workload imbalance sharing* characteristic is similar to the grouping processing tasks that aim at receiving the same data as in Lin *et al.* (2015). Furthermore, the random routing strategy in P_{random} can better ensure the workload balance.

4.4.3.2 *Routing strategies*

To clarify the delivery route for incoming points in ART, we first define several routing actions as follows.

- **Range-routing:** Given a workload area A and its sub-area set $\{a_i\}$ with $A = \{a_i | \cup_{a_i} = A, \cap_{a_i} = \emptyset\}$, the tasks of an operation G and its group set $\{g_i\}$ with $|A| = |G|$, then, the function that records the one-to-one mapping relationships between A and G is defined as *Range-routing*, denoted by $f_{\text{range}}(p) \mapsto g_i$.
- **Random-routing:** Given an incoming point p, a task set $\mathcal{D}_i$ with D tasks in group g_i, the process that a function randomly picks a task d_j ($d_j \in \mathcal{D}_i$) as p's task destination is defined as *Random-routing*, denoted by $f_{\text{random}}^{\mathcal{D}_i}(p) \mapsto d_j$.
- **Broadcast-routing:** Given a incoming point p, a task set $\mathcal{D}_i$ with D tasks in group g_i, the process that a replication function sends p to all tasks in $\mathcal{D}_i$ is defined as *Broadcast-routing*, denoted by $f_{bc}(p) \mapsto \mathcal{D}_i$.
- **Filter-screening:** Given a incoming point p, a set of determining criteria $\mathfrak{R}$, we define the process that judging whether p is in keeping with $\mathfrak{R}$ for g_i as *Filter-screening*, denoted by $\mathfrak{R}^{g_i}(p)$, where the value of $\mathfrak{R}^{g_i}(p)$ is either true or false.

Based on the actions defined above, the workflow of ART's routing strategy can be divided into two parts: *routing for storage* and *routing for join*. As shown in Algorithm 4.2, ART first locates the task group for the incoming point for storage in line 2, using the defined *Range-routing* strategy. Then, a task is selected from that group by the *Random-routing* strategy, and ART takes this task as the storage destination for the incoming point in line 3. Meanwhile, ART broadcasts the incoming point to all

---

Algorithm 4.2 Routing Strategy of *ART*

---

input: Point: p

output: Destination Task for Storage: d, Destination Task Set for Join: $\mathcal{D}$

1: ▶ (Routing for Storage)

2: $g_i \leftarrow f_{Range}(p)$ ▷'$\leftarrow$' means Assignment

3: $d \leftarrow f_{random}^{\mathcal{D}_i}(p)$

4: ▶ (Routing for Join)

5: **for** each $g_i \in G$ **do**

6:     **if** $\mathfrak{R}^{g_i}(p)$ **then**

7:         $\mathcal{D} \Leftarrow g_i$ ▷'$\Leftarrow$' means Loading

   return d and $\mathcal{D}$;

---

task groups. In each task group, *Filter-screening* is responsible for checking whether p should be joined with the trajectories stored in the current group. If the answer from *Filter-screening* is positive, all trajectories in this group will join with the incoming point p, else, p will be discarded directly.

Figure 4.6 illustrates ART's routing strategy for an incoming point p. For storage, the *Range-routing* assigns p into g_1 according to p's location. Then, d_{11} in g_1 is selected for p's storage according to *Random-routing*. For join action(s), p is sent to all groups ($g_{1\sim o}$), and the *Filter-screening* of each task group, respectively determines whether to pass it on or to simply discard. The regulations of *Filter-screening* include two aspects. First, if the value of $f_{range}(p)$ equals to the current group's ID, p will be discarded directly, like the *Filter-screening* of g_1 due to $f_{range}(p) = g_1$. Another rule of *Filter-screening* is about the distance relationship of p and trajectories that are stored in the current group, which will be described in Section 4.6.3. If p passes through the screening, it will be broadcast to each task of the current group for similarity computation.

4.5 Migration Plan Generation

After we generate the new scheme, we should calculate a migration plan from the old scheme to the new scheme. In this section, we will first introduce how to route the input data stream which is designed to promise the correctness of join results, and then we describe how to map

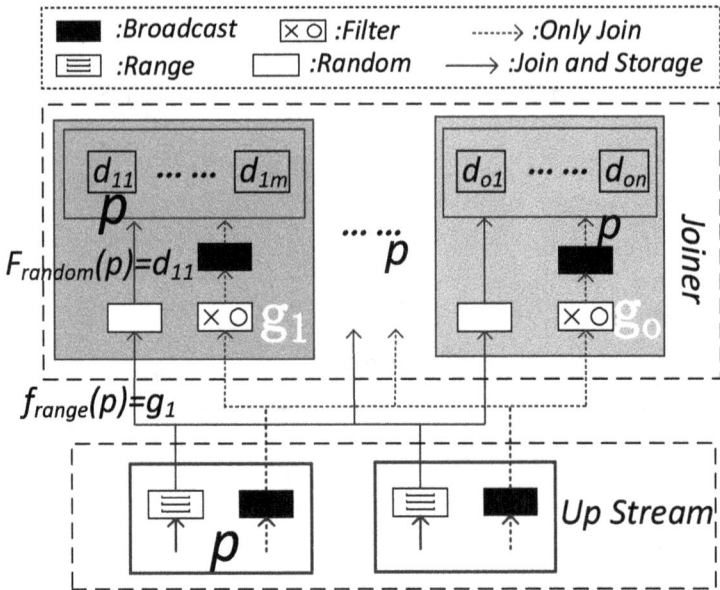

Fig. 4.6.   Example of ART's routing strategy.

tasks between the new and old schemes with the target of reducing the migration cost.

In this section, we introduce how to route tuples in the basic matrix model with a random tuple distribution manner. As described in Section 4.3.1.1, the matrix model randomly routes tuples to cells of each stream corresponding to one side of the matrix. Hence, it can handle data skewness perfectly. The whole procedure of basic tuple routing is described in Algorithm 4.3.

We use $\Gamma(\Gamma \in \{row,\ column\})$ to represent which side of the matrix the input tuple corresponds to and use ϵ ($\epsilon \in [0, (\alpha - 1)]$ or $\epsilon \in [0 \sim (\beta - 1)]$) which represent to which line in the side of Γ the tuple should be sent. Then the return pair (Γ, ϵ) of Algorithm 4.3 means the input tuple should be sent to the ϵth line in the Γ side of the matrix. In Algorithm 4.3, line (2 and 3) and line (5 and 6) identify which side of the matrix the input tuple belongs to, then, lines 4 and 7 accordingly generate a random position. Finally, for the routing of matrix model, the input tuple will be sent to all the processing tasks which are located in the line ϵ along the side of Γ.

Algorithm 4.3 Basic Tuple Routing

---

input: R stream , S stream
output: Matrix side:Γ, Line:ϵ
1: **foreach** tuple τ **do**
2:    **if** $\tau \in R$ **then**
3:       $\Gamma \leftarrow row$
4:       $Random[0 \sim (\alpha - 1)] \rightarrow \epsilon$
5:    **else if** $\tau \in S$ **then**
6:       $\Gamma \leftarrow column$
7:       $Random[0 \sim (\beta - 1)] \rightarrow \epsilon$
8: **return** Γ, ϵ

4.5.1 *Task-load mapping generation*

Supposing m_{ij} and m_{kl} corresponds to two cells in the matrix which are M_o in the old schema and M_n in the new schema, respectively, and each cell corresponds to one join processing task. In order to reduce the data migration among cells during schema change, it is crucial to find the optimal task for each cell in M_n. Less migration cost means there are more data overlap for the cells between the old and new schemes. We then define a correlation coefficient λ_{kl}^{ij} for each pair of tasks corresponding to m_{ij} and m_{kl}, which are in M_o and M_n, respectively. λ_{kl}^{ij} is a measurement for the cell data overlapping between m_{ij} and m_{kl} calculated as Eq. (4.7):

$$\lambda_{kl}^{ij} = (h_{ij}^R \cap s_{kl}^R) \cdot |R| + (h_{ij}^S \cap s_{kl}^S) \cdot |S|. \tag{4.7}$$

A new indicant $npi = \langle m_{ij}, m_{kl}, \lambda_{kl}^{ij} \rangle$ (task mapping item) is defined to represent the effort for migration $(|s_{kl}^R| + |s_{kl}^S| - \lambda_{kl}^{ij})$ when using the task in charge of m_{ij} for the data in m_{kl}. The whole procedure of task pairing is described in Algorithm 4.4 and can be divided into two parts:

(1) **Part I** enumerates all the possible npis shown in lines 2–5 in Algorithm 4.4;
(2) **Part II** generates a task pairing relationship with the purpose of minimizing migration by selecting npi with the biggest λ_{kl}^{ij} into NP set. This NP set will generate the task-load mapping with the least migration cost according to Theorem 4.5.

Algorithm 4.4 Generation Task-Load Mapping

---

input: Old scheme M_o, New scheme M_n

output: Task mapping NP

1: Initialize $NP = Null$

2: **foreach** m_{ij} in Old scheme M_o **do**

3:    **foreach** m_{kl} in New scheme M_n **do**

4:       Calculate λ_{kl}^{ij} according to Equ. 4.7

5:       Add the item $< m_{ij}, m_{kl}, \lambda_{kl}^{ij} >$ to a temporary set NPI

6: **foreach** task mapping item with max λ_{kl}^{ij} in NPI **do**

7:    **if** m_{ij} or m_{kl} in npi not exist in NP **then**

8:       $< m_{ij}, m_{kl} > \rightarrow NP$

9:    Delete $< m_{ij}, m_{kl} >$ from NPI

10: **return** NP

Theorem 4.5. *Among task pairings between the old and new schemes, NP set produced by Algorithm* 4.4 *leads to the minimal migration cost.*

Proof. For part I in Algorithm 4.4, it generates npis with the size of $|M_o| \cdot |M_n|$. In other words, $\alpha_o \cdot \beta_o \cdot \alpha_n \cdot \beta_n$ items are generated where α_o and β_o are the number of rows and columns in the old scheme M_o and α_n and β_n are the number of rows and columns in the new scheme M_n. Obviously, $|NP|$ is a smaller one and each m_{ij} or m_{kl} appears in NP only once at most. Then we can conclude that the current maximal λ_{kl}^{ij} is independent of others. That is to say, part II described as lines 6–9 in Algorithm 4.4 produces the maximal cumulative sum of λ_{kl}^{ij}. It means there is the maximal volume of non-migrating data in NP, also implying that the task mapping NP leads to the minimal migration cost. Based on the preceding discussion, we can conclude that Theorem 4.5 is established.   □

4.5.2 *Migration plan generation*

As described earlier, a migration plan defines how to migrate data among tasks when the scheme changes. In order to make it easy for explanation, we describe data moving among tasks with Stream R, and it will be the same for Stream S. We use n_{kl}^R to denote the range of data that should be moved into area m_{kl} from stream R, calculated as shown in Eq. (4.8):

$$n_{kl}^R = s_{kl}^R - (s_{kl}^R \cap h_{kl}^R). \tag{4.8}$$

Migration plan $mp = \langle m_{ij}, m_{kl}, N_{ij}^R \rangle$ represents the data moving between the two areas m_{ij} in the old scheme M_o and m_{kl} in the new scheme M_n, with N_{ij}^R representing the data moving from area m_{ij} to area m_{kl} for R. We define two kinds of actions for moving: duplicating and migrating. Duplicating happens among tasks along the same row/column; otherwise, it is data migrating. Supposing for each cell m_{kl} in the new scheme M_n, h_{kl}^R and s_{kl}^R are the tuples in it for the last schema and should be kept in the current schema. Then cell m_{kl} deletes the migrated data in set $h_{kl}^R - s_{kl}^R$ for stream R, which is represented as $mp = \langle \odot, m_{kl}, h_{kl}^R - s_{kl}^R \rangle$. All the calculations are the same for stream S.

Migration plan generation is described in Algorithm 4.5 and is divided into two steps as follows:

Step-1 — Splitting stream data for matrix cells: According to matrix characteristics described in Section 4.3.1.1, it is easy for us to get the whole dataset of stream R or S by combining the data

---

Algorithm 4.5 Migration Plan Generation

input: Old scheme M_o, New scheme M_n, Task mapping NP
output: Migration plan MP

1: **foreach** row i with column 0 in old scheme M_o **do**
2:    **foreach** m_{kl} in new scheme M_n **do**
3:        **if** $h_{i0}^R \cap n_{kl}^R \neq Null$ **then**
4:            $< m_{i0}, m_{kl}, h_{i0}^R \cap n_{kl}^R > \rightarrow MP$
5: **foreach** column j with row 0 in old scheme M_o **do**
6:    **foreach** m_{kl} in new scheme M_n **do**
7:        **if** $h_{0j}^S \cap n_{kl}^S \neq Null$ **then**
8:            $< m_{0j}, m_{kl}, h_{0j}^S \cap n_{kl}^S > \rightarrow MP$
9: **foreach** task m_{kl} in new scheme M_n **do**
10:    $< \odot, m_{kl}, h_{kl}^R - s_{kl}^R > \rightarrow MP$
11:    $< \odot, m_{kl}, h_{kl}^S - s_{kl}^S > \rightarrow MP$
12: **return** MP

---

from the first row or the first column in M_o. According to the new scheme M_n, we can divide the streams evenly to fill each cell as in lines 1–8.

Step-2 — Deleting migrated tuples: It deletes migrated data under the new scheme M_n in lines 9–11.

Let's take Fig. 5.8 as an example. A partitioning scheme changes from 2×1 to 2×2. In the old scheme M_o, each area manages one half of the data volume from R and the total volume of the data from S is shown in Fig. 5.8(a): $h_{00}^R = [0, \frac{1}{2}]$, $h_{10}^R = [\frac{1}{2}, 1]$ and $h_{00}^S = [0, 1]$, $h_{10}^S = [0, 1]$. When the workload of the streams increases, the system may scale out by adding one more column with two tasks forming a 2×2 scheme as shown in Fig. 5.8(b). In this case, data partitions of R are unchanged where tasks in the first row still manage one half of the data volume ($s_{0j}^R = [0, \frac{1}{2}]$, $j \in \{0, 1\}$) and tasks in the second row manage the other half ($s_{1j}^R = [\frac{1}{2}, 1]$, $j \in \{0, 1\}$). Stream S should be split into two partitions for two columns, each of which manages $\frac{1}{2}$ range of data, that is, $s_{i0}^S = [0, \frac{1}{2}]$, $s_{i1}^S = [\frac{1}{2}, 1]$, with $i \in \{0, 1\}$.

NP is $\{\langle m_{00}^o, m_{00}^n \rangle, \langle m_{10}^o, m_{10}^n \rangle\}$ as shown in Fig. 5.8(b). In Fig. 5.8(b), we label the relevant task pairs between M_o and M_n by assigning the same numbers to the tasks. The tasks tagged with red *new* in m_{01} and m_{11} are new additive tasks. m_{01} needs data $n_{01}^R = [0, \frac{1}{2}]$ and $n_{01}^S = [\frac{1}{2}, 1]$; m_{11} needs data $n_{11}^R = [\frac{1}{2}, 1]$ and $n_{11}^S = [\frac{1}{2}, 1]$. According to Algorithm 4.5, s_{01}^R and s_{11}^R are generated by duplicating R data from m_{00} and m_{10}, respectively. m_{01} and m_{11} generate S by duplicating $[\frac{1}{2}, 1]$ from m_{00}. Since S has been reallocated according to the preceding discussion, the range of data in $[\frac{1}{2}, 1]$ from S is depleting from m_{00} and m_{01}.

4.5.3 *Discussion*

In this section, we will discuss further optimization for the matrix model to pursue a more cost-effective model. And then, we describe the tuple routing approach in the variant model which may have better resource usage.

4.5.3.1 *Optimized matrix*

In Fig. 4.2, if we take R as the primary stream P and the number of divisions generated by the primary stream is $P_\gamma = \lceil \frac{|R|}{V_h} \rceil$, then the matrix scheme of example in Fig. 4.2(a) should have only one column with two cells. However, N_c calculated in Eq. (4.6) will have fragment tasks if its rounding

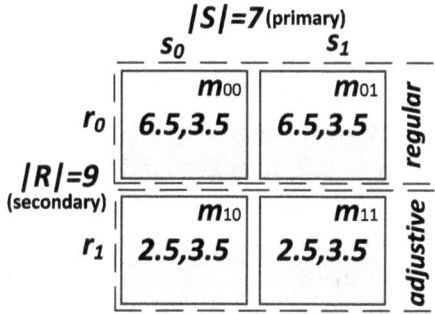

Fig. 4.7.   Example of the further optimization for matrix.

up value is not equal to the rounding down value. For example, in Fig. 4.7, given $V = 10\,\text{GB}$, $|R| = 9\,\text{GB}$, and $|S| = 7\,\text{GB}$, a matrix M with $\alpha = 2$ and $\beta = 2$ will be generated. Sine S is the primary stream, each task first gets data assignment from S by $\frac{|S|}{\beta} = 3.5\,\text{GB}$ and the remaining $6.5\,\text{GB}$ space can be used for divisions from R. The memory utilization percentage of the two tasks in the last row is 60%.

In Fig. 4.7, since the data for both m_{11} and m_{10} join with r_1, it is feasible to move the tuples in s_1 to m_{10} to complete the join work, still satisfying the memory threshold $V = 10\,\text{GB}$ ($2.5 + 3.5 + 3.5 = 9.5 < 10$), and promise the completeness of results. Then, an optimized partition scheme with only three tasks for $R \bowtie S$ can be generated, which is much more resource economic. We will study the optimization strategy of the matrix model, the definition of tuple routing, and the specific migration procedure in further studies.

4.5.3.2   *Optimized routing*

For tuple routing in the matrix model, we load data to rows and columns in a top-down manner. Since we have divided the load along the primary stream randomly, we have to assign the load from the other one evenly to each cell. In such a case, each cell may have free resources. In this section, we propose an optimized routing method to make full use of our resources.

We differentiate the two streams as a primary stream P and a secondary stream D to find an optimal processing scheme. Here, we propose to differentiate the routing policy for the primary stream and the secondary stream, that is, the tuples in the primary stream will be sent into the row or column randomly while tuples in the secondary stream will be sent selectively instead of randomly.

Our algorithm is shown in Algortithm 4.6 and we consider the cells in Fig. 4.2. For the primary stream, lines 2–8 randomly split the incoming data into a number of non-overlap substreams. Then, we process the secondary stream. We use $Random[0 \sim \psi]^{\omega} \to \epsilon$ ($\epsilon \in [0, \psi]$) to represent that a tuple randomly selects a line ϵ between 0 and ψ in the probability of ω. Then, $\chi^{\omega} \to \epsilon$ means the input tuple will be sent to the χth in the probability of ω. In our design, we expect to fill the secondary stream as much as possible to the cells except the last row (S is primary one) or column (S is the secondary

---

Algorithm 4.6 Tuple Routing in the Varietal Model

---

input: R stream , S stream

output: Matrix side:Γ, Line:ϵ

 1: **foreach** tuple τ **do**

 2:    **if** τ belongs to the primary stream **then**

 3:        **if** R stream the primary stream **then**

 4:            $\Gamma \leftarrow row$

 5:            $\epsilon \leftarrow Random[0 \sim (\alpha - 1)]$

 6:        **else if** S stream the primary stream **then**

 7:            $\Gamma \leftarrow column$

 8:            $\epsilon \leftarrow Random[0 \sim (\beta - 1)]$

 9:    **else if** τ belongs to the secondary stream **then**

10:        **if** S stream the primary stream **then**

11:            $\Gamma \leftarrow row$

12:            $\epsilon \leftarrow Random[0 \sim (\alpha - 2)]^{\frac{(V-\frac{P}{P_\gamma})\cdot(\alpha-2)}{D}}$

13:            $\epsilon \leftarrow (\alpha - 1)^{1-\frac{(V-\frac{P}{P_\gamma})\cdot(\alpha-2)}{D}}$

14:        **else if** R stream the primary stream **then**

15:            $\Gamma \leftarrow column$

16:            $\epsilon \leftarrow Random[0 \sim (\beta - 2)]^{\frac{(V-\frac{P}{P_\gamma})\cdot(\beta-2)}{D}}$

17:            $\epsilon \leftarrow (\beta - 1)^{1-\frac{(V-\frac{P}{P_\gamma})\cdot(\beta-2)}{D}}$

18: **return** Γ, ϵ

---

one), which is $V - P/P_\gamma$. Lines 10–13 in Algorithm 4.6 show the tuple routing process when the input tuple τ belongs to the secondary stream and the S stream is the primary stream. Line 12 means the first $(\alpha - 1)$ rows will have the probability of $\dfrac{(V - \frac{P}{P_\gamma}) \cdot (\alpha - 2)}{D}$ to receive the input tuple randomly. Line 13 assigns the input tuple into the last row with the probability of $1 - \dfrac{(V - \frac{P}{P_\gamma}) \cdot (\alpha - 2)}{D}$. Lines 14–17 show the process of tuple routing when the input tuple belongs to the secondary stream and the primary stream is R. This procedure is similar to the process in lines 10–13. We may find that the cells in the last row or column managed by the secondary stream will be underloaded. Those cells can be combined to save system resources and then we may get the irregular matrix as discussed in Section 4.5.3.1.

4.5.3.3 *Others for optimized scheme*

Besides scheme generation and routing tuples as discussed earlier, there are also other problems that need to be studied for the irregular matrix scheme, such as migration actions and guaranteeing the correctness. Specifically, because the content that stored in each cell of the irregular matrix is different to the regular one, the migration action will be challenge. Furthermore, the correctness of a system during the process of migration should also be redesigned. We will keep this as our future work.

4.6 Balance Data Partition

4.6.1 *Computation requirements*

To accomplish the task defined in Definition 4.1 for Hausdorff criteria, we first introduce the computation requirements of RTTS in this section. Then, we describe the processing architecture according to the designed model. Finally, a workload shedding strategy is devised to optimize the processing procedure.

Hausdorff distance between trajectory P and trajectory Q is a maxmin function, defined as $H(P, Q) = \max\{h(P, Q), h(Q, P)\}$, where $h(P, Q) = \max_{p_i \in P}\{\min_{q_i \in Q}\{d(p_i, q_j)\}\}$. In the above expressions, p_i and q_j are points of sets P and Q, respectively, and $d(p_i, q_j)$ is any metric between these points. For simplicity, we define $d(p_i, q_j)$ as the Euclidean distance between p_i and q_j in this section.

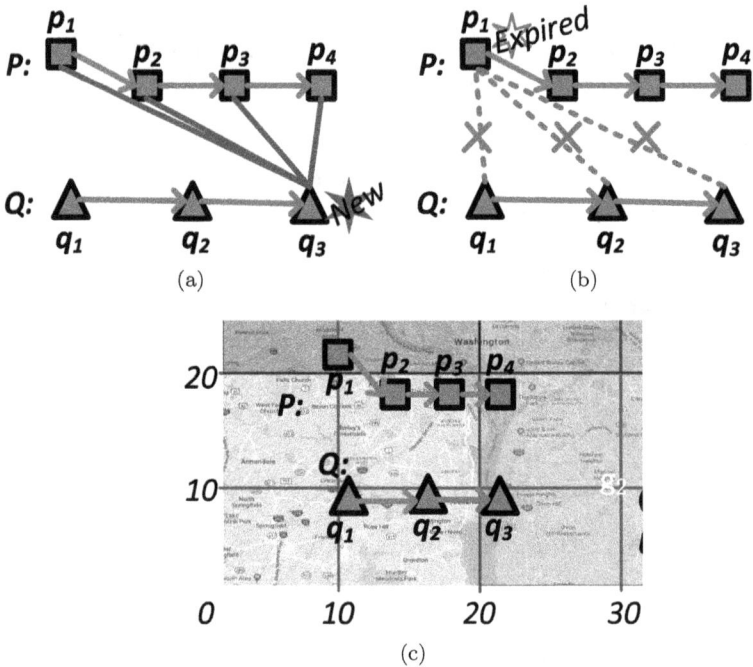

Fig. 4.8. A toy example of trajectory updates. (a) New point appearance, (b) expired point disappearance and (c) trajectories' distribution.

For each trajectory, both the appearance and disappearance of its point(s) directly affect the results of the distance computation. As depicted in Fig. 4.8, there are two trajectories P and Q with points p_{1-4} and q_{1-3}, respectively. In Fig. 4.8(a), q_3 of trajectory Q is a new point. With the arrival of q_3, distances $d(p_1, q_3)$, $d(p_2, q_3)$, $d(p_3, q_3)$, and $d(p_4, q_3)$ are generated. Although the distances may not be the final result at the moment, they should also be recorded for future use. As an extreme example, if the points q_1 and q_2 are both expired, the distances containing q_3 certainly become the candidate results, even though they are the most unlikely pairs to be selected in the end. Likewise, since p_1 in Fig. 4.8(b) is an expired point, the distances related to it should no longer be taken into account.

The preceding discussions draw a conclusion that the pairwise distances between trajectory points should be updated synchronously when a trajectory changes. Furthermore, in the parallel processing architecture, points that belong to the same trajectory may be distributed to different groups and tasks. In the example shown in Fig. 4.8(c), trajectory $P(Q)$ spans three(two) groups that are certainly distributed to different tasks. Therefore, compared to the centralized solutions, trajectory similarity calculation on distributed platform incurs more computation, storage and data transmission cost. For instance, the memory consumption of N trajectories reaches up to $\frac{n^2 \cdot N^2 \cdot \varphi}{2}$, where n is the average point number of each trajectory and φ is the average (state) size of each point for storage. Since the volume of transmission is proportional to memory, the transmission cost can be expressed as $\frac{n^2 \cdot N^2 \cdot \psi}{2}$, where ψ is the average (state) size of each point for transmission. Moreover, the computation complexity can be expressed as $\frac{n^2 \cdot N^2}{2}$.

In practice, the numbers for both trajectory and point are considerably large. Therefore, deploying calculations directly in the data stream processing system will inevitably cause an unbearable huge pressure on all resources. Alternatively, we propose a concise processing architecture to meet the computation requirements. Then, we describe how to ease the unnecessary workload while providing more flexibility to handle RTTS at a lower cost.

4.6.2 *Processing architecture*

There is no free lunch in the world. An explicit information table can handle key distributions perfectly. However, it has a cost on both memory consumption and management. To make our processing architecture cheap and light, we design a new 5D vector structure for the distance information of two trajectories. The vector can be expressed as (P, p, Q, q, v), in which P, Q denote two trajectories and p, q are two points of the trajectories, respectively. Also, v is the distance between points p and q. For example, a vector $(P, p, Q, q, 1)$ indicates that the distance of p in P and q in Q is 1.

An important observation is that there is no need to record the specific distance value among points in those vectors to satisfy the query requirement defined in Definition 4.1. For this reason, v just needs to provide judgment as to whether the distance between p and q is greater than the set threshold ϑ. Hence, we set the value type of v as *Boolean*: 0 means the distance $d(p, q) > \vartheta$, and *1* means $d(p, q) \leq \vartheta$. Based on this, a universal set of the 5D vectors of the two trajectories can form a bitmap, which integrates the distance information of all points of P and Q. An example of the bitmap is shown in Fig. 4.9, where three points of trajectory Q and four points of P form a 3×4 bitmap. The cell c_{ij} of the bitmap denotes

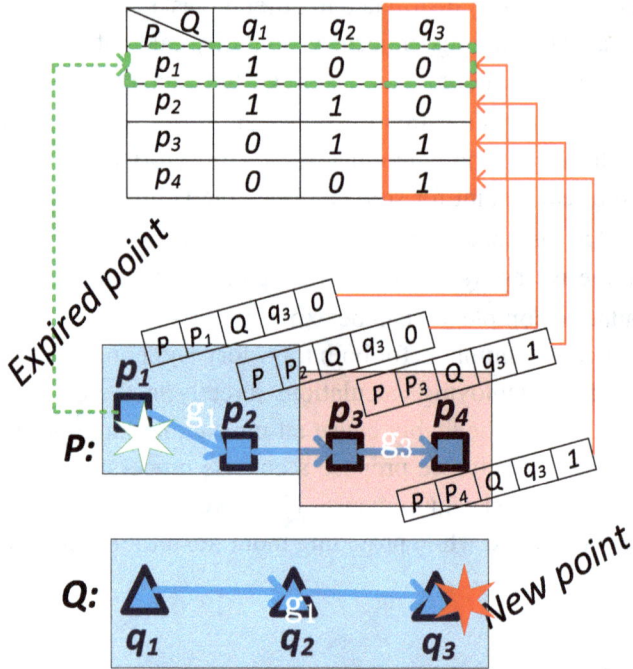

P \ Q	q_1	q_2	q_3
p_1	1	0	0
p_2	1	1	0
p_3	0	1	1
p_4	0	0	1

Fig. 4.9.   Example of bitmap and its updates.

whether the distance of the ith point of P and the jth point of Q exceeds the threshold ϑ. Then, the changes of trajectories can be reflected by adding or deleting rows or columns in the bitmap. In Fig. 4.9, after a new point q_3 of trajectory Q appears, four vectors containing q_3 and all points of trajectory P are generated. Those vectors form a new column in bitmap (enclosed by red rectangle). Similarly, when the point p_1 of trajectory P expires, the first row of bitmap (enclosed by green rectangle in Fig. 4.9) will be deleted for information synchronization.

According to the above bitmap structure, the trajectory similarity process can be reflected by Fig. 4.10 and Algorithm 4.7. After the routing actions in Algorithm 4.2, each task obtains their points and generates the corresponding distances. For each changed trajectory stored in the current processing task, Algorithm 4.7 first generates the distance vectors for it in lines 2–12. Specifically, for each new point, Algorithm 4.7 records the judgment information of the relationship between it and the points that

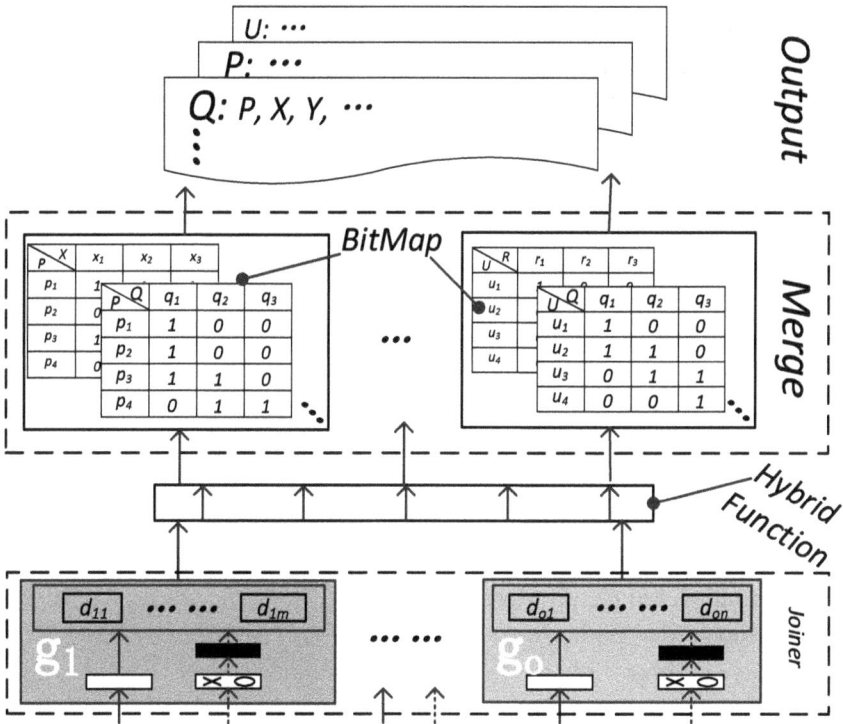

Fig. 4.10.   The processing architecture using bitmap structure.

belong to the other trajectories (lines 3–10). Then, Algorithm 4.7 performs a similar process for the expired point (lines 11–12). Thereafter, Algorithm 4.7 merges the vectors generated by all parallel processing tasks to generate the matching results in lines 13–18. In routing for those vectors, Algorithm 4.7 uses a hybrid function to differentiate the various mapping functions. Specifically, a key-based function based on the trajectories' ID is used for the adding vectors to aggregate the new distance information (lines 15 and 16). Conversely, vectors of those expired points are broadcast into all tasks in the merge operator (lines 17 and 18).

4.6.3   *Workload shedding*

Obviously, the performance of Algorithm 4.7 is susceptible to the number of trajectories and points. However, the similarity operator is usually

---

Algorithm 4.7 Results Generation

---

input: Trajectories: $\mathbb{P}$
output: Matching Result $\mathbb{B} = \{B_i\}$
 1: ▶ (Distance Calculation)
 2: **for** each $P \in \mathbb{P}$ **do**
 3:    **if** p $\in P$ is a new point **then**
 4:        **for** each $Q \in \mathbb{P}$ **do**
 5:            **for** each $q \in Q$ **do**
 6:                **if** $d(p, q) \le \vartheta$ **then**
 7:                    $v \leftarrow \langle P, p, Q, q, 1 \rangle$
 8:                **else**
 9:                    $v \leftarrow \langle P, p, Q, q, 0 \rangle$
10:                    $V \Leftarrow v$
11: **if** p $\in P$ is a expired point **then**
12:    $V \Leftarrow \langle P, p \rangle$
13: ▶ (Routing and Result Merge)
14: **for** each v $\in$ V **do**
15: **if** $|v| = 5$ **then**
16:    $f(v) \Rightarrow \mathbb{B}$
17: **else**
18:    delete row(s) or column(s) with v form $\mathbb{B}$
19: **return** the matching result $\mathbb{B}$

---

performed on millions of trajectories and points in real-world applications. The huge size of points inevitably degenerates the scalability of the system due to the enormous computational complexity and memory consumption, which can also be concluded according to the discussions in Section 4.6.1. To alleviate this problem, the key observation that similar trajectories always pass through similar spatial regions can provide the foundation for pruning workload.

Next, we introduce the workload pruning theorem based on the above observation.

Theorem 4.6. *Given the distance threshold ϑ and two trajectories P and Q, if there exists a point $p(q) \in P(Q)$ such that $\min_{q_i \in Q}\{d(p, q_j)\} > \vartheta$ ($\min_{p_i \in P}\{d(p_i, q)\} > \vartheta$), then $H(P, Q) > \vartheta$.*

Proof. Since the Hausdorff distance of trajectories P and Q is a maxmin function, which can be expressed as $H(P, Q) = \max\{\max_{p_i \in P}\{\min_{q_i \in Q}\{d(p_i, q_j)\}\}, \max_{q_i \in Q}\{\min_{p_i \in P}\{d(q_j, p_i)\}\}\}$, then the larger distance has a higher priority to be selected. Assume there exists a point $p(q) \in P(Q)$ such that $\min_{q_i \in Q}\{d(p, q_j)\} > \vartheta \, (\min_{p_i \in P}\{d(p_i, q)\} > \vartheta)$ and the Hausdorff distance of trajectories P and Q is measured as a value which is smaller than ϑ. Then, the distance result generation must violate the Hausdorff definition. Theorem 4.6 is established.   □

Theorem 4.6 is similar to that proposed by Xie *et al.* (2017), which focuses on how an entire trajectory can be pruned by just examining the individual segments given a distance threshold for the trajectory distance. Applying the above mentioned theorem, we can reduce the broadcast volume of tuples greatly from the headstream. In other words, we only need to assign tuples to their adjacent task group(s). Specifically, the filter function in Fig. 4.6 can first judge whether to discard the incoming point according to the minimal distance of the point and the sub-area of the current group. If the distance is smaller than ϑ, we send the incoming point downstream or discard it directly otherwise.

4.7 Practical Verification and Study

All the approaches in our experiment are implemented and run on top of *Apache Storm*. The adaptive processing architecture is shown in Fig. 4.11 and the overall workflow of the adjustment components for distributed stream join is as follows. At the end of each time interval (such as 5 s), the tasks report the information about the current resource usages (such as memory load) to a *controller* module. Then the *controller* decides whether to change the processing scheme; if the processing scheme needs change, the *controller* first produces a new scheme; accordingly, it expects to explore the task-load mapping function for mapping tasks in an old scheme to the ones in a new scheme. Finally, it schedules the data migration among tasks.

The *Storm* system (version 0.10.1) is deployed on a 21-instance HP blade cluster with CentOS 6.5 operating system. Each instance in the cluster is equipped with two Intel Xeon processors (E5335 at 2.00 GHz) having four cores.

In this section, we evaluate our proposals by comparing with a handful of baseline approaches. All these approaches are implemented and run

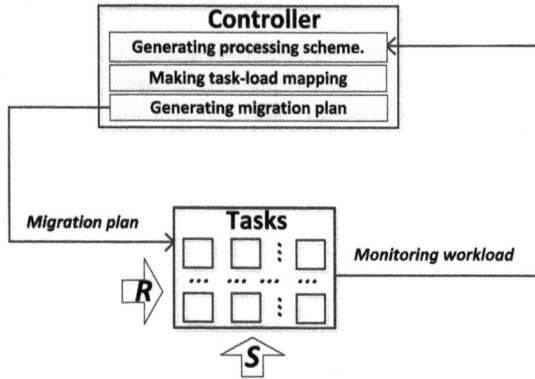

Fig. 4.11. Architecture of adaptive processing for matrix model.

on top of *Apache Storm* under the same task configuration. To collect the workload measurements, we add a load reporting module into the processing logics when implementing them in Storm's topologies. By controlling the pressure on tuple processing, we force the distributed system to reach a saturation point of CPU resource. The Storm system (in version 0.9.3) is deployed on a HP blade cluster with CentOS 6.5 operating system. Each node in the cluster is equipped with two Intel Xeon processors (E5335 at 2.00 GHz) having four cores and 16 GB RAM. Each core is exclusively bounded with a worker thread during our experiments.

4.7.1 *Environment setting*

4.7.1.1 *Datasets*

We evaluate all the approaches using the existing benchmark TPC-H and generate databases using the *dbgen* tool shipped with TPC-H benchmark. Before feeding data to the stream system, we pre-generate and pre-process all the input datasets. Specifically, we adjust the degree of skew on the join attributes by defining a skew parameter z for the Zipf function and we set $z = 1$ by default. Furthermore, we also use 10 GB real social data[1] from Weibo, which is the biggest Chinese social media data to test each approach.

---

[1] http://open.weibo.com/wiki/2/statuses/user_timeline.

We conduct the experiments on three join queries, namely E_{Q_5}, B_{NCI} and B_{MR}, among which the first two were used by Elseidy *et al.* (2014) and Lin *et al.* (2015). E_{Q_5} is an equi-join which represents the most expensive operation in query Q_5 from TPC-H benchmark. B_{NCI} and B_{MR} are both band-joins, which are different in memory usage by different data selectivity on the attribute *Quantity*.

We test the proposed algorithms using two datasets:

The first *Taxi* workload includes 11-day feeds from a popular *Didi* service, in which each feed is regarded as a point. The point in trajectory is a 4D vector structure, including the information of its trajectory's ID, generation timestamp, longitude, and latitude. Overall, the dataset contains over 10^8 points in 10^5 trajectories. During our experiment, we set the window size as 1 minute.

To test the scalability and robustness of various methods, we also generate a large set of trajectories. Our synthetic workload generator creates snapshots of points for discrete time intervals for the defined trajectory set. The distribution of points among sub-areas follows Zipf distribution, which is controlled by the skewness parameter z. In addition, we use parameter f to control the rate of distribution fluctuation across time intervals. At the beginning of a new interval, our generator keeps swapping frequencies between different sub-areas until the change on the workload is significant enough.

4.7.1.2 *Baseline comparison*

For the purpose of comparison, we implement four different distributed stream join algorithms: *MFM, Square, Dynamic* [Elseidy *et al.* (2014)] and *Readj* [Gedik (2014)]. *MFM* and *Square* are proposed in this section. *MFM* denotes our flexible and adaptive algorithm that generates the scheme with less tasks according to Eq. (4.6). *Square* adopts a naive method to obtain the task number defined in Eq. (4.4). *Dynamic* [Elseidy *et al.* (2014)] assumes the number of tasks in a matrix must be a power of two. If one stream doubles its volume, *Dynamic* adjusts the matrix scheme by doubling the cells along the side corresponding to this stream. Meanwhile, it halves cells along the other side of the matrix. Besides, *Dynamic* scales out by splitting the states of every task to four tasks if a task stores a number of tuples exceeding specified memory capacity (here, we do not consider the division of matrix scheme). *Readj* [Gedik (2014)] is designed to minimize the load by redistributing tuples based on a hash function on keys.

For the purpose of comparison, we evaluate four different distributed stream join algorithms, namely ART, R_{BF} [Xie *et al.* (2017)], *Dynamic* [Elseidy *et al.* (2014)] and *Bi* [Lin *et al.* (2015)]. Specifically, ART is proposed in this section. R_{BF} is a brute force index, which takes each point as both the search and update request in the real-time system. It is an improved index based on R-tree with the following procedure. The whole area first split into multiple sub-areas and each sub-area is carried by one task. Then we build a local R-tree for points in each partition. We set the parallelism of the spout as 1 and the incoming points task it as the root node of R_{BF}. Similar to Xie *et al.* (2017), each internal node in R_{BF} contains the complete set of trajectory IDs for all points contained by its branches. *Dynamic* [Elseidy *et al.* (2014)] assumes the number of tasks in a matrix must be a power of two. If one stream doubles its volume, *Dynamic* adjusts the matrix scheme by doubling the cells along the side corresponding to this stream. Meanwhile, it halves cells along the other side of the matrix. Besides, *Dynamic* scales out by splitting the states of every task to four tasks if a task stores a number of tuples exceeding the specified memory capacity. *Bi* handles band-joins using a complete bipartite graph. On one side of the bipartite graph, a data stream R is decomposed into substreams by a key-based hash function, each partition of which is stored and maintained by a computation node. Tuples from the other data stream S are pushed to the corresponding nodes for stream R, based on the hash key values of the tuples. Similar operations are applied on the other side of the bipartite graph at the same time, with nodes maintaining tuples from S and joining with tuples from R, using the same hash matching strategy. Here, we set only one group in each side of the bipartite graph to meet our query's requirement.

4.7.1.3 *Evaluation metrics*

We measure resource utilization and system performance through the following metrics:

- *Task Number* is the total number of tasks used in the system and each task is equipped with a constant quota of memory V;

- *Throughput* is the average number of tuples that are processed by a system per time unit (second or minute);
- *Migration Volume* is the total amount of tuples migrated to other tasks during a scheme change;
- *Migration Plan Time* is the average time spent on generating a migration plan;
- *Load Ratio* is the ratio of the average load of tasks and the task current load.

We focus on evaluating the following metrics in our experiments: *Throughput* is the average number of tuples the system processes in a unit second. *Computation request volume* is the average number of tuples that should be joined within each task. *Migration cost* reveals the percentage of states associated with the keys involved in migration over the states maintained by all task instances. In the rest of the chapter, we report the average values for these metrics over complete processing procedure, as well as the minimal and maximal values when applicable, to demonstrate the stability of different balance processing algorithms.

To understand the phenomenon of workload skewness, we report the workload imbalance phenomenon on the task instances by routing keys with the traditional hash-based mechanism. The results of load imbalance (route 1000 keys into 15 tasks) are shown in Fig. 4.12. Figure 4.12(a) shows the probability distribution of the keys under the skew of $z = 0.9$. Figure 4.12(b) reflects the load ratio of each task. Among those tasks, the load skewness phenomenon is obvious where the maximal workload is around four times larger than the minimal one.

4.7.2 *Scalability*

The task consumption of each scheme under different loading data volume is shown in Fig. 4.13. As data loading in Fig. 4.13, our algorithms MFM and Square have a stable performance while Dynamic shows a sharp increase in task number, for Dynamic has a strict requirement that the number of tasks must be a power of two. In contrast, our algorithms *MFM* and *Square* generate the processing scheme based on the current workload. Furthermore, *Optimized* produces a smaller scheme than *MFM* and *Square*. This is because it generates the irregular matrix scheme as discussed in

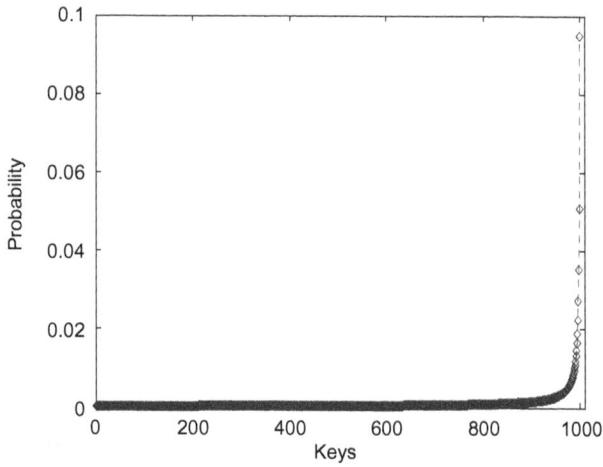

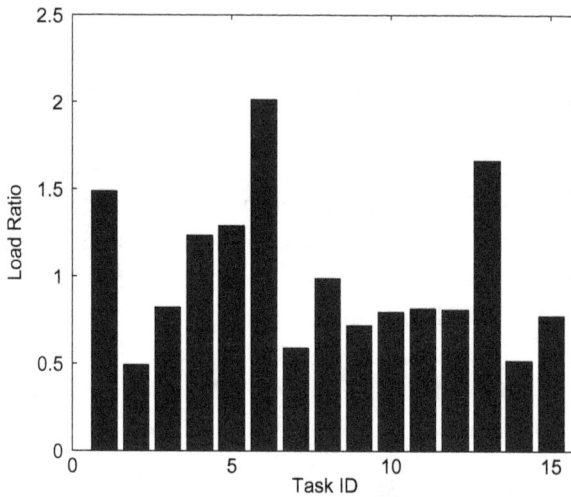

Fig. 4.12. Performance on workload skew. (a) Skew of key granularity and (b) skew of task workload.

Section 4.5.3.1. However, how to define the migration action and ensure the correctness of system for irregular matrix scheme are challenges, and we will focus on this work in our future work.

To testify the scalability of our join algorithm, we set $V = 8 \cdot 10^5$ and continue to load all $6 \cdot 10^6$ tuples into our system by executing B_{NCI}.

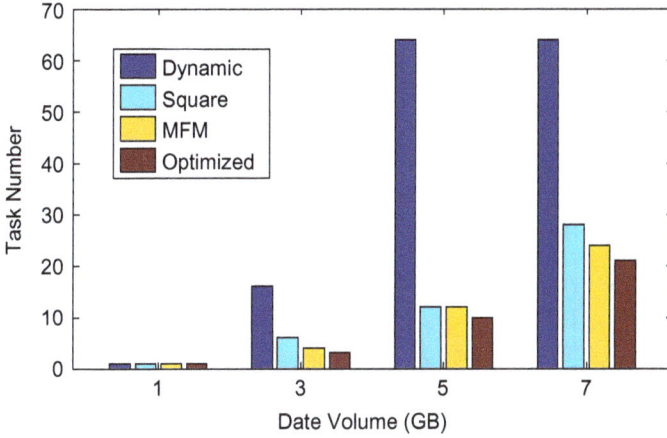

Fig. 4.13.   Task consumption of different schemes while loading different sizes of data.

Figure 4.14 shows an increase in the task number and migration cost which loading data into the system. With the increase of task number shown in Fig. 4.14(a), the memory utilization consumed by *Dynamic* also increases dramatically, which is proportional to the task number. The naive method *Square* consumes more memory compared to *MFM* since its task number increases slightly. Our algorithm *MFM* performs the best among those methods, which can scale out with a minimal number of tasks and apply for resources on its real demand. Figure 4.14(b) illustrates the changes in the migration cost with query B_{NCI} when loading the whole dataset into our system. Consistently, *Dynamic* causes the highest migration cost than all other algorithms, because *Dynamic* suffers from massive replications to maintain its matrix structure. Furthermore, *Square* and *MFM* yield low migration volume in that they involve less tasks. From Fig. 4.14, we find that the migration volume increases along with data loading. This is because all matrix schemes progressively get larger.

In addition, we examine the latency for generating migration plan and throughput for equi-join E_{Q_5} with different algorithms. For the purpose of load balance, we define the balance indicator θ_t for task instance d during time interval T_t as $\theta_t = |\frac{L_t(d) - \bar{L}_t}{\bar{L}_t}|$, where $\bar{L}$ is the average load of all task instances. For this group of experiments, we set $\theta_t \leq 0.05$. Figure 4.15(a) provides the latency for generating migration plan. Obviously, the latency of

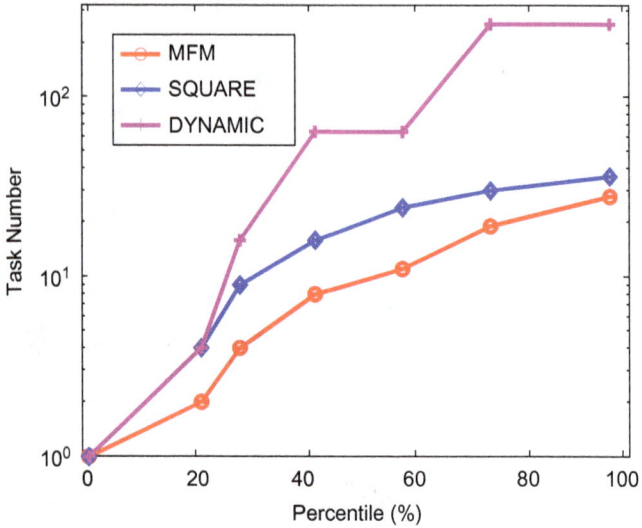

(a)

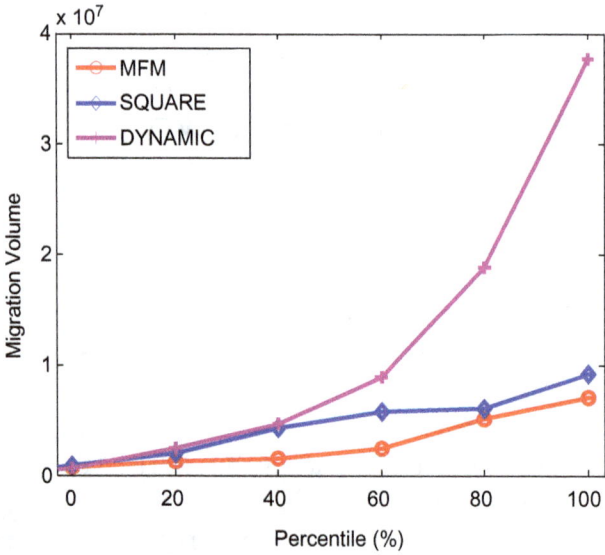

(b)

Fig. 4.14.   Performance of full-history join with B_{NCI}. (a) Task number consumption and (b) migration cost.

Readj is much larger than all other algorithms for *Readj*, which is designed to minimize the load difference among tasks by redistributing data on keys with a hash function and it must recalculate the balance states for each scale-out processing. The other algorithms including *Dynamic* use random distribution as a routing policy, so they need not do calculation for balance scheduling. Figure 4.15(b) draws the throughput of each algorithm under different data skewness. Throughput of *Readj* decreases with severer skewness because it spends more time for generating migration plan. Although the tasks used by *Dynamic* are much more than our methods, our throughput is more than *Dynamic* due to its massive migration cost.

4.7.3 *Dynamic*

This group of experiments shows the performance with window-based join, which bounds the memory consumption based on the window size. For this experiment, we set the window size as 5 minutes and the average input rate is about $1.8 \cdot 10^4$ tuples per second. We provide maximum 32 tasks for this group testing. The dynamics is simulated by altering the relative stream volume ratio $|R|/|S|$ between stream R and S [Elseidy *et al.* (2014)] with a total volume of $2 \cdot 10^7$ tuples, where the ratio fluctuates between f and $\frac{1}{f}$ with f defined as the fluctuation rate.

Figures 4.16(a) and 4.16(b) depict the throughput and number of tasks used for query B_{MR}. Figure 4.16(a) shows that our methods have better throughput compared to *Dynamic*. For our algorithms *MFM* and *Square*, the given 32 tasks are far more than our needs as shown in Fig. 4.16(b), while *Dynamic* exhausts all the tasks at any time. This determines the difference of throughputs between *Dynamic* and other methods as shown in Fig. 4.16(a).

Figure 4.16(c) shows the throughputs of different algorithms under different dynamic ratios f for query B_{NCI}. As described in this section, the effectiveness of generating a migration plan and the network cost of migration determine the efficiency of different algorithms. As shown in Fig. 4.16(c), the overall throughput obtained by us is stable for dynamic ratios f.

Figure 4.16(d) illustrates the throughput of different queries under the workload $2 \cdot 10^7$ tuples. Because the intermediate results are materialized before being stored in memory, different queries generate different volume

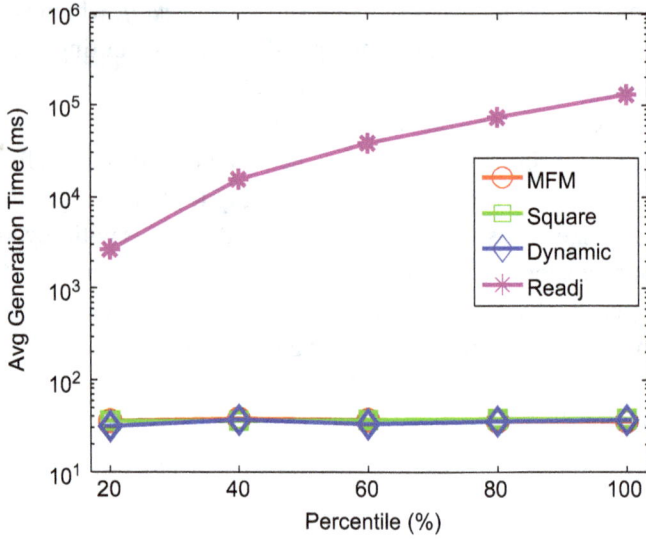

(a)

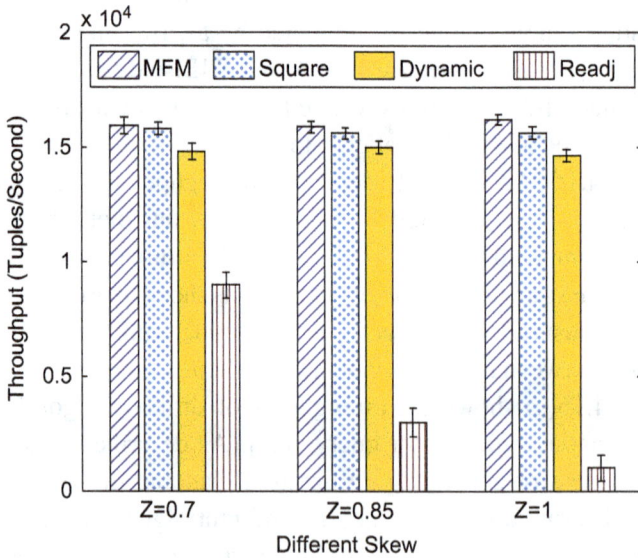

(b)

Fig. 4.15. Performance of full-history with E_{Q_5}. (a) Migration plan time and (b) average throughput in different skew.

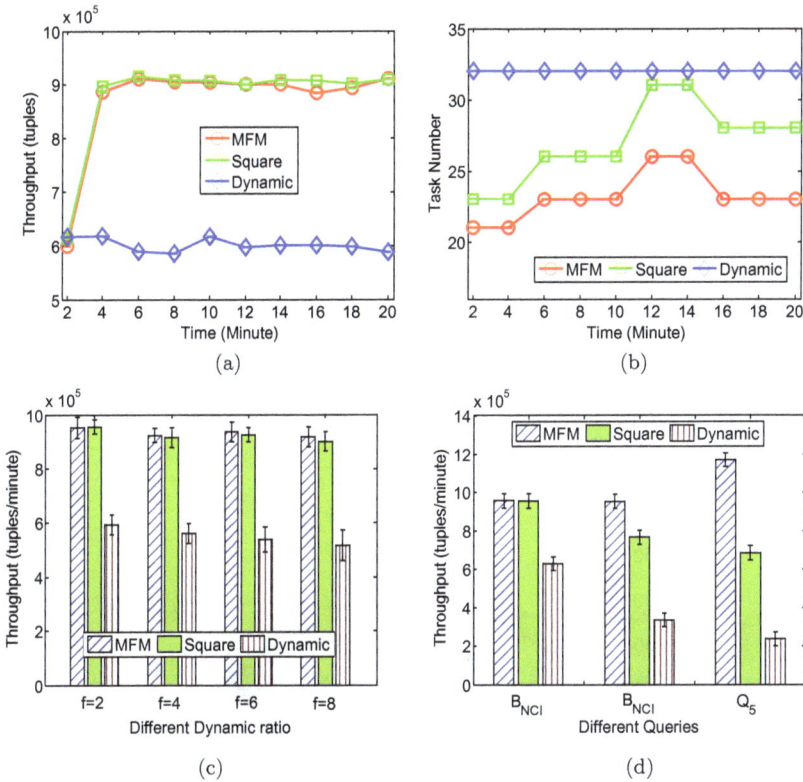

Fig. 4.16. Performance of window-based join. (a) Real-time throughput, (b) task number consumption, (c) average throughput of different dynamic ratio and (d) throughput of different query.

of states which are to be stored in the memory. Since E_{Q_5} is lack of filters on predicate, it should store all tuples within a window for join processing and then it requires more memory. In this way, throughput of *Dynamic* decreases dramatically due to its memory requirement for E_{Q_5}. For the two band-joins, B_{NCI} will have more throughput for its filters; *Quantity* > 48 can filter out more tuples than *Quantity* > 10 in B_{MR}. This also indicates that B_{MR} requires more tasks than B_{NCI} and it has lower throughput when the total memory size is predefined.

To prove the usability of our algorithm, we do band-join *Social data query* on a 10 GB Weibo dataset. We load the 10 GB dataset

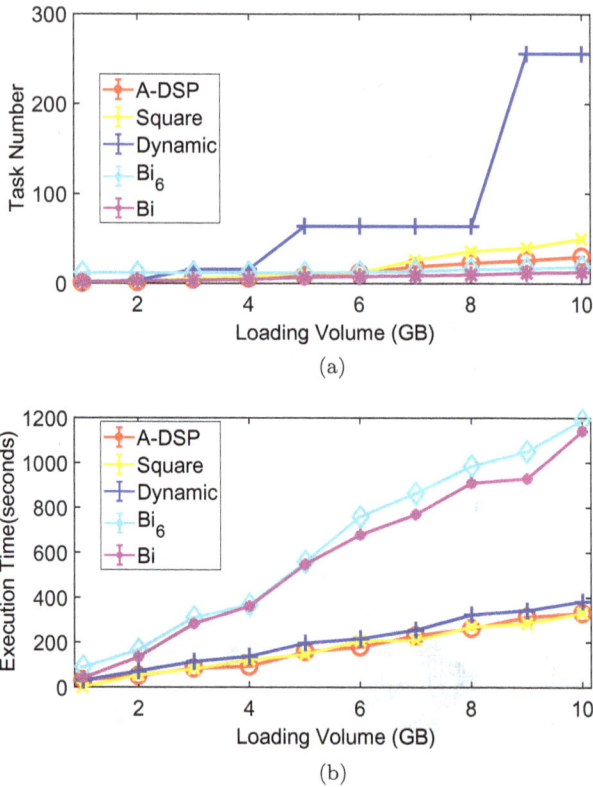

Fig. 4.17. Performance on real data. (a) Task consumption and (b) execution time.

continuously and measure the resource consumption of different algorithms. In Fig. 4.17(a), *Readj* uses less tasks; however, it is the slowest for its lack of CPU resources as shown in Fig. 4.17(b). Our method *MFM* provides a flexible matrix scheme which applies for new tasks according to its real load while *Dynamic* scales out in a generous way.

4.7.4 *Throughput*

To test the relationship between throughput and resource consumption, we run all approaches under the different number of task instances to report their performance of throughput and computing request volume. Specifically, results in Figs. 4.18(a) and 4.18(b) are generated under the condition of adequate resources while Figs. 4.18(c) and 4.18(d) are under

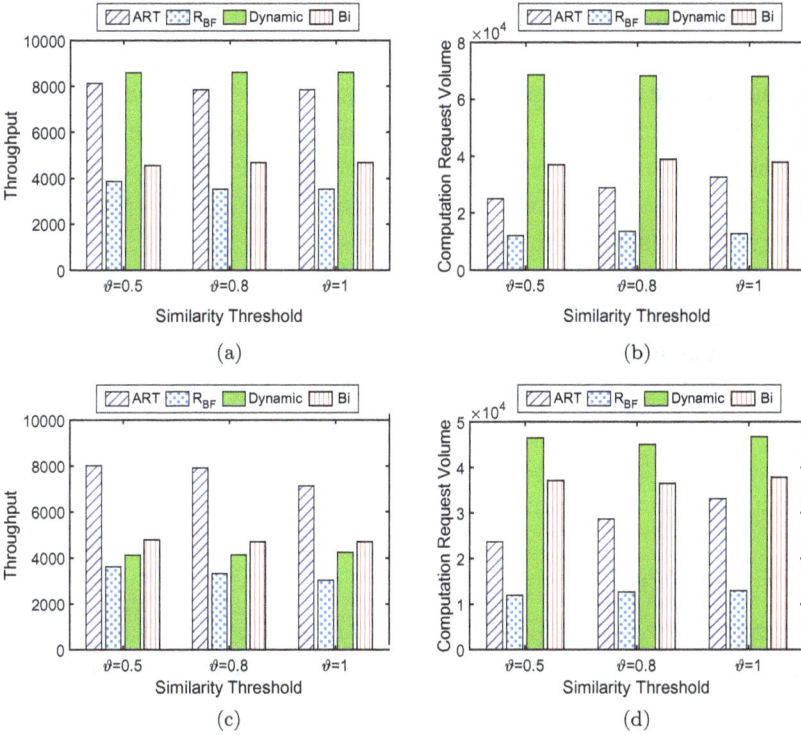

Fig. 4.18. Throughput and number of computing request. (a) Throughput under enough tasks, (b) computing request volume under enough tasks, (c) throughput under limitative tasks and (d) computing request volume under limitative tasks.

restricted resources. We set the window size as 60 s and the stream flow-in rate at about 10^4 points per second to make full use of CPU resources.

Figures 4.18(a) and 4.18(b), respectively, show the system throughput and the average computing request volume that are received by each task for different processing schemes under various ϑ. The value of ϑ can be regarded as the extended size of each point to compute with other trajectories, which is also directly proportional to computational outreach. R_{BF} produces the the lowest throughput and it is ϑ-sensitive. This is because it takes each incoming point as both search and update request item and the bigger ϑ setting means the more computing demands. The throughput of *Dynamic* algorithm in Fig. 4.18(a) is obviously higher than other approaches. However, it is at the cost of data broadcasting among groups. As shown in Fig. 4.18(b), it incurred the most computing request. In essence, it consumes the maximum number of tasks. *Bi* is a resource-saving method with no duplication, and its routing strategies also use the simple random and broadcast manner. However, its broadcast volume is too massive to ensure the system's performance. The main reason is that it has only one task group for each stream and it broadcasts the same amount of data regardless of the different setting of ϑ as shown in Fig. 4.18(b). In the case that the available tasks are limited as 25, ART, R_{BF}, and *Bi* are unaffected as 25 tasks is enough for them. Instead, since *Dynamic* must consume more tasks to maintain its 2D processing architecture, this limited resource reduces its performance. From Fig. 4.18 we can conclude that our algorithm ART is more efficient, for it can guarantee the system in a high-throughput performance while incurring smaller resource consumption.

4.7.5 *Scalability*

To better understand the performance of the different approaches in action, we present the robustness of the throughput over time on the various matching range, especially when the system scales out the resource by adding new computation resources to the operator. Figure 4.19 demonstrates the trend on task throughput during the loading of all 3 GB data into the Storm system, under the configuration that the available tasks for similarity computation are 25. Meanwhile, we maximize the input rate by fully utilizing all the computing power.

Figures 4.19(a) and 4.19(b) show that the throughputs of our algorithms ART and *Bi* are both almost unaffected by the volume of loading data. This is because these limited tasks are enough for them. Actually, the task used by ART and *Bi* are 13 and 8, respectively. *Dynamic* suffers a sharp decrease of throughput in both Figs. 4.19(a) and 4.19(b) during the process of data loading, for it has a strict requirement that the number of tasks in a similarity computation operator must be a power of two. When a system scales out, *Dynamic* must quadruple its tasks and may waste resources. Furthermore, it also requires the additional computational resources to merge those intermediate results. In contrast, our algorithm ART generates the processing scheme based on the current workload. Since R_{BF} uses a global R-tree index to route each incoming point, it is susceptible to the tree size and the

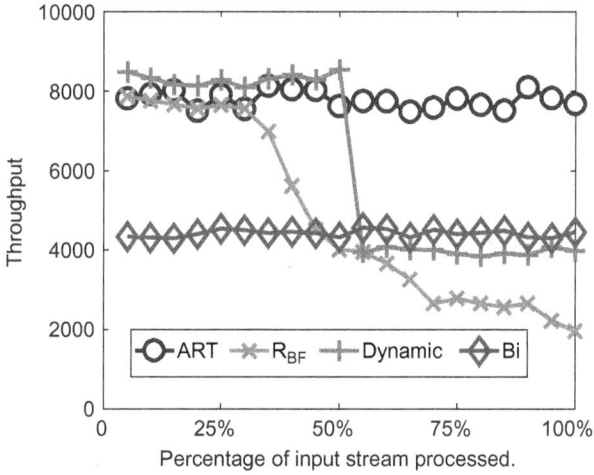

(a)

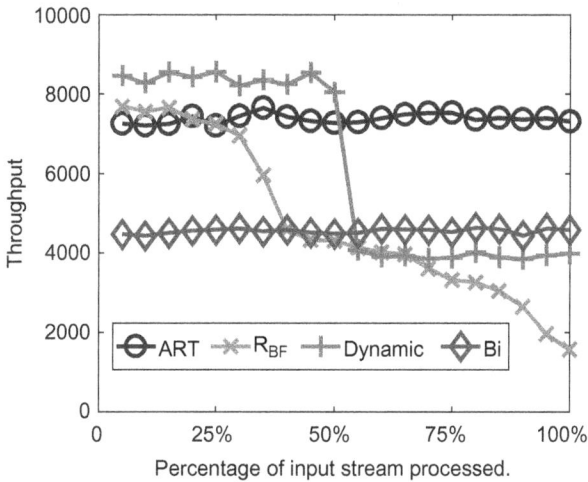

(b)

Fig. 4.19. Throughput of full-history similarity under various matching scopes: (a) $\vartheta = 0.5$ and (b) $\vartheta = 0.8$.

query's range. Along with points flowing into the system, R_{BF} suffers more when the workload of both update and retrieval increases. The workload, especially the update operation severely affects the system's performance. These effects are reflected in the downward trend of the throughput in both Figs. 4.19(a) and 4.19(b).

4.7.6 *Robustness*

We test the algorithms on synthetic datasets using different dynamic magnitude, i.e., $f = 0.1, 0.2, \ldots, 1$, in order to validate the adaptivity of our processing scheme. To facilitate the description, we directly report the volume

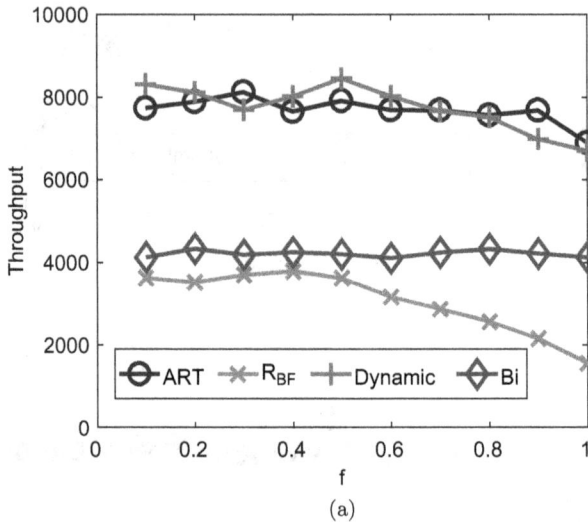

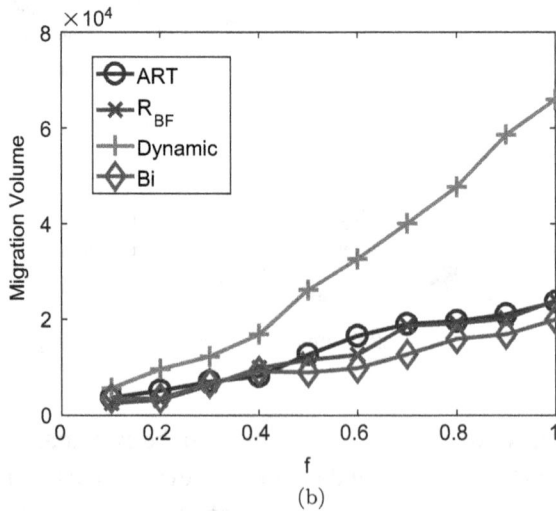

Fig. 4.20. Throughput and migration cost with varying distribution change frequency: (a) $\vartheta = 0.5$ and (b) $\vartheta = 0.8$.

of states associated with the points involved in migration over the states maintained by all the task instances as migration cost. To further validate the effects of different band-joins and data skewness on system performance, we run window-based joins to testify the throughput under a sufficient number of tasks. It should be noted especially that the dynamic magnitude of *Dynamic* refers to the change ratio of the two incoming streams.

Figure 4.20(a) shows that our algorithms ART and *Dynamic* can enable the system to produce more throughput. However, *Dynamic* is at the cost of consuming more resources, which can be reflected by its higher migration volume in Fig. 4.20(b). Furthermore, the migration action also reduces the performance and increases the operational complexity of the system to some extent. *Bi* algorithm has less migration cost due to the less redundant storage. However, as discussed earlier, it may pay a lot on CPU cost and broadcasting, which in turn may reduce the throughput. This phenomenon also can be proved by our experimental results, that is, although it incurs the least migration in Fig. 4.20(a), it produces less throughput in Fig. 4.20(b). For R_{BF}, a larger dynamic magnitude means it costs more to maintain its fixed indexing structure. In our scheme, the arrangement of processing tasks according to the location of input points can serve as the first step of workload shedding. Furthermore, the combination of these data partition functions in Section 4.4.3.2 acts as an adaptive data partition designed to cut off unnecessary network workload. The task groups of ART can relieve workload dynamics to a large extent. Meanwhile, the random distribution strategy within each group can reduce the cost of migration action. From Fig. 4.20 we can conclude that our algorithm is more efficient in dynamic environments.

4.8 Summary

This chapter presents a new mechanism for trajectory similarity in distributed stream processing engines. Our ART provides an easy-to-use and lightweight processing scheme enabling high flexibility to the system to handle the dynamic trajectory input. Our proposed scheme supports allocating resources on demand. Additionally, we design a routing algorithm with the moderate complexity to generate task mapping schemes to fulfill the objective of operational cost reduction. New workload shedding techniques are also introduced to improve the efficiency of our approach, to enable practical implementation over the state-of-the-art stream processing engines. Our experiments on *Apache Storm* platform show excellent performance improvement on a variety of workloads from real applications and also present a huge advantage over other solutions on both system throughput and response latency.

Chapter 5

Cost-Effective Stream Join Model

5.1 Motivation and Basic Idea

As people pay more attention to the potential value in big data analysis, real-time processing becomes a popular trend in various application domains, such as stock trading analysis, traffic monitoring and network measurement. Introduction of distributed and parallel processing frameworks enables the efficient processing of massive streams. However, the load balancing issue [Liu *et al.* (2005); Xing *et al.* (2006); Xu *et al.* (2008); Gufler *et al.* (2012); Kwon *et al.* (2012)] emerges soon, which obviously obstructs performance. Extensive efforts are devoted to tackling the load balancing issue for different operators, including summarization [Cormode and Muthukrishnan (2005)], aggregation [Nasir *et al.* (2016)] and join [Xu *et al.* (2008); Bruno *et al.* (2014); Vitorovic *et al.* (2016)]. Among these operations, θ-join [Elseidy *et al.* (2014); Lin *et al.* (2015); Okcan and Riedewald (2011)] is recognized as the most challenging one.

There are a handful of approaches designed for join load balancing over fast and continuous streams, which can be divided into two categories: the one-dimensional space processing model(1-DSP) [Gedik (2014); Bruno *et al.* (2014); Cheng *et al.* (2014); Nasir *et al.* (2015, 2016)] and the two-dimensional space processing model(2-DSP) [Elseidy *et al.* (2014); Vitorovic *et al.* (2016); Okcan and Riedewald (2011); Lin *et al.* (2015)]. We use m to denote the number of task instances in a DSPE. For 1-DSP,

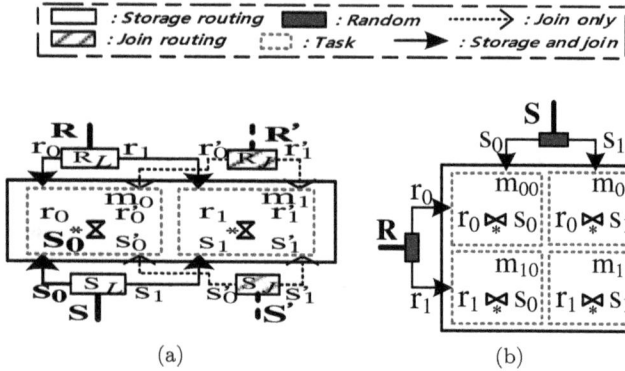

Fig. 5.1. Two typical paradigms of existing stream join models. (a) 1-DSP model and (b) 2-DSP model (matrix).

we map the key space K in any stream to m tasks by a dividing function F, such as a hash function, defined as $F(k_i) \longmapsto m_k$, where $k_i \in K$ and $0 \leq m_k \leq m - 1$. As shown in Fig. 5.1(a), it has three tasks numbered by m_{0-2}. Any key from either stream R or S is supposed to be assigned to one of the tasks. In contrast, 2-DSP arranges tasks into two-dimensional space, where each dimension represents the division of one stream. As shown in Fig. 5.1(b), it organizes the tasks as a matrix, represented as m_{ij}, with $0 \leq i \leq 1$ and $0 \leq j \leq 1$. Streams S and R are divided along the horizontal and vertical dimension, respectively. Let us take a deep look at the routing strategies for these two models.

- **1-DSP:** In Fig. 5.1(a), stream R or S is split into two substreams r_i (s_i) for join processing and stored locally in m_i, with $0 \leq i \leq 1$. However, for non-equi-join, since a join tuple may get involved in multiple local join tasks according to join predicates(*), in addition to the locally stored substream r_i in task m_i, additional substreams r_i' are sent to m_i for join purposes with locally stored tuples s_i, which contain tuples to be joined but not included in r_i. So 1-DSP has two routing methods, one for local storage (*storage routing*, e.g., R_L) and the other one for join routing (*join routing*, e.g., R_J) defined by the join predicate, as shown in Fig. 5.1(a). During the join process, the destination of the incoming tuple, e.g., r_i, is determined by two different routing strategies: *storage routing* R_L decides its storage task, while *join routing* R_J determines the task(s) to which r_i shall be assigned to produce join results. In other words, the $R_J(S_J)$ acts only when $R_L(S_L)$ cannot return complete results for any join predicate; otherwise, *join routing* is useless where $R_J = \emptyset (S_J = \emptyset)$.

- **2-DSP:** The join-matrix model is a typical representation for 2-DSP, in which a partitioning scheme is employed on each dimension to split the incoming stream data randomly into a set of mutually exclusive sub-streams to guarantee the balance requirement. As shown in Fig. 5.1(b), stream R is split into two substreams r_0 and r_1 along the vertical side, with $r_0 \cap r_1 = \emptyset$ (s_0 and s_1 for S, respectively). Therefore, $R \bowtie_\theta S$ is decomposed into four sub-tasks, each of which, m_{ij} ($0 \le i, j \le 1$), takes a pair of substreams from R and S. The join-matrix model can always return complete results for any join predicate as it can promise that each pair of tuples from two data streams meets once.

It is easy to figure out that 1-DSP is a value-sensitive partitioning scheme because of the existence of the partition function, while 2-DSP uses some random partition strategy which is value-insensitive one. Then 1-DSP is more suitable for Equal-joins involving chapter scale of data with a relatively stable data distributions. For θ-join, it may involve excessive broadcast by 1-DSP; furthermore, distribution dynamics and skewness will inevitably increase the routing complexity. Although the value-insensitive partitioning scheme in 2-DSP enables its support for θ-join and can handle data skewness perfectly, this is at the cost of high computing, which becomes considerably severe when the join operator is of low selectivity. However, the resource cost of distributed computing plays a crucial role in solution evaluations, especially for cloud-based applications, because of its popularly used pricing model, such as the pay-as-you-go scheme.

To get along with such a pricing mechanism, the join model is expected to be resource sensitive as well as high throughput. In this chapter, we propose an adaptive join processing scheme, denoted as A-DSP, which can adaptively change processing models and gain full advantage of 1-DSP and 2-DSP. In summary, the major contributions of this work are as follows: (1) We propose the A-DSP join model to reduce the operational cost with full support to arbitrary join predicates while guaranteeing the completeness of join results. (2) We devise scheme generation algorithms for A-DSP, which minimize the use of task instances acquired for join computation while preserving the high processing throughput. (3) We design a lightweight scheme adjustment algorithm which generates low overhead migration plans in an efficient manner, enabling smooth runtime migration during resource addition and reduction. (4) We empirically evaluate our model against the state-of-the-art solutions on both standard benchmarks and real-world stream data workloads with detailed explanations on experimental results.

The remainder of this chapter is organized as follows. Section 5.2 reviews the existing studies on stream join processing and workload balancing in distributed systems. Section 5.3 introduces the preliminaries. Section 5.4 presents the basic principle of the model design. Section 5.5 describes how to generate the processing scheme. Section 5.6 explains the detailed implementation of our proposed method and shows the experimental results. Section 5.7 finally concludes the chapter and discusses future research directions.

5.2 Related Work and Literature

In the early 21st century, considerable research has unfolded on designing efficient stream join operators in a distributed environment with a cluster of machines. There are two common classes of strategies that enable join operation in distributed stream processing systems, namely 1-DSP and 2-DSP.

- **1-DSP:** Photon [Ananthanarayanan *et al.* (2013)] is designed by Google to join data streams such as web search queries and user clicks on advertisements. It utilizes a central coordinator to implement fault tolerance and scalable joining through key-value matching, but cannot handle θ-join. D-Streams [Zaharia *et al.* (2013)] adopts mini-batch for continuous data streams in a blocking way on Spark. Though it upholds θ-join well, under the constraint of window size, some tuples may miss each other and such batch-mode computing can only give approximate results. TimeStream [Qian *et al.* (2013)] equipped with resilient substitution and dependency tracking mechanisms provides both MapReduce-like batch processing and non-blocking stream processing. However, it suffers from excessive communication cost due to maintenance of distributed join state. Join-biclique [Lin *et al.* (2015)] based on the bipartite-graph model supports full-history and window-based stream joins. Compared to the join-matrix model used in DYNAMIC [Elseidy *et al.* (2014)], it reduces data backup redundancy and improves resource utilization. In the meantime, considerable efforts have been put into the elasticity feature of the distributed stream processing systems [Ding *et al.* (2015); Fu *et al.* (2015)], dealing with when and how to efficiently scale in or out computing resources. This is an important research direction; however, it is orthogonal to what we are focusing on in this chapter.

- **2-DSP:** In recent years, the join-matrix model for parallel and distributed joins has been studied again. Intuitively, it models a join between two datasets R and S as a matrix, where each side corresponds to one relation. Stamos and Young (1993) proposed a symmetric fragment and replicate method to support parallel θ-joins. This method relies on replicating input tuples to ensure result completeness and extending the fragment and replicate algorithm [Epstein *et al.* (1978)], which suffers from high communication and computation cost. Okcan and Riedewald (2011) proposed techniques in MapReduce that adopt the join-matrix model and support parallel θ-joins. They designed two partitioning schemes, that is, 1-Bucket and M-Bucket. The 1-Bucket scheme is content insensitive but incurs high data replication; the M-Bucket scheme is content sensitive in that it maps a tuple to a region based on the join key. Because of the inherent nature of MapReduce, these two algorithms are offline and require all the data statistics to be available beforehand, which is not suitable for stream join processing. In data stream processing, Elseidy *et al.* (2014) presented a *(n,m)-mapping scheme* partitioning the matrix into $J (J = n \times m)$ equal regions and proposing algorithms which adjust the scheme adaptively to data characteristics in real time. However, Elseidy *et al.* (2014) assumed that the number of partitions J must be to the power of two. Moreover, the the matrix structure suffers from bad flexibility because when the matrix needs to scale out(down), it must add(remove) the entire row or column cells.

Due to the characteristics of data streams, e.g., infiniteness and instantaneity, conventional join algorithms using blocking operations, e.g., sorting, cannot work any more. For stream join processing, much effort has been put into designing non-blocking algorithms. Wilschut presented the symmetric hash join SHJ [Wilschut and Apers (1993)]. It is a special type of hash join and assumes that the entire relations can be kept in the main memory. For each incoming tuple, SHJ progressively creates two hash tables, one for each relation, and probes them mutually to identify joining tuples. XJoin [Urhan and Franklin (2001)] and DPHJ [Ives *et al.* (1999)] both extend SHJ by allowing parts of the hash tables to be spilled out to the disk for later processing, greatly enhancing the applicability of the algorithm. Dittrich *et al.* (2002b) designed a non-blocking algorithm called PMJ that inherits the advantages of sorting-based algorithms and also supports inequality predicates. The organic combination of XJoin and PMJ is conductive to the realization of HMJ [Mokbel *et al.* (2004)], presented by Mokbel. However, all the previous algorithms belong to centralized algorithms and rely on a central entity doing join computation, which cannot be applied in distributed computing directly.

5.3   Preliminaries

5.3.1   *Problem description*

Skewness and dynamics are common phenomena in DSPEs, which always cause trouble in workload imbalance among parallel processing tasks and could lower performance of data processing significantly. As defined in Vitorovic *et al.* (2016), system workload is composed of its *input* and *output*, each of which can be measured by the number of tuples received or generated in a unit time interval. Processing of an *input* tuple incurs the network, memory and join computation costs, and the cost of *output* tuples mainly comes from the post-processing phase where the *output* results are transferred to the downstream operator over the network.

Table 5.1 shows the functional difference between 1-DSP and 2-DSP regarding resource consumption and balance consideration. Generally speaking, 1-DSP is a resource-saving join model with a poor workload balance ability, while 2-DSP can guarantee the workload balance perfectly at the cost of more resource consumption. Furthermore, the specialized join type of 1-DSP and 2-DSP is different. Namely, 1-DSP is more suitable for chapter-scale join while 2-DSP perfectly supports the arbitrary join predicate.

Table 5.1. Comparison with 1-DSP and 2-DSP.

Methods		1-DSP	2-DSP	A-DSP(ours)
Resource saving		✓	×	✓
Balance	*Input*	✓	✓	✓
	Output	×	✓	✓
	Input & Output	×	✓	✓

To make up the technical gap between 1-DSP and 2-DSP, questions on how to generate the join processing model transformation in a transparent and lightweight manner should be handled. Based on this, our A-DSP model aims to balance the workload among parallel tasks while minimizing the operational cost over elastic clusters by addressing the following: (1) how to generate an appropriate join scheme to guarantee the balanced status for both input and output; (2) how to generate the join scheme quickly while minimizing resource utilization and (3) when the scheme is changed, how to adaptively repartition workloads among tasks while minimizing migration cost.

5.3.2 *Solution overview*

In real-time scenarios, the stream has its inherent feature of dynamism of both the volume and distribution, which means the analysis of workload variance among parallel processing tasks is not a mathematical theorem. Specifically, the predefined and fixed routing strategies to pursue workload balance for parallel processing tasks are usually non-effective under dynamic scenarios. Inspired by the above idea, our join model (A-DSP) provides a convenient adaptive join algorithm for arranging the dynamic workload.

From the perspective of content, we define the area coverage as $\lceil c_{(i,j)}, c_{(i',j')} \rfloor$, where $\lceil c_{(i,j)}, c_{(i',j')} \rfloor$ means a rectangle in the tuple matrix whose upper left corner is $c_{(i,j)}$ and lower right is $c_{(i',j')}$. Cells $c_{(r,c)} \in \lceil c_{(i,j)}, c_{(i',j')} \rfloor$ can be expressed as $\{c_{(r,c)} | i \leq r \leq i', j \leq c \leq j'\}$. Table 5.3 lists the notations commonly used in the rest of the chapter.

Before discussing the specific processing schemes, we first introduce some definitions which are related to area coverage. Essentially, *CA* is a *loose* area which will always be equivalent to C, while $\widetilde{CA}$ is a *tight* area which can bring results together. Both CA and $\widetilde{CA}$ should cover all the input and output tuples of the join operation. Based on this, it is important to note that even as there is no join candidate in another stream in $\widetilde{CA}$, the input tuples should also be taken into account. We use c_i^r or c_i^s to denote the tuple, located in the ith row or column in the tuple matrix, that has no output result. Then, the universal set of c^r and c^s, denoted by C^R and C^S, should also be covered by $\widetilde{CA}$ for the following calculation, e.g., c_{4-7}^s in Fig. 5.2(b).

Based the processing architecture in Fig. 5.1, the partition way for join-matrix can be expressed as in Table 5.2. The overall workflow of A-DSP can be seen as a two-phase method: A-DSP first takes $\widetilde{C}$ containing the *tight* set of candidate cells $\widetilde{CA}$ as input, partitioning as 1-DSP strategy, to generate a set of $\tilde{ca}$. For the process of partitioning $\tilde{ca}$ into *TaskAs*, A-DSP takes $\tilde{ca}$ as the unordered coverage area ca and 2-DSP is used to assign the specific workload for task instance.

Accordingly, the imbalance-resistant process of A-DSP also can be divided into two phases: $P_{\widetilde{CA}}$ *workload imbalance sharing* and P_{ca} *random routing*. In $P_{\widetilde{CA}}$, A-DSP splits $\widetilde{CA}$ according to a content-sensitive routing rule. It is noteworthy that, although the $P_{\widetilde{CA}}$ uses a key-based routing strategy, each $\tilde{ca}$ is usually carried by multiple tasks which can smooth the workload imbalance. In other words, $\tilde{ca}$ in A-DSP always acts as a cushioning layer resisting the workload imbalance. This *workload imbalance sharing* characteristic is similar to the grouping processing tasks aimed at receiving the same key in Lin *et al.* (2015). As shown in Table 5.2, in P_{ca},

Table 5.2. Summary of methods. $\widetilde{C} \xrightarrow[P_{\widetilde{CA}}]{\widetilde{CA}} \tilde{ca}$ means partition tuple matrix $\widetilde{C}$ into multi-$\tilde{ca}$s, covering all candidate cell(s) in $\widetilde{CA}$. This partition process is named $P_{\widetilde{CA}}$.

Methods	Partition way	Example
1-DSP	$\widetilde{C} \xrightarrow{\widetilde{CA}} TaskAs$	Fig. 5.2(b)
2-DSP	$C \xrightarrow{CA} TaskAs$	Fig. 5.2(a)
A-DSP(Our)	$\widetilde{C} \xrightarrow[P_{\widetilde{CA}}]{\widetilde{CA}} \tilde{ca} \xrightarrow[P_{ca}]{ca} TaskAs$	Figs. 5.2(c) and 5.2(d)

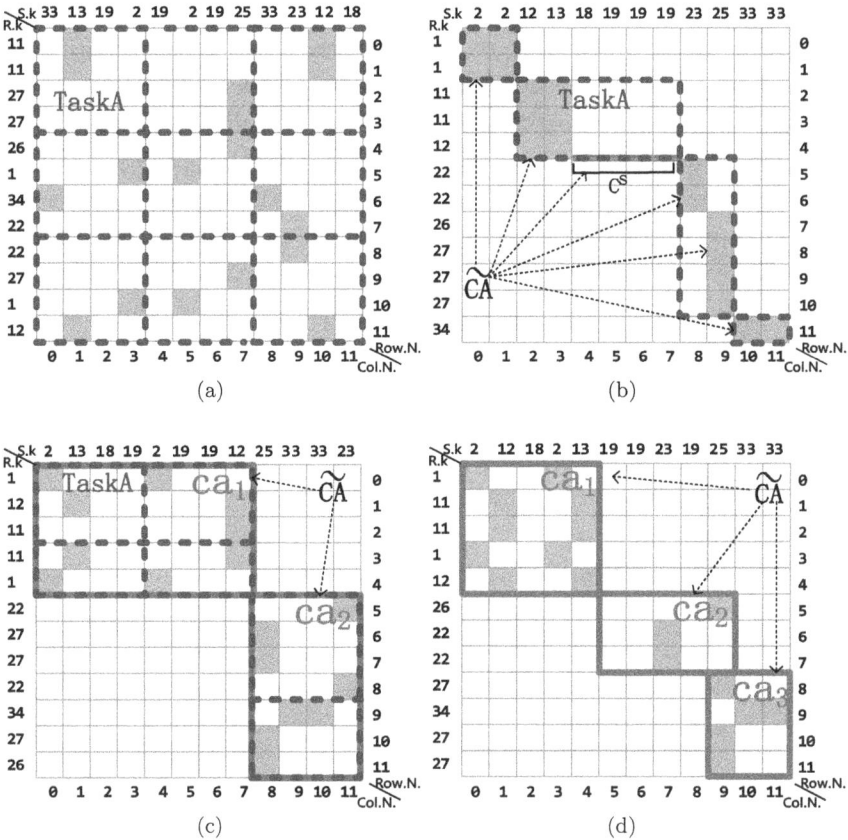

Fig. 5.2. Example of 2-DSP (a) and A-DSP strategy (b–d). (a) Partition *CA* by *TaskA*s, (b) partition $\widetilde{CA}$ by *TaskA*s, (c) partition $\widetilde{CA}$ by *ca* & *ca* by *TaskA*s and (d) other region partition.

A-DSP takes $\widetilde{ca}$ as the coverage area *ca* without order and splits it into multiple *TaskA*s, and then the incoming tuples are randomly distributed among those *TaskA*s.

Compared with 2-DSP, A-DSP can use less tasks while guaranteeing workload balance. As the join example shows in Fig. 5.2, each stream(R/S) has 12 tuples and each tuple pair has the candidate tuple(s) according to its join key($R.k$/$S.k$). The join condition is $|R.k - S.k| \leq 2$, and cells which produce join results are shaded in the tuple matrix. For each task, we assume the maximum workload $\overline{L} = 8$. Figure 5.2(a) shows the traditional strategy, which takes the whole tuple matrix as *CA*, and partitions *CA* by *TaskA*s directly. By using an optimized partition method [Fang *et al.* (2017)], nine tasks are needed to execute this join operation. This random partition scheme for incoming tuples can always ensure workload balance among parallel processing tasks. Figure 5.2(b) shows the process of using 1-DSP to partition $P_{\widetilde{CA}}$ into *TaskA*s, leading to imbalance workload among tasks. Figure 5.2(c) illustrates the phases of $P_{\widetilde{CA}}$ and P_{ca} in A-DSP: it first splits $\widetilde{CA}$ into two *ca*s(ca_1 and ca_2) according to the ordered key sequence, and then takes each *ca* as an independent join-matrix area and splits it into *TaskA*s. By splitting ca_1 into four *TaskA*s and ca_2 into two *TaskA*s, A-DSP needs less tasks (six tasks) to execute the join job than Fig. 5.2(a) (nine tasks).

However, the partition result in Fig. 5.2(c) is not optimal. Figure 5.2(d) shows another alternative, which generates a join scheme with four tasks (ca_1 with 2, ca_2 and ca_3 both with 1). Essentially, the shape of each *ca* is the decisive factor in the performance of our A-DSP. We will first introduce the basic principle of *ca*'s partition to determine its shape. Furthermore, the correctness in calculation area initialization and during the running process should also be taken into account. To propose a better processing scheme, the issues to be solved in this chapter include the following:

(1) How to ensure the correctness of matrix partition?
(2) In P_{ca}, how to partition *ca* into *TaskA*s so as to handle the dynamics of streams, in terms of the volume and distribution changes?
(3) In $P_{\widetilde{CA}}$, how to partition $\widetilde{CA}$ into *ca* to generate a flexible and adaptive processing scheme?
(4) During system running, how to migrate data among tasks under the consideration of minimizing the migration cost while ensuring the correctness?

5.3.3   *Constraints in partition process*

Beyond all doubt, the most fundamental performance requirement of the system is to ensure the correctness of the join process, while ensuring that the system has high throughput, low latency and a low-cost processing manner. Accordingly, there are still a few restrictions that our A-DSP model should comply with.

Table 5.3. Notations for cost-effective join.

Notations	Description
R, S	R, S stream
M	Matrix based on *TaskA*
m_{ij}	*TaskA* located at the ith row, jth column in M
$c_{(i,j)}$	Cell located at the ith row, jth column in tuple matrix
cr_x	The xth cr in CR form upper left to down right
ϕ^r/ϕ^s	Tuples in row/column for area ϕ, ($\phi \in \{c_{(i,j)}, cr, CA\}$)
$\alpha/\beta(\alpha^x/\beta^x)$	The number of rows/columns of M in $cr(cr_x)$
m_{ij}^x	Element of ith row and jth column in cr_x, corresponding to a single *TaskA*
h_{ij}^{xR}/h_{ij}^{xS}	The substream R/S that has been stored in m_{ij}^x, represented as a range $[b,e]$
$V(V_h)$	Memory size of tasks V $\left(\text{half size } V_h = \frac{V}{2}\right)$
$|o|$	The volume of set o
$F_*(k)$	Mapping function for tuples with join key k according to join predicate expression $*$

5.3.3.1 Correctness of $P_{\widetilde{CA}}$

To ensure the correctness of the process, all crs combined should cover the whole calculation area CA, and none of crs should overlap. This can be expressed as follows:

• **Completeness:** For join results, the completeness of partition can be expressed as

$$\mathbb{C} \subset \bigcup_{x\in[0,\gamma-1]} cr_x, \tag{5.1}$$

where cr_x refers to the xth calculation range in CR. For tuples without joined results,

$$C^r \subset \left(\bigcup_{x\in[0,\gamma-1]} cr_x\right)^r, \quad C^s \subset \left(\bigcup_{x\in[0,\gamma-1]} cr_x\right)^s. \tag{5.2}$$

This also echoes the description of CA coverage that CA not only contains the tuples that produce the output result but also tuples that have no join candidate.

- **Independence:** This means that cells in join-matrix do not occur in other cr, which can be expressed as

$$\forall x, x' \in [0, \gamma - 1], x \neq x' \Rightarrow cr_x \cap cr_{x'} = \emptyset. \tag{5.3}$$

Furthermore, it is possible that one of the row or column tuples exists in more than one cr, but there will be no result generated if it only happens in one side. This point can be interpreted by the routing strategy of the incoming tuple in Section 5.5.1.

5.3.3.2 Correctness of P_{ca}

The main challenge of stream join is to identify all pairs of tuples from stream R and stream S meeting the user's join predicate. By randomly dividing the stream $cr_x^r(cr_x^s)$ into $\alpha^x(\beta^x)$ non-overlapping substreams, the final join result is the union of the join results in all pairs of substreams. We use $h_{ij}^{xR} / h_{ij}^{xS}$ to denote the substream R/S that has been stored in m_{ij}^x in cr_x. Based on the definition, the matrix model in cr has the following properties, which prove the correctness of the join-matrix model.

- **Duplication:** The same row/column has the same subset of data from R/S:

$$\forall x \in [0, \gamma - 1], \forall j, j' \in [0, \beta^x - 1], \forall i \in [0, \alpha^x - 1],$$
$$\Rightarrow h_{ij}^{xR} = h_{ij'}^{xR};$$
$$\forall x \in [0, \gamma - 1], \forall i, i' \in [0, \alpha^x - 1], \forall j \in [0, \beta^x - 1],$$
$$\Rightarrow h_{ij}^{xS} = h_{i'j}^{xS}. \tag{5.4}$$

- **Intersection:** Tuples in stream R/S from different row/columns should be disparate:

$$\forall x \in [0, \gamma - 1], \forall j \in [0, \beta^x - 1], \forall i, i' \in [0, \alpha^x - 1], i \neq i',$$
$$\Rightarrow h_{ij}^{xR} \cap h_{i'j}^{xR} = \emptyset;$$
$$\forall x \in [0, \gamma - 1], \forall i \in [0, \alpha^x - 1], \forall j, j' \in [0, \beta^x - 1], j \neq j',$$
$$\Rightarrow h_{ij}^{xS} \cap h_{ij'}^{xS} = \emptyset. \tag{5.5}$$

- **Integrity:** Tuples from the same row/column can be combined to generate one branch of the complete stream for cr:

$$\forall x \in [0, \gamma - 1], \forall j \in [0, \beta^x - 1] \Rightarrow \bigcup_{i \in [0, \alpha^x - 1]} h_{ij}^{xR} = cr_x^r;$$

$$\forall x \in [0, \gamma - 1], \forall i \in [0, \alpha^x - 1] \Rightarrow \bigcup_{j \in [0, \beta^x - 1]} h_{ij}^{xS} = cr_x^s. \tag{5.6}$$

5.3.3.3 *Cost efficiency of resource utilization*

By using matrix M to decompose the calculation range cr_x into $\alpha^x \times \beta^x$ tasks, the resource utilization is modeled as follows.

- **Memory:** Since tuples are duplicated along rows or columns, values of α and β determine the memory consumption C_m of the join operator, as

$$C_m = \sum_{cr_x \in CR} |cr_x^r| \cdot \beta^x \cdot R_{\text{size}}^{\text{state}} + |cr_x^s| \cdot \alpha^x \cdot S_{\text{size}}^{\text{state}}, \tag{5.7}$$

where $R_{\text{size}}^{\text{state}}$ and $S_{\text{size}}^{\text{state}}$ are the sizes of memories used to maintain useful information over streams R and S, respectively.
- **Network:** By duplicating tuples on partitioning over rows and columns in M, it consumes network bandwidth C_n, i.e., the number of bytes transferred during data transmission. C_n is defined as

$$C_n = \sum_{cr_x \in CR} |cr_x^r| \cdot \beta^x \cdot R_{\text{size}}^{\text{tuple}} + |cr_x^s| \cdot \alpha^x \cdot S_{\text{size}}^{\text{tuple}}, \tag{5.8}$$

where $R_{\text{size}}^{\text{tuple}}$ and $S_{\text{size}}^{\text{tuple}}$ are the tuple sizes in streams R and stream S, respectively. Since join operator satisfies $R_{\text{size}}^{\text{tuple}} \propto R_{\text{size}}^{\text{state}}$ and $S_{\text{size}}^{\text{tuple}} \propto S_{\text{size}}^{\text{state}}$ [Gedik (2014)], we therefore have $C_n \propto C_m$. In other words, optimization over memory consumption always minimizes the bandwidth consumption at the same time.
- **CPU:** For θ-join in cr, we define its computation complexity as

$$C_{cr_x} = |cr_x^r| \cdot |cr_x^s| = \sum_{i \in [0, \alpha^x - 1]} \sum_{j \in [0, \beta^x - 1]} (|h_{ij}^{xR}| \cdot |h_{ij}^{xS}|). \tag{5.9}$$

Obviously, C_{cr_x} is a constant value($|cr_x^r| \cdot |cr_x^s|$) and is independent of α^x and β^x. Therefore, the whole computation complexity can be expressed as $C_c = \sum_{cr_x \in CR} C_{cr_x}$.

In order to simplify the explanation, we assume that the average (state) size of each tuple from stream R or S is identical, denoted by a unit load "1". In the rest of this chapter, $|R|/|S|$ denotes the overall load of the memory C_m or the network consumption C_n of stream R/S; $|h_{ij}^{xR}|/|h_{ij}^{xS}|$ represents the load of memory or network consumption in m_{ij}^x for stream R/S.

5.3.4 *Optimization goal*

Based on the model of data and workload, we are ready to define the optimization goal of our A-DSP, with the objectives of (i) load balance among all task instances, (ii) correctness of the process and (iii) minimization of the resource cost. Suppose the maximum memory size for each task is V. We formulate our objective as an optimization problem defined as

$$\min \sum_{x \in [0, \gamma - 1]} \alpha^x \cdot \beta^x, \tag{5.10}$$

s.t. expression (5.1)–(5.3) in Partition CA into CR;

expression (5.4)–(5.6) in Partition cr into $TaskAs$;

$$\forall x \in [0, \gamma - 1], |c_x^r| \cdot \beta^x + |c_x^s| \cdot \alpha^x \leq \alpha^x \cdot \beta^x \cdot V; \tag{5.11}$$

$$\forall x \in [0, \gamma - 1], i \in [0, \alpha^x - 1], j \in [0, \beta^x - 1],$$

$$|m_{ij}^{xr}| + |m_{ij}^{xc}| \leq \overrightarrow{L}, \quad |m_{ij}^x| \leq \underset{\rightarrow}{L}. \tag{5.12}$$

In above formulations, expression (5.1)–(5.3) and (5.4)–(5.6) ensure the correctness of join operation, and expression (5.11)–(5.12) describe the limitation of workload balance. Specifically, expression (5.11) limits the total resource usage while expression (5.12) prescribes that both the input and output workloads should not be more than their average workload. In the next section, we discuss the way of finding proper values of α^x and β^x for cr^x, which is the basis of our follow-up design.

5.4 Model Design for Resource-Sensitive Join Processing

As shown in Section 5.3.3, properties of *intersection* and *integrality* ensure the correctness of partition *cr* to *TaskA*s. Specifically, *intersection* guarantees that duplicated results do not exist and *integrality* ensures that there are no missing results. In this context, *intersection* and *integrality* act as the principles in designing join scheme generation and scheme changing.

5.4.1 *Basic principle*

For the matrix model, the half perimeter of this area can be seen as the consumption of memory and network. As shown in Fig. 5.3(a), the stream volumes for R and S in *cr* are $|cr^r| = 6\,\text{GB}$ and $|cr^s| = 6\,\text{GB}$, and then the calculation area is $|cr^r| \times |cr^s|$ and its memory cost is $|cr^r| + |cr^s|$. As defined by Eqs. (5.7)–(5.9) in Section 5.3.3, the total resource consumption is the resource accumulation of each cell in the matrix. Then it is critical to determine the data division in each cell and the shape of calculation matrix so as to pursue a cost-effective model.

Assuming the length and width of the cell area are a and b, respectively, we have the following expression:

$$a \cdot b \le \frac{(a+b)^2}{4}. \tag{5.13}$$

Equation (5.13) can be modified as the following expression:

$$a + b \ge 2 \cdot \sqrt{a \cdot b}. \tag{5.14}$$

In Eq. (5.13), if the memory volume of each task(cell) is limited, that is, the right part of Eq. (5.13) being a constant value, then $a = b$ will maximize cell area, that is, $a \cdot b$. In this way, the total calculation area can be segmented into less cell area and each cell can have better resource usage. Similarly, Eq. (5.14) can represent a situation wherein when the calculate ability of each cell is predefined, $a = b$ will minimize the memory consumption. We have the following theorem.

Theorem 5.1. *Assuming we use matrix model to handle stream join operation and $V_h = \frac{V}{2}$, if there exist α and β in cr with $\frac{|cr^r|}{\alpha} = \frac{|cr^s|}{\beta} = V_h$, then the processing cost for $R \bowtie S$ is minimized.*

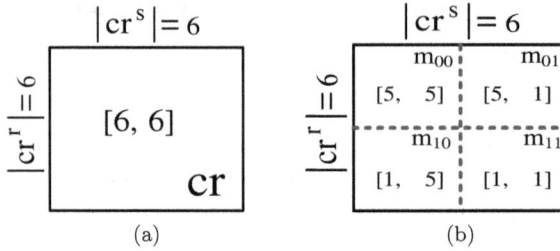

Fig. 5.3. A toy example of scheme partition at $|cr^r| = 6$ and $|cr^s| = 6$. (a) Calculation area of matrix and (b) 2×2 partition scheme M.

Proof. Each task has the predefined CPU and memory resources. According to Eq. (5.14), for the given CPU resource C_c (represented by the calculation area $a \cdot b$), square($a = b$) has the least memory usage C_m. For the given memory C_m, the square will produce the least cells and maximize the computation ability according to Eq. (5.13). The network cost C_n can be represented by memory usage C_m. Overall, we can get the maximum cells and the minimum memory consumption while $\frac{|cr^r|}{\alpha} = \frac{|c^s|}{\beta} = V_h$. □

5.4.2 Partition CR to TaskAs

The matrix model will take up less tasks (cells) while each cell in the matrix is squared according to Theorem 5.1. This means that the length and width of each cell should be V_h. Then the numbers of rows and columns should be $\lceil \frac{|cr^r|}{V_h} \rceil$ and $\lceil \frac{|cr^s|}{V_h} \rceil$, respectively. Then the total number of tasks used in matrix M can be expressed as

$$N = \left\lceil \frac{|cr^r|}{V_h} \right\rceil \cdot \left\lceil \frac{|cr^s|}{V_h} \right\rceil. \tag{5.15}$$

We continue to use Fig. 5.3(a) as an example, given task memory $V = 10\,\text{GB}$ and $V_h = 5\,\text{GB}$, and the calculation area of $R \bowtie S$ can be divided as shown in Fig. 5.3(b). The generated scheme in Fig. 5.3(b) takes up four tasks with two rows and two columns (four divisions: s_0, s_1, r_0 and r_1) for its matrix M. Among those cells, we load data to rows and columns by V_h in a top-down manner. In the last row and column of matrix M, the cells may have less data divisions compared to previous cells and are called fragment tasks filled with fragment data. In this example, m_{00} is first fed by V_h for both R and S streams and then $m_{00} = (5\,\text{GB}, 5\,\text{GB})$. However, the last column and row cannot be filled up. According to Eq. (5.15), though we can calculate the number of tasks needed for joining processing, workload is not evenly distributed among tasks because of the fragment data. Then tasks for fragment data may have free resources compared to other tasks, and it will be more obvious for the large matrix.

In order to facilitate the subsequent description, we name the two join streams as a primary stream P and a secondary stream D. Then we take the primary stream P as the basis volume to calculate how much memory should be assigned for it in each task and, accordingly, the secondary stream D gets the remaining portion of memory in each cell. Specifically, we use P_γ to represent the number of divisions generated by the primary stream, and then for the secondary stream, its division number D_γ^c can be calculated as

$$
D_\gamma^c = \left\lceil \frac{|D|}{V - \frac{|P|}{P_\gamma}} \right\rceil.
\tag{5.16}
$$

P may be either R or S. We use N_c to represent the number of tasks for processing join between P and D in matrix M which is calculated as

$$
N_c = P_\gamma \cdot D_\gamma^c = P_\gamma \cdot \left\lceil \frac{|D|}{V - \frac{|P|}{P_\gamma}} \right\rceil.
\tag{5.17}
$$

In Fig. 5.3, if we take R as the primary stream P and the number of divisions generated by primary stream is $P_\gamma = \lceil \frac{|cr^r|}{V_h} \rceil$, then the matrix scheme of the example in Fig. 5.3(a) should have only one column with two cells. However, D_γ^c calculated in Eq. (5.16) will have fragment tasks if its rounding up value is not equal to the rounding down value. For example in Fig. 5.4(a), given $V = 10\,\text{GB}$, $|cr^r| = 9\,\text{GB}$, and $|cr^s| = 7\,\text{GB}$, a matrix M with $\alpha = 2$ and $\beta = 2$ will be generated. Sine S is the primary stream, each task first gets data assignment from S by $\frac{|cr^s|}{\beta} = 3.5\,\text{GB}$ and the remaining space 6.5 GB can be used for divisions from R. The memory utilization percentage of the two tasks in the last row is 60%.

An optimized partition scheme of Fig. 5.4(a) is shown as Fig. 5.4(b), which takes up only three tasks for $R \bowtie S$. In Fig. 5.4(b), the replica $|s_1| = 3.5\,\text{GB}$ of S in m_{01} is sent to m_{10} to join with subset $|r_1| = 2.5\,\text{GB}$ of R to ensure the correctness and completeness of join results. It is feasible to

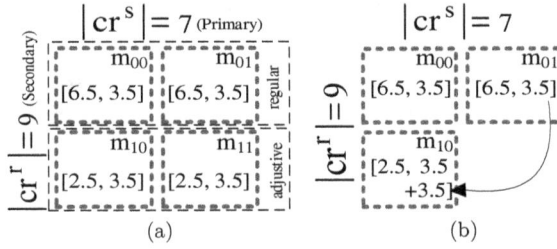

Fig. 5.4. Example with the optimized scheme. (a) Regular matrix and (b) optimal matrix.

move tuples in s_1 to m_{10} to complete the join work if the memory threshold $V = 10\,\text{GB}$ remains satisfied.

Compared to the regular matrix scheme in Fig. 5.4(a), the optimal workload assignment in Fig. 5.4(b) can make better use of resource among tasks. Let us take Fig. 5.4(b) to explain the generation of the irregular line, which is the last row. Given the divisions for primary stream S, which is $\beta = P_\gamma = 2$ in Fig. 5.4(a), we divide those α rows for secondary stream R into two types: regular ones (the first row) and adjustive ones (the second row). For regular ones, we have $\alpha^f = D_\gamma^f$ lines of segments (labeled as *regular* in Fig. 5.4(a)), where $D_\gamma^f = \lfloor \frac{|D|}{V - \frac{|P|}{P_\gamma}} \rfloor$. By using the regular division, we may not manage all the workload for secondary stream R, since $D_\gamma^f \cdot (V - \frac{|P|}{P_\gamma}) \le |D|$. For the remaining loads D^L from D calculated as Eq. (5.18), it is expected to add additional P_δ (as in Eq. (5.18)) number of columns along the last row with $P_\delta < P_\gamma$.

$$D^L = |D| - D_\gamma^f \cdot \left(V - \frac{|P|}{P_\gamma}\right),$$
$$P_\delta = \left\lceil \frac{|P|}{V - D^L} \right\rceil. \tag{5.18}$$

The difference from the previous regular matrix is that we will not add one whole row (column) of tasks for the join work with the purpose of making full use of system resources. Accordingly, the optimal number of tasks N_o for $R \bowtie S$ can be calculated as Eq. (5.19):

$$N_o = \begin{cases} P_\gamma \cdot D_\gamma^f, & |D| = D_\gamma^f \cdot \left(V - \frac{|P|}{P_\gamma}\right), \\ P_\gamma \cdot D_\gamma^f + P_\delta, & \text{otherwise.} \end{cases} \tag{5.19}$$

As described in Theorem 5.1, we use V_h as the divisor to find P_γ for generating an optimal scheme by probing all four cases. Specifically, we make $P_\gamma \in \{\lceil \frac{|cr^r|}{V_h} \rceil, \lfloor \frac{|cr^r|}{V_h} \rfloor, \lceil \frac{|cr^s|}{V_h} \rceil, \lfloor \frac{|cr^s|}{V_h} \rfloor\}$ in Eq. (5.19).

The method of finding an optimal partition scheme is described in Algorithm 5.1. First, the minimal number of tasks is determined in line 1 according to Eq. (5.19); then in lines 2–5, the number of rows α and columns β can be calculated according to values of P and P_γ. If $P_\gamma \in \{\lceil \frac{|cr^r|}{V_h} \rceil, \lfloor \frac{|cr^r|}{V_h} \rfloor\}$, R is the primary stream, or else S is the primary one. The scheme of varietal matrix generated from Algorithm 5.1 can be expressed as $\langle \alpha, \beta, P_\delta, \boxtimes \rangle$ which means that the varietal matrix has α rows, β columns and has P_δ additional cells in $\boxtimes$ ($\boxtimes \in row, column$).

We still use Fig. 5.4(b) to explain Algorithm 5.1. According to Eq. (5.18), Eq. (5.19) and line 1 in Algorithm 5.1, S is the primary stream and R is the secondary one, in which $\beta = 2$, $D_\gamma^f = \lfloor \frac{9}{10-7/2} \rfloor = 1$. m_{00} and m_{01} are supposed to have regular workload assignments with 3.5 GB from S, and the remaining memory is used for R, which will be $10 - 3.5 = 6.5$ GB. Since R has more load than 6.5 GB, we add one more row which is the adjustive division for the remaining data of R that $D^L = 9 - 6.5 = 2.5$ GB. In such a case, the cells in regular division lines have full usage of memory $6.5 + 3.5 = 10$ GB as in m_{00} and m_{01}. For adjustive purposes, we add $P_\delta = 1$ cell to join the remaining data D^L in R with S, which belongs to cell m_{10} and m_{11} in Fig. 5.4(a). In this adjustive row, D^L will join with the subset of S for m_{10} and m_{11} (3.5 GB) and then the workload in m_{10}

Algorithm 5.1 Partition *CR* to *TaskAs* Algorithm

input: Stream R, Stream S, Memory size V

output: Row number α, Column number β, additional cells P_δ, additional position $\boxtimes$

1: $N_o \leftarrow$ Get the minimum task consumption according to Eq. (5.19) where $P_\gamma \in \{\lceil \frac{|cr^r|}{V_h} \rceil, \lfloor \frac{|cr^r|}{V_h} \rfloor, \lceil \frac{|cr^s|}{V_h} \rceil, \lfloor \frac{|cr^s|}{V_h} \rfloor\}$.

2: **if** $P_\gamma \in \{\lceil \frac{|cr^r|}{V_h} \rceil, \lfloor \frac{|cr^r|}{V_h} \rfloor\}$ **then**

3:      $\alpha \leftarrow P_\gamma, \beta \leftarrow D_\gamma^f, P_\delta \leftarrow N_o - P_\gamma \cdot D_\gamma^f, \boxtimes \leftarrow column$

4: **else**

5:      $\alpha \leftarrow D_\gamma^f, \beta \leftarrow P_\gamma, P_\delta \leftarrow N_o - P_\gamma \cdot D_\gamma^f, \boxtimes \leftarrow row$

6: **return** $\alpha, \beta, P_\delta, \boxtimes$

comes to be 9.5 GB. The varietal matrix scheme shown in Fig. 5.4(b) can be expressed as $\langle 1, 2, 1, row \rangle$.

Theorem 5.2. *Algorithm 5.1 will consume the minimal number of tasks and ensure the correctness of operation when using matrix model for $R \bowtie S$ with the memory size of each task V.*

Proof. Assume that there exists another varietal matrix M' with scheme $\langle \alpha', \beta', P'_\delta, \boxtimes' \rangle$. It could be used for $R \bowtie S$ and the number of tasks N' used in M' is lesser than N_o. To find the N_o, Algorithm 5.1 tries all possible values that make $\frac{|P|}{P_\gamma}$ nearest to V_h according to Eq. (5.18), Eq. (5.19) and line 1. In other words, it is impossible for $\frac{|cr^r|}{\alpha'}$ and $\frac{|cr^s|}{\beta'}$ to get more closer to V_h than $\frac{|cr^r|}{\alpha}$ and $\frac{|cr^s|}{\beta}$. According to Theorem 5.1, a squared cell shape consumes minimal resources. Then, the assumption of existing regular matrix M' does not hold.

In order to ensure the correctness of join, Algorithm 5.1 can ensure join correctness when it generates a regular matrix scheme. When Algorithm 5.1 produces an irregular scheme, the irregular scheme can be split into a partial regular scheme and the P_δ tasks in the last row or column. The partial regular scheme can ensure *intersection* and *completeness* for a part of secondary stream D and all primary stream P. According to Eqs. (5.18) and (5.19), the P_δ tasks will hold the remaining part of D and all the primary stream P. So our algorithm can promise and guarantee the correctness of stream join.   □

Though the previous description takes memory as the limited resource, for CPU-intensive workload, e.g., C_c for each task, we take similar processing by using $\sqrt{C_c}$ instead of V_h to find the optimal α and β.

5.4.3 *Scheme generation*

In this section, we present the method of generating the processing scheme for join operation. Specifically, we first introduce the basic idea of processing scheme generation. Then, we further improve the performance of the scheme generation by using density-based clustering for cells in $\mathbb{C}$ and how to make our A-DSP fault tolerant.

Monotonicity is a property of the join output distribution which holds for many interesting joins, including equi-, band- and inequality joins. It states that if $c_{(i,j)}$ is not a candidate cell, then all cells (k, l) with $k \leq i$ and $l \geq j$ or all cells (k, l) with $k \geq i$ and $l \leq j$ are not candidate cells.

Definition 5.1. An *area dichotomy* is defined as splitting a coverage area into two sub-areas based on a split point d, meeting the condition that there are no candidate cells simultaneously located in $c_{(i,j')}$ and $c_{(i',j)}$ where $i < i'$ and $j < j'$, and $c_{(i,j)}$ is the location of d.

The reason for limiting the location of d described in the above Definition 5.1 is because we want to ensure that no more than two sub-areas will be generated. Based on this, the minimal task consumption can be expressed as

$$N_{\widetilde{CA}} = \text{Min}_{d \in \widetilde{CA}} \{N_{\widetilde{CA}^d}, N_{\widetilde{CA}_d}\}, \tag{5.20}$$

where $\widetilde{CA}^d$ and $\widetilde{CA}_d$, respectively, represent the first and second coverage areas that are divided based on $\widetilde{CA}$ using split point d.

Lemma 5.1. *Assuming that the distribution of candidate cells in tuple matrix is monotonous, $\forall d \in D_{\widetilde{CA}}$, if $N_{\widetilde{CA}} \geq N_{\widetilde{CA}^d} + N_{\widetilde{CA}_d}$, then the cells*

$$\{c_{(k,l)} | (\alpha - 1) \cdot V_h + 1 \geq k \geq V_h, (\beta - 1) \cdot V_h + 1 \geq l \geq V_h\}$$
$$-c_{(\alpha-1)\cdot V_h+1, \beta-1)\cdot V_h+1)}$$

should all be candidate cells.

Proof. Without splitting

$$N = \left\lceil \frac{|R|}{V_h} \right\rceil \cdot \left\lceil \frac{|S|}{V_h} \right\rceil.$$

With splitting by d which located in $c_{(i,j)}$

$$N' = \left\lceil \frac{i}{V_h} \right\rceil \cdot \left\lceil \frac{j}{V_h} \right\rceil + \left\lceil \frac{|R| - i'}{V_h} \right\rceil \cdot \left\lceil \frac{|S| - j'}{V_h} \right\rceil,$$

where $c_{(i',j')}$ is the beginning cell of ca_2. The location of candidate cell $c_{(i',j')}$ should meet the conditions $i' = i + 1$, $j' \leq j + 1$ or $i' \leq i + 1$, $j' = j + 1$, for all rows and columns covered by the coverage area.

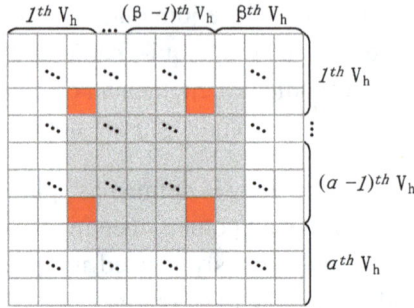

Fig. 5.5.   The illustration of the worst case using area dichotomy.

Because of the precondition that $N \leq N'$, cells $\{c_{(k,l)} | k\%V_h = 0, l\%V_h = 0, k \neq |R|, l \neq |S|\}$ must not be the splitting points (e.g., the red cells in Fig. 5.5).

According to the definition of *area dichotomy* in Definition 5.1 wherein the splitting point should meet the condition, if $c_{(i,j)}$ is the candidate cell, then $c_{(i,j')}$ and $c_{(i',j)}$, $i < i'$ and $j < j'$, cannot be the candidate cells at the same time. Here, while setting $c_{(i,j)}$ cannot be taken as a candidate cell, we regard both $c_{(i,j+1)}$ and $c_{(i+1,j)}$ as candidate cells, as tight candidate cell distribution is more conducive to generate less coverage area. Based on the above, the candidate cells can be expressed as

$$\{c_{(k,l)}, c_{(k,l+1)}, c_{(k+1,l)} | k\%V_h = 0, l\%V_h = 0, k \neq |R|, l \neq |S|\}.$$

If both the i-th cell and the $(i+2)$-th cell are candidates, the monotonicity of the distribution of candidate cells determines the $(i+1)$-th cell also be a candidate cell. And then, the candidate cells can be expressed as

$$\{c_{(k,l)} | (\alpha-1) \cdot V_h + 1 \geq k \geq V_h, (\beta-1) \cdot V_h + 1 \geq l \geq V_h\}$$
$$-c_{(\alpha-1)\cdot V_h+1, \beta-1)\cdot V_h+1)},$$

located in the central gathering area of the join-matrix in Fig. 5.5.   □

Theorem 5.3. *Assuming the distribution of candidate cells in tuple matrix is monotonous, $\forall d \in D_{\widetilde{CA}}$, if $N_{\widetilde{CA}} \geq N_{\widetilde{CA}^d} + N_{\widetilde{CA}_d}$, then the low bound of $N_{\widetilde{CA}}$ based on the minimal task consumption is $1 - \frac{\alpha+\beta-3}{\alpha\beta}$, where $\alpha \geq 2$ and $\beta \geq 2$.*

Proof. According to Lemma 5.1, the minimal task consumption consists of three parts: $\lceil c_{(0,0)}, c_{(V_h-1,V_h-1)} \rfloor$ consumes 1 task, $\lceil c_{(V_h,V_h)}, c_{((\alpha-1)\cdot V_h+1,(\beta-1)\cdot V_h+1)} \rfloor$ consumes $(\alpha - 1) \cdot (\beta - 1)$ task and $\lceil c_{((\alpha-1)\cdot V_h+2,(\beta-1)\cdot V_h+2)}, c_{(|R|,|S|)} \rfloor$ consumes 1 task. Then, the low bound can be expressed as $\frac{1+(\alpha-1)\cdot(\beta-1)+1}{\alpha \cdot \beta}$, which can be simplified as the result of Theorem 5.3. $\qquad \square$

Based on the above theorem, we provide the method of area dichotomy in Algorithm 5.2. For each cell, it first judges if it should be the split point according to Definition 5.1 (lines 4 and 5). Then, Algorithm 5.2 iteratively

---

Algorithm 5.2 Partition $\widetilde{CA}$ to cas Algorithm

input: $\widetilde{CA}$
output: cas
 1: $\square \leftarrow \widetilde{CA}$
 2: **function** PARATITIONAREA($\square$)
 3:      **foreach** $c_{(i,j)}$ from upper left to lower right in $\square$ **do**
 4:         **if** $c_{(i,*)}$ && $c_{(*,j)}$ **then**
           /*there are candidate cells both in the right and down of $c_{(i,j)}$*/
 5:           CONTINUE
 6:         **if** $N_o(\lceil c_{(b,b)}, c_{(i,j)} \rfloor) + N_o(\lceil c_{(i',j')}, c_{(e,e)} \rfloor) < N_o(\square)$ **then**
           /* $c_{(b,b)}$: the top-left cell in $\square$, $c_{(e,e)}$: the bottom-right cell in $\square$,
                           $c_{(i',j')}$: the next candidate cell after $c_{(i,j)}$*/
 7:           PARATITIONAREA($\lceil c_{(b,b)}, c_{(i,j)} \rfloor$)
 8:           PARATITIONAREA($\lceil c_{(i',j')}, c_{(e,e)} \rfloor$)
 9:         **else**
10:           $cas_{(i,j)} \leftarrow \lceil c_{(b,b)}, c_{(e,e)} \rfloor$
11:           $CAs \leftarrow cas_{(i,j)}$
          /* $cas_{(i,j)}$: the set of coverage area be derived from the first splitting
                         point $c_{(i,j)}$, CAs: the set of $cas_{(i,j)}$*/
12:      **foreach** cas in CAs **do**
13:         get cas_k which has the minimal value of $\sum_{ca \in cas_k} N_o(ca)$
14:         $cas \leftarrow cas_k$
15:      **return** cas

---

splits all the processable partitions according to Theorem 5.3 (lines 6–8) and gathers corresponding split results (lines 9 and 10). Finally, it picks out the partition result with minimal task consumption as its output (lines 12–15).

We continue using the example in Fig. 5.2 to illustrate the process of Algorithm 5.2. As shown in Fig. 5.2(d), the first splitting point selects $c_{(4,4)}$ as its location and splits $\widetilde{CA}$ into two parts: $\lceil c_{(0,0)}, c_{(4,4)} \rfloor$ and $\lceil c_{(5,5)}, c_{(11,11)} \rfloor$. For $\lceil c_{(0,0)}, c_{(4,4)} \rfloor$, Algorithm 5.2 stops splitting this coverage area because its split action will not bring about task consumption reduction. Conversely, $\lceil c_{(5,5)}, c_{(11,11)} \rfloor$ is split into two parts $\lceil c_{(5,5)}, c_{(7,9)} \rfloor$ and $\lceil c_{(8,9)}, c_{(11,11)} \rfloor$ as this split action brings about two task savings. Furthermore, as shown in coverage area ca_1 in Fig. 5.2(d), the routing strategy for tuples assigned to $\lceil c_{(0,0)}, c_{(4,4)} \rfloor$ is based on random.

5.5 Handling Workload Dynamics

The adaptive processing architecture is shown in Fig. 5.6 and can be decomposed into the following five steps:

Step-1 — Monitoring workload: It collects information about current resource usage (e.g., memory) and decides whether to change the processing scheme, which is realized by sampling.

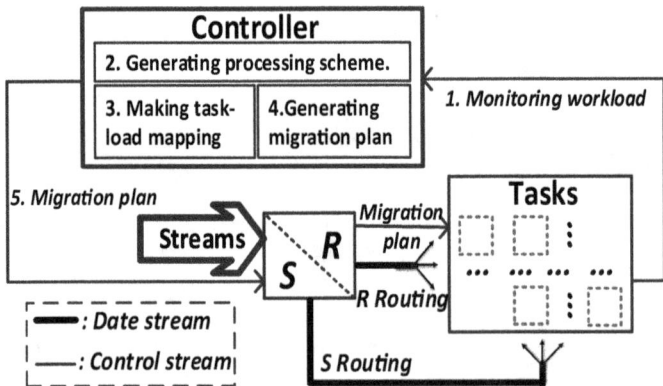

Fig. 5.6. Architecture of adaptive processing.

Step-2 — Generating processing scheme: It produces a new scheme according to workload and resource information.

Step-3 — Making task-load mapping: It expects to find the task-load mapping function so as to maximize non-moving data volume when transforming from the old scheme to the new scheme.

Step-4 — Generating migration plan: It schedules the data migration among tasks according to the task-load mapping scheme.

Step-5 — Defining consistent protocol according to migration plan: This step defines consistent protocols to ensure the correctness of the system.

We omit a detailed description of Step 5 in this chapter as it is the same as that given by Elseidy *et al.* (2014). As it is an essential step to indicate the destination for each tuple in the incoming stream, we first introduce the routing strategy for A-DSP in Section 5.5.1.

5.5.1 *Routing strategy*

One option for workload distribution is to explicitly assign the tuples based on a carefully optimized routing table, which specifies the mapping of each tuple to a designated node. It is a simple way of handling key skewness and workload variances. However, as there is no free lunch in the world, the number of distinct keys is usually enormous, and probably increases unboundedly in practice. Such an enormous routing table will result in huge memory consumption and maintenance cost. With the help of the processing architecture, A-DSP can provide an extremely simple routing plan for the incoming streams while ensuring the workload balance among parallel processing tasks. The pseudo code of the routing strategy is listed in Algorithm 5.3.

As described in Section 5.3.2, A-DSP is a nested structure including a content-sensitive and content-insensitive level. Therefore, the processing flow of routing algorithm can be divided into the following two steps:

Step-1 — Routing tuples in CA: This step is responsible for routing tuples into a content-related cr according to the basic mapping function $F_*(k)$. It is important to note that the join predicate expression $*$ determines which pair of tuples should meet with each other. It also means that different crs may need to receive the same tuple(s). Based on this, Algorithm 5.3 first

---

Algorithm 5.3 Routing Strategy

---

input: Input tuple: τ, Mapping function: F_*
output: Routing destination RD: $\{(cr, \ddagger, th)\}$
1: $k \leftarrow \mathcal{E}(\tau)$ ◁ extract the key of incoming tuple τ
2: / $***$Step-1: Routing tuples in CA $***$/.
3: $Cr \leftarrow$ ROUTINGINCA(CR, k, F) /* Cr is set of cr*/
4: / $***$Step-2: Routing tuples in CR $***$/.
5: RD $\leftarrow$ ROUTINGINCR(Cr, τ)
6: **return**
7: **function** ROUTINGINCA(CR, k, F_*)
8: $\quad K^* \leftarrow F_*(k)$
9: $\quad$ **foreach** $k^* \in K^*$ **do**
10: $\quad\quad th^* \leftarrow BasicPartition(k^*), Cr^* \leftarrow cr^{th^*}$
11: $\quad$ **return** Cr^*
12: **function** ROUTINGINCR(Cr, τ)
13: $\quad$ **foreach** $cr^* \in Cr$ **do**
14: $\quad\quad$ **if** $\tau \in R$ **then**
15: $\quad\quad\quad \ddagger^* \leftarrow row, th^* \leftarrow RandomInt[0 \sim (\alpha - 1)]$
16: $\quad\quad$ **else**
17: $\quad\quad\quad \ddagger^* \leftarrow column, th^* \leftarrow RandomInt[0 \sim (\beta - 1)]$
18: $\quad\quad$ RD$^* \leftarrow (cr^*, \ddagger^*, th^*)$
19: $\quad$ **return** RD*

---

extracts the set of candidate join keys K^* according to $F_*(k)$ in line 8. Then, the set of $cr(Cr^*$ in line 11) which the input tuples τ should be sent to can be determined by a basic routing function (line 10, e.g., consistent hash) as shown in lines 9–11.

Step-2 — Routing tuples in *CRs*: After processing in Step 1, the input tuples are clear about which $cr(s)$ in *CRs* should be sent to the destination. Therefore, this step is responsible for further determining which $TaskA(s)$ in cr is the destination of the tuples. The routing strategy in cr is based on a random assignment since the processing scheme in cr is content insensitive. Specifically, Algorithm 5.3 randomly generates a row or column number according to which stream the input tuple comes from and determines its destination (lines 15–20). The destination can be expressed as ($cr, \ddagger, th$, which means the input tuple should be send to all tasks located in ‡th ($‡ \in (row, column)$)) cr.

We continue using the previous example to illustrate Algorithm 5.3. When a tuple with join key 2 comes into the system, it first determines the first cr as its direction according to the join predicate expression ($|R.k - S.k| \leq 2$) and basic routing strategy (consistent hashing). Since this cr is divided into 2 rows and 2 columns, Algorithm 5.3 randomly generates a row number in (0,1) to determine the destination task, and the routing destination for this tuple can be expressed as ($cr^1, row, 0$) or ($cr^1, row, 1$). For simplicity, we only show the routing strategy of regular join-matrix in Algorithm 5.3.

5.5.2 *Scheme changing*

There are two criteria which should be guaranteed during the process of cr's scheme changing. The first one is to ensure the correctness of the process and the second one is to lower migration cost during the process of scheme changing as far as possible. To simplify our description, some additional notations used in the following chapters are summarized in Table 5.4.

We use m_{ij} and m_{kl} to represent the cells in M_o and M_n, respectively, where $i(k)$ and $j(l)$ are the row number and column number of $M_o(M_n)$. We define the correlation coefficient λ_{kl}^{ij} to reflect the volume of data overlap between m_{ij} and m_{kl}, which can be calculated as $\lambda_{kl}^{ij} = |h_{ij}^R \cap s_{kl}^R| + |h_{ij}^S \cap s_{kl}^S|$.

Algorithm 5.4 shows the task mapping method, which aims to minimize the states' migration when using the new scheme M_n. Specifically,

Table 5.4.   Table of additional notations.

Notations	Description
M_o/M_n	Old matrix and new matrix for cr
k/l	kth row and lth column in new scheme
h_{ij}^R/h_{ij}^S	Data have been stored in m_{ij} in cr
s_{kl}^R/s_{kl}^S	Data for m_{kl} in new scheme M_n in cr, represented as a range $[b, e]$ on stream cr^r/cr^s
tpi	The mapping of tasks between old and new scheme
mp	The migration plan
TP/MP	The set of tpi/mp

Algorithm 5.4 Task Mapping TP Generation

---

input: Old matrix scheme M_o, New matrix scheme M_n

output: Task mapping set TP

1: **foreach** m_{ij} in Old scheme M_o **do**

2:     **foreach** m_{kl} in New scheme M_n **do**

3:         $\lambda_{kl}^{ij} \leftarrow (h_{ij}^R \cap s_{kl}^R) \cdot |cr^r| + (h_{ij}^S \cap s_{kl}^S) \cdot |cr^s|$

4:         $TPI \leftarrow < m_{ij}, m_{kl}, \lambda_{kl}^{ij} > / * TPI$ is a temp set $*/$

5: Initialize $TP = Null$

6: **foreach** tpi in TPI in descending order based on λ_{kl}^{ij} **do**

7:     **if** m_{ij} or m_{kl} in tpi has been appeared in TP **then**

8:         Continue

9:     $< m_{ij}, m_{kl} > \rightarrow TP$

10: **return** TP

Algorithm 5.4 first enumerates all the possible mappings in form of $tpi = \langle m_{ij}, m_{kl}, \lambda_{kl}^{ij} \rangle$ as shown in lines (1–4); then it selects the optimal mappings which have larger λ_{kl}^{ij} among all mapping sets in lines (6–10). Task mapping TP generated by Algorithm 5.4 gathers the largest cumulative values of λ_{kl}^{ij}. Because each m_{ij} or m_{kl} appears in TP only once at most, the correlation coefficient λ_{kl}^{ij} is independent of others. Our algorithm always selects the mapping pair with the biggest λ_{kl}^{ij}, and then it will generate the maximum cumulative value of λ_{kl}^{ij}. In other words, Algorithm 5.4 finally produces minimal migration cost during the process of scheme changing.

Considering scheme generation and task mapping generation discussed above, we design advanced scheme mapping for reducing migration cost. In order to make it easy to explain, we take a one-dimensional scheme division as an example and treat its total volume as unit "1", as shown in Fig. 5.7, where $h_i(s_i)$ represents the range processed by task i.

A naive method is to divide the stream into even ranges and assign each range to one task as shown in Fig. 5.7(a). In the old scheme, there are four tasks (No. 0–3) and each task manages 25% of the whole stream, represented as h_i ($i \leq 3$). When it is scaled out to five tasks, five ranges are generated evenly and each range s_j ($j \leq 4$) maps to one task. Based on Algorithm 5.4, we can figure out the best mapping from $\{h_i\}$ to $\{s_j\}$ as

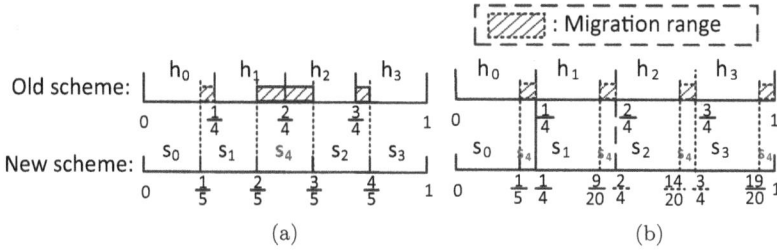

Fig. 5.7. Advanced scheme generation and task mapping. (a) Original and (b) optimized.

shown in Fig. 5.7(a), represented by the dotted line. The shaded range in the old scheme will be migrated among tasks, and the newly added task will be assigned the data in range $[2/5, 3/5]$ labeled as s_4. The total volume of data migration is $\frac{1}{20} + \frac{1}{5} + \frac{1}{20} = \frac{3}{10}$.

Join correctness is independent of the order of tuples as long as we can guarantee that the same row (column) has the same states. In this context, we can conduct optimization based on the start point alignment method for task mapping as follows. We first align the same range start points for $\{s_j\}$ in the new scheme to those from $\{h_i\}$ in the old scheme, if any. In Fig. 5.7(b), the old scheme is scaled out to five tasks. We align the same start range points between four tasks such as s_0–s_3 from the new scheme and h_0–h_3 from the old scheme. Each h_i cuts down the shaded $1/20(=1/4 - 1/5)$ of the range and moves them to the newly inserted task that is s_4. In such a case, the total migration volume is $\frac{1}{20} + \frac{1}{20} + \frac{1}{20} + \frac{1}{20} = \frac{1}{5}$, which is less than the migration cost generated by Algorithm 5.4. For scaling down, it is almost the same. We align the start points of the new tasks with some of the old ones, and split the ranges managed by the removing nodes (to be deleted) to the tasks kept in the new scheme.

5.5.3 *Workload transfer among processing tasks*

Figuring out the part of the data which should be migrated among tasks is necessary information in the process of scheme changing. We use $\diamond$ to represent the join stream such that $\diamond \in \{cr^r, cr^s\}$ and $n_{kl}^{\diamond}$ means the data that are lacked in m_{kl}, and then the range of data $n_{kl}^{\diamond}$ is

$$n_{kl}^{\diamond} = s_{kl}^{\diamond} - (s_{kl}^{\diamond} \cap h_{kl}^{\diamond}). \tag{5.21}$$

Then we define the migration plan as $mp = \langle m_{ij}, m_{kl}, v^\diamond \rangle$ that can be read as follows: for stream $\diamond$, the data $v^\diamond$ should be copied for m_{ij} in the old scheme M_o to m_{kl} in the new scheme M_n, where $v^\diamond$ is

$$v^\diamond = h^\diamond_{ij} \cap n^\diamond_{kl}. \tag{5.22}$$

For each m_{kl}, we use $d^\diamond_{kl}$ to represent the data which are no longer needed and should be moved out, and $d^\diamond_{kl}$ can be calculated as

$$d^\diamond_{kl} = h^\diamond_{kl} - (s^\diamond_{kl} \cap h^\diamond_{kl}). \tag{5.23}$$

In this case, the migration plan can be represented as $mp = \langle \odot, m_{kl}, d^\diamond_{kl} \rangle$. The migration plan with mark $\odot$ can be read as follows: for stream $\diamond$, delete data $d^\diamond_{kl}$ from m_{kl}.

The generation of the migration plan is described in Algorithm 5.5 and can be divided into four steps as follows:

Step 1 — Discarding states that are no longer needed in M_n: As shown in line 1 in Algorithm 5.5, this step is used to clean useless states generated by the old scheme M_o. Specifically, some states will be discarded when the scheme change happens.

Step 2 — Filling stream data for cells in the new scheme: We can get the whole dataset in stream R or S by combining the data from the first row or the first column in M_o. As in lines 2–11, we can fill each cell with data in M_n using tuples which are stored in the first row or column in M_o.

Step 3 — Handling the last row or column with irregular scheme: This step plays the role of making a scheme with full use of resources. It redistributes the subset of data of the primary stream located in cells $P_\delta \sim P_\gamma$ in lines 12–18.

Step 4 — Deleting useless tuples: It deletes data with $\odot$ mark in mp under the new scheme M_n in lines 19–21.

In above steps, step 1 will be triggered when the old scheme M_o is an irregular matrix and step 3 will be triggered when the new scheme M_n is irregular. To make it comprehensible, we first walk through an example with a regular scheme transformation (just use step 2 and step 4 in Algorithm 5.5) and then discuss the details of the irregular scheme generation.

Algorithm 5.5 Migration Plan Generation

---

input: Old scheme M_o, New scheme M_n, Task mapping TP

output: Migration plan MP

1: Discard states with mark $\boxdot$ state for each task in new scheme
2: **foreach** row i with column 0 in old scheme M_o **do**
3:    **foreach** task m_{kl} in new scheme M_n **do**
4:      **if** $h_{i0}^R \cap n_{kl}^R \neq \varnothing$ **then** $/ * According\ to\ Equ.5.21\&5.22 * /$
5:        $< m_{i0}, m_{kl}, h_{i0}^R \cap n_{kl}^R > \rightarrow MP$
6:        Update n_{kl}^R

7: **foreach** column j with row 0 in old scheme M_o **do**
8:    **foreach** task m_{kl} in new scheme M_n **do**
9:      **if** $h_{0j}^S \cap n_{kl}^S \neq \varnothing$ **then**
10:       $< m_{0j}, m_{kl}, h_{0j}^S \cap n_{kl}^S > \rightarrow MP$
11:       Update n_{kl}^S

12: **foreach** task x located between P_δ and P_γ **do**
13:   **if** $P = R$ **then** $/ * y \in [0, P_\delta - 1] * /$
14:     $< \boxdot, m_{xD_\gamma^f}, m_{yD_\gamma^f}, s_{xD_\gamma^f}^R > \rightarrow MP$
15:     Set task in $m_{xD_\gamma^f}$ in M_n as inactive
16:   **else if** $P = S$ **then**
17:     $< \boxdot, m_{D_\gamma^f x}, m_{D_\gamma^f y}, s_{D_\gamma^f x}^S > \rightarrow MP$
18:     Set task in $m_{D_\gamma^f x}$ in M_n as inactive

19: **foreach** task m_{kl} in new scheme M_n **do**
20:   $< \odot, m_{kl}, d_{kl}^R > \rightarrow MP$ $/ * According\ to\ Equ.5.23 * /$
21:   $< \odot, m_{kl}, d_{kl}^S > \rightarrow MP$

22: **return** MP

A scheme changes from 2×2 to 2×3 as depicted in Fig. 5.8 and we also treat the total volume of cr^r/cr^s as unit "1". In the old scheme M_o, each cell manages half size of stream data from cr^r and cr^s as shown in Fig. 5.8(a): each row manages half size of cr^r with $h_{00}^R = h_{01}^R = [0, \frac{1}{2}]$ and $h_{10}^R = h_{11}^R = [\frac{1}{2}, 1]$; each column manages half size of cr^s with $h_{00}^S = h_{10}^S = [0, \frac{1}{2}]$ and $h_{10}^S = h_{11}^S = [\frac{1}{2}, 1]$. When the workload of stream cr^s increases, the system may scale out by adding one more column

(a) $crs_{1/2}$, cr^r with $1/2$:

$h^S_{00}=[0,\frac{1}{2}]$, $h^R_{00}=[0,\frac{1}{2}]$ — ①: m_{00}	$h^S_{01}=[\frac{1}{2},1]$, $h^R_{01}=[0,\frac{1}{2}]$ — ②: m_{01}
$h^S_{10}=[0,\frac{1}{2}]$, $h^R_{10}=[\frac{1}{2},1]$ — ③: m_{10}	$h^S_{11}=[\frac{1}{2},1]$, $h^R_{11}=[\frac{1}{2},1]$ — ④: m_{11}

(a)

(b) crs with $1/3$, $2/3$; cr^r with $1/2$:

$h^S_{00}=[0,\frac{1}{2}]$, $h^R_{00}=[0,\frac{1}{2}]$, $s^S_{00}=[0,\frac{1}{3}]$, $s^R_{00}=[0,\frac{1}{2}]$ — ①: m_{00}	$n^S_{01}=[\frac{1}{3},\frac{2}{3}]$, $s^R_{01}=[0,\frac{1}{2}]$, $s^S_{01}=[\frac{1}{3},\frac{2}{3}]$, $n^R_{01}=[0,\frac{1}{2}]$ — ⑤: m_{01}	$h^S_{02}=[\frac{1}{2},1]$, $h^R_{02}=[0,\frac{1}{2}]$, $s^S_{02}=[\frac{2}{3},1]$, $s^R_{02}=[0,\frac{1}{2}]$ — ②: m_{02}
$h^S_{10}=[0,\frac{1}{2}]$, $h^R_{10}=[\frac{1}{2},1]$, $s^S_{10}=[0,\frac{1}{3}]$, $s^R_{10}=[\frac{1}{2},1]$ — ③: m_{10}	$n^S_{11}=[\frac{1}{3},\frac{2}{3}]$, $s^R_{11}=[\frac{1}{2},1]$, $s^S_{11}=[\frac{1}{3},\frac{2}{3}]$, $n^R_{11}=[\frac{1}{2},1]$ — ⑥: m_{11}	$h^S_{12}=[\frac{1}{2},1]$, $h^R_{12}=[\frac{1}{2},1]$, $s^S_{12}=[\frac{2}{3},1]$, $s^R_{12}=[\frac{1}{2},1]$ — ④: m_{12}

(b)

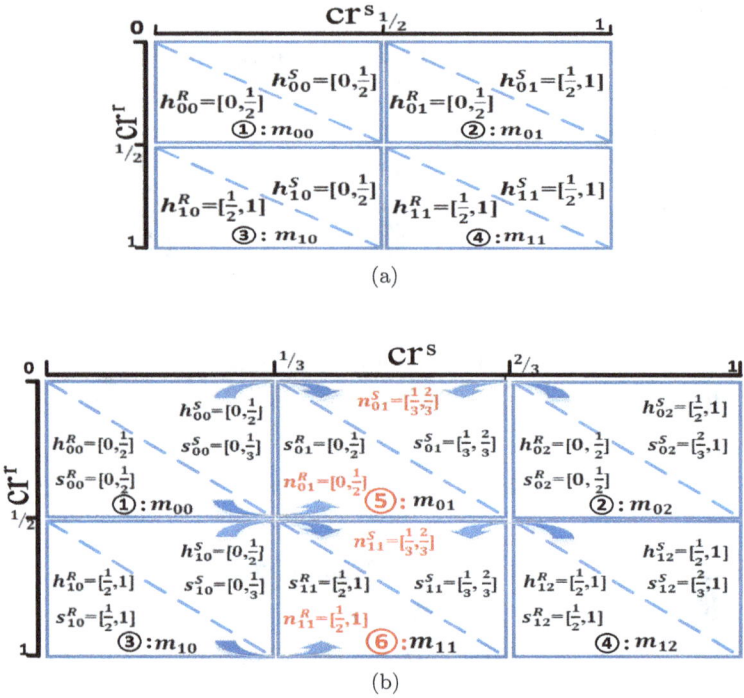

Fig. 5.8.   Stream distribution example. (a) Old scheme: stream distribution and (b) new scheme: stream distribution.

with two tasks using a 2×3 scheme as shown in Fig. 5.8(b). In this case, data partitions to cr^r are unchanged where tasks in the first row still manage half size of volume ($s^R_{0j} = [0, \frac{1}{2}]$, $j \in \{0, 1, 2\}$) and tasks in the second row manage the other half ($s^R_{1j} = [\frac{1}{2}, 1]$, $j \in \{0, 1, 2\}$). Stream cr^s should be split into three partitions for three columns, each of which manages $\frac{1}{3}$ range of data, that is, $s^S_{i0} = [0, \frac{1}{3}]$, $s^S_{i1} = [\frac{1}{3}, \frac{2}{3}]$ and $s^S_{i2} = [\frac{2}{3}, 1]$, with $i \in \{0, 1\}$.

According to the discussion, if we have the optimal partitioning scheme with minimal migration cost, TP is $\{\langle m^o_{00}, m^n_{00}\rangle, \langle m^o_{01}, m^n_{02}\rangle,$ $\langle m^o_{10}, m^n_{10}\rangle, \langle m^o_{11}, m^n_{12}\rangle\}$. In Fig. 5.8(b), we pair the relevant tasks between M_o and M_n by assigning the same numbers for tasks. The tasks tagged with red numbers ⑤ and ⑥ in m_{01} and m_{11} are not paired. m_{01} is supposed to manage data $n^R_{01} = [0, \frac{1}{2}]$ and $n^S_{01} = [\frac{1}{3}, \frac{2}{3}]$; m_{11} is supposed to manage data $n^R_{11} = [\frac{1}{2}, 1]$ and $n^S_{11} = [\frac{1}{3}, \frac{2}{3}]$. According to Algorithm 5.5, in m_{01}, s^R_{01} is generated by duplicating cr^r data from m_{00}. Since cr^s is reallocated by splitting into three parts for the insertion of a new column, it first generates the complete dataset by combining h_{00}^S and h_{01}^S in scheme M_o, and then s_{01}^S is generated by replicating cr^s data from m_{00}^S with h_{00}^S by range $[\frac{1}{3}, \frac{1}{2}]$ and from m_{01}^S with h_{01}^S by range $[\frac{1}{2}, \frac{2}{3}]$. Then the data for s_{01}^S are deleted from these cells. m_{11} in M_n will be assigned data in the same way as m_{01}.

Since the last row or column may not be regular for the sake of resource usage, we randomly assign the tuples from the primary stream, which are expected to locate from the areas managed by the last $(P_\gamma - P_\delta)$ tasks to the areas managed by the first P_δ tasks and set the last $(P_\gamma - P_\delta)$ tasks as inactive. Let us continue with the example in Fig. 5.8 to illustrate how irregular scheme processing should be handled. We assume the memory size of each task is 10 GB. At time t, the stream volumes are $|cr^r| = 10$ GB and $|cr^s| = 15$ GB. We use the scheme shown in Fig. 5.8(b) where each task manages 10 GB data and each stream contributes 5 GB data. At time $t + 1$, the volume of stream cr^r shrinks to 7 GB, and the scheme generator produces a new scheme with five tasks as shown in Fig. 5.9. In Fig. 5.9, cr^s is the primary stream and cr^r is the secondary stream with $P_\gamma = 3$, $P_\delta = 2$ and $D_\gamma^f = 2$. Then we randomly distribute h_{02}^S to m_{10} and m_{11} to ensure the join correctness, which are called *sojourners* to m_{10} and m_{11}. Those sojourn tuples will be tagged with ⊡ and deleted from the sojourn area as soon as the scheme change happens. This step is a necessary and easy way to manage those random distributed tuples.

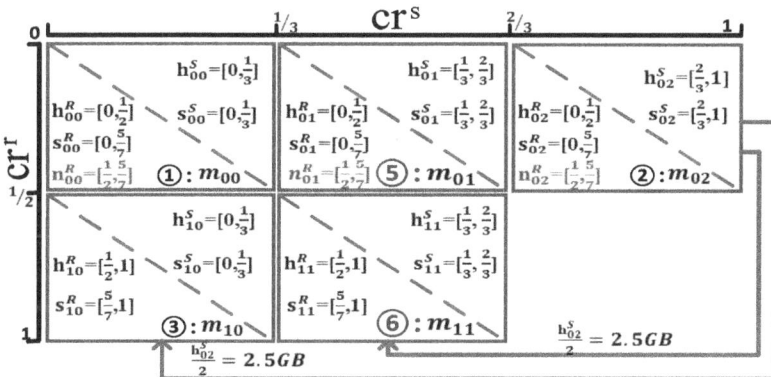

Fig. 5.9. Example with the irregular scheme.

As described above, the data distribution for irregular scheme change is almost the same as the regular one except that an additional state ⊡ is defined to handle a subset of tuples from the primary stream and this subset will be deleted as soon as the scheme change happens. The process of irregular scheme change is also shown in Algorithm 5.5. Its first step is to discard states tagged with label ⊡; then fill data to each task with the new scheme as described in line 2–11 in Algorithm 5.5; lines 12–18 show how to redistribute the subset of tuples (*sojourners*) from primary stream P and route those to the first $P_\delta \sim P_\gamma$ tasks. In Fig. 5.9, $P = S$ in line 13 of Algorithm 5.5 and a temporary variable y decide the *sojourn* task for *sojourner* tuples, where $y \in \{0, 1\}$ for $P_\delta = 2$. This means that it randomly redistributes s_{02}^S to m_{10} and m_{11}. The last lines 19–21 take the same actions as the regular scheme change happens.

5.6 Practical Verification and Study

5.6.1 *Environment setting*

- **Environment:** We implement the approaches and conduct all the experiments on *Apache Storm*. The *Storm* system is deployed on a cluster of 21 HP blade instances, each of which runs on a CentOS 6.5 operating system and is equipped with two Intel Xeon processors (E5335 at 2.00 GHz) with four cores and a 32 GB RAM. Overall, there are 300 virtual machines available exclusively for our experiments, each with dedicated memory resources.
- **Datasets:** We test the proposed algorithms using two types of datasets. The first TPC-H dataset is generated by the *dbgen* tool shipped with a TPC-H benchmark. Before feeding the data to the stream system, we pre-generate and pre-process all the input datasets. We adjust the datasets with different degrees of skew on the join attributes under *Zipf* distribution by choosing a value for skew parameter z. By default, we set $z = 1$. The second dataset is 10 GB social data[1] (coming from Weibo which is the biggest Chinese social media data) which consist of 20,000,000

---

[1]http://open.weibo.com/wiki/2/statuses/user_timeline.

real-feed tuples. We run self-join on social data to find the correlation degree among tuples.

- **Queries:** We experiment on four join queries, namely one equi-join from the TPC-H benchmark and three synthetic band-joins. The equi-join, E_{Q_5}, represents the most expensive operation in query Q_5 from the benchmark. B_{NCI}, B_{MR} and *Social data query* are all band-joins, which are different in the range of join. Specifically, B_{NCI} is the θ-join query that corresponds to a chapter range, while B_{MR} is the θ-join query that represents a big range. B_{MR} and *Social data query* are full band-joins which require that each tuple from one stream meets all the tuples from the other stream. The E_{Q_5} and B_{NCI} were used in Elseidy *et al.* (2014) and Lin *et al.* (2015).

- **Baseline Approaches:** For the purpose of comparison, we evaluate four different distributed stream join algorithms as follows.

    Square figures out the number of tasks through a simple and easy way as defined in Eq. (5.15).

    Dynamic [Elseidy *et al.* (2014)] takes join-matrix as its processing model and assumes that the number of tasks in a matrix must be a power of 2. Since the model needs to maintain its matrix structure, if the workload of one stream increases twofold, *Dynamic* will double cells along the side corresponding to this stream. Meanwhile, cells along the other side will get reduced by half. In addition, during system scaling out, *Dynamic* splits the states of every node into 4 nodes if storage of any task exceeds half of the specified memory capacity.

    Readj [Gedik (2014)] is designed to minimize the load of restoring the keys based on the hash function, implemented by rerouting over the keys with maximal workload. The migration plan of keys for load balance is generated by pairing tasks and keys. For each task–key pair, their algorithm considers all possible swaps to find the best move alleviating the workload imbalance.

    Bi_6 and Bi [Lin *et al.* (2015)] handle θ-join using a complete bipartite graph. On one side of the bipartite graph, a data stream R is decomposed into substreams by a key-based hash function, each partition of which is stored and maintained by a computation node. Tuples from the other data stream S are pushed to corresponding nodes for stream R, based on the hash key values of the tuples. Bi represents there is only one sub-group for each side of join-biclique and Bi_6 means there are six sub-groups for each side.

- **Performance Metrics:** We evaluate resource utilization and system performance through the following metrics:

  Task number is the total number of tasks consumed by the system and each task is assigned with a specified quota of memory space V.

  Execution Time is consumption time tasked to deal with a certain amount of data.

  Throughput is the average number of tuples that are processed by the system per second (time unit). *Average join request account* is the average number of tuples which should be joined within each task.

  Migration volume is the total number of tuples which should be moved to other tasks during scheme changing.

  ResourceCost(RC) is the cumulative usage volume of a certain resource which can be expressed as $RC = \sum_{r \in \mathbb{R}} r \cdot t_r$, where r is the measurement of resource consumption, which may be memory, network or CPU, $\mathbb{R}$ is the set of r and t_r is the duration time for the resource r.

5.6.2   *Full-history stream joins*

Figure 5.10 demonstrates the trend on task consumption and execution time during loading of all 16 GB data into the Storm system. The maximum input rate can be set to consume all the computing power of each task, using enough parallelism for spout in Storm.

During data loading as shown in Fig. 5.10(a), our algorithm A-DSP has stable performance while *Dynamic* meets a sharp increase in task number. This is because *Dynamic* has a strict requirement that the number of tasks must be a power of two, and then *Dynamic* must quadruple its tasks and may waste resources when the system scales out. Contrarily, our algorithm A-DSP generates the processing scheme based on current workload. *Square* limits the *TaskA* which must be square shaped and divides *CA* directly making it use more computing resources. Since *Bi* is designed for memory optimization, it is obvious that *Bi* uses a minimal number of tasks. Specifically, Bi_6 sets up six sub-groups for each stream and every sub-group contains one task initially. As data flow in, tasks inside sub-groups will scale out dynamically. Figures 5.10(b)–5.10(d) depict processing efficiency under different

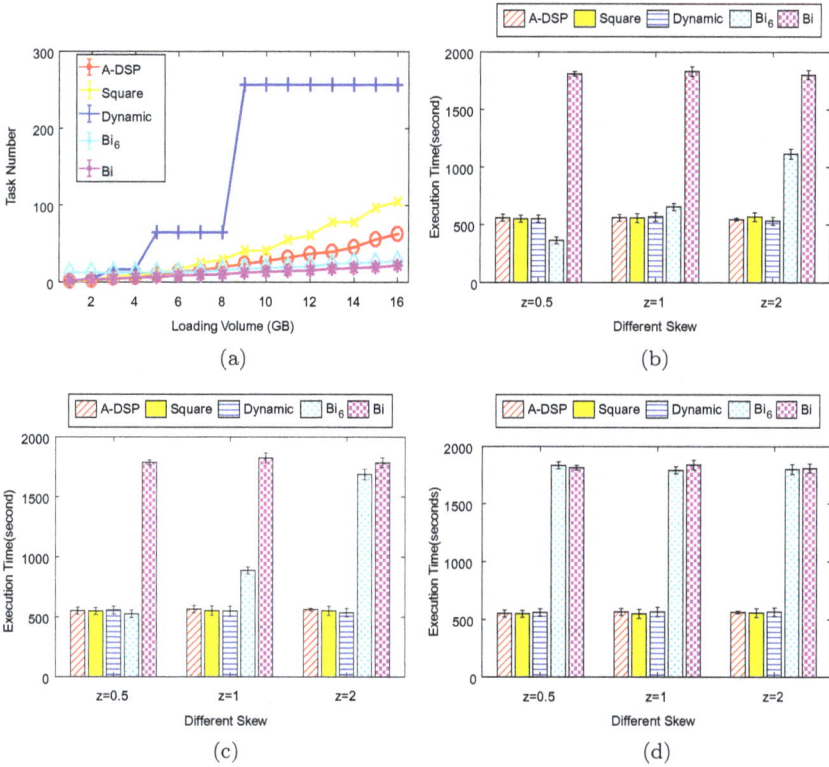

Fig. 5.10. Task consumption and execution time of full-history join. (a) Task number consumption, (b) execution time for E_{Q_5}, (c) execution time for B_{NCI} and (d) execution time for B_{MR}.

data skewness executing E_{Q_5}, B_{NCI} and B_{MR}. A-DSP and matrix-join methods, including *Square* and *Dynamic*, can process join stably since data are distributed to tasks randomly. Although *Bi* takes up fewer tasks, its efficiency is almost three times lower than others due to its lack of computing resources. Specifically, when $z = 2$, severer skewness may cause tuple broadcast among groups. B_{MR} is a wide range of band-joins, and the advantages of sub-grouping in Bi_6 completely disappear as shown in Fig. 5.10(d). Due to the random tuple distribution on join-matrix models, the execution time of *Square* and *Dynamic* is immune to data skewness. Furthermore, our A-DSP uses a hybrid routing strategy which can also benefit from random distribution.

In Fig. 5.10, the execution time of *Dynamic* is similar to our methods, but it is at the expense of more tasks. Since *Bi* and *Bi*$_6$ take minimizing memory usage as the optimization goal, it may decrease processing efficiency when it lacks CPU resources as shown in Fig. 5.10(d). From Fig. 5.10 we can conclude that our algorithms are more scalable and efficient.

5.6.3   *Window-based stream joins*

For this group of experiments, we have 64 GB data with window size of 180 s. We set stream flow-in rate at about $3 \cdot 10^5$ tuples per second to make full use of CPU resources. To facilitate the description, we define the tuple that is distributed to the storage side for join as the join request. To further validate the effects of different band-joins and data skewness on system performance, we run window-based joins to testify throughput under different models.

Figure 5.11 shows system throughput and average number of join requests received by the task in different processing schemes for queries E_{Q_5}, B_{NCI} and B_{MR} under different data skewness. Figure 5.11(a), 5.11(c) and 5.11(e) compare throughput of each algorithm. Throughput of matrix-based algorithms is obviously higher than those of bipartite-graph-based ones which result from data broadcasting among groups and are lacking CPU resources. While executing E_{Q_5} under low-skew data, Bi_6 can route join requests more selectively to sub-groups, guaranteeing the execution efficiency within each task. With severer skewness, however, the amount of data broadcasting among sub-groups lowers system performance greatly. While executing B_{NCI} and B_{MR}, the band-join operations incur more broadcasts among sub-groups and aggravate the CPU loads compared to E_{Q_5}. This is obvious in Fig. 5.11(f), where the wide-range band-join requests make Bi_6 lose the advantage of selection operation on grouping data, because *Bi* has only one sub-group for each stream and it broadcasts the same amount of data for these three kinds of queries as shown in Fig. 5.11(b), 5.11(d) and 5.11(f). Matrix-based algorithms share the CPU load equally among tasks, but suffer from consuming more tasks. In this group of experiments, the task usages of A-DSP, *Square*, *Dynamic*, *Bi*$_6$ and *Bi* are as follows: 13, 16, 64, 12 and 6, respectively.

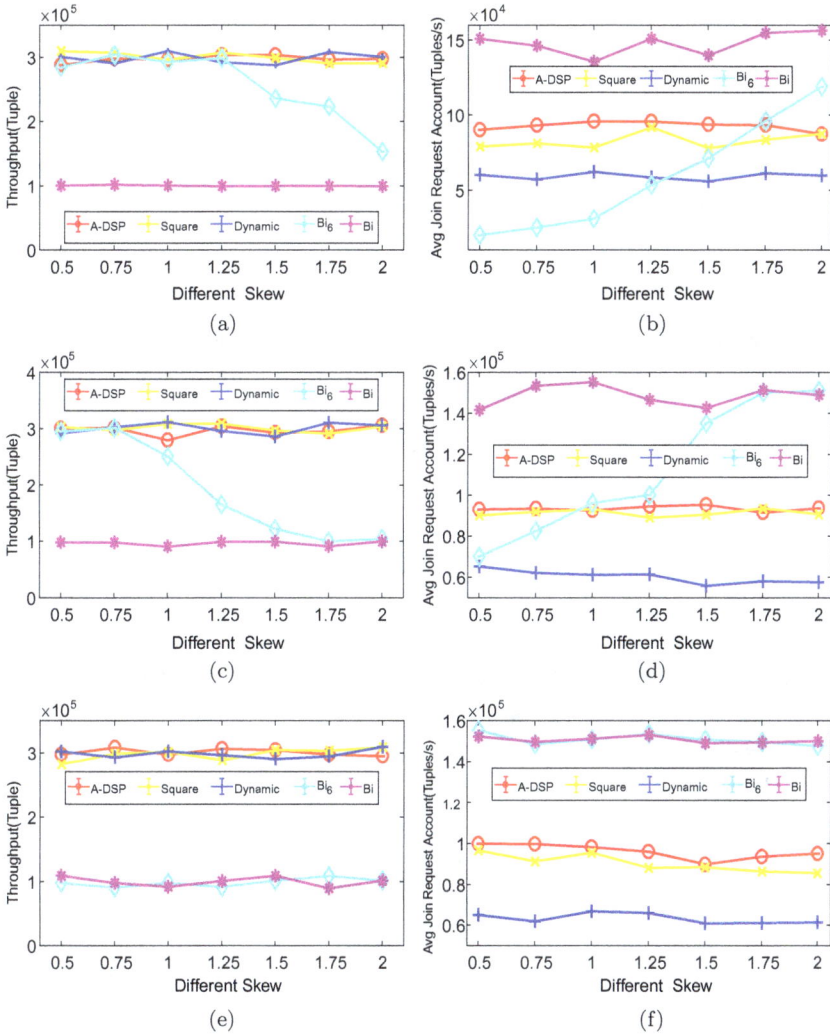

Fig. 5.11. Throughput and tuple account of window-based join for different queries. (a) Throughput for E_{Q_5}, (b) join request account for E_{Q_5}, (c) throughput for B_{NCI}, (d) join request account for B_{NCI}, (e) throughput for B_{MR} and (f) join request account for B_{MR}.

5.6.4 *Adaptivity*

In order to validate the adaptivity of our processing scheme, we simulate two scenarios as follows: (1) We do selectivity transmission for join operation by altering the calculation range of the join predicate. (2) We keep varying the stream volume ratio by $\varrho = \frac{|R|}{|S|}$ under the specified total stream volume of 40 GB. Both those experiments are run based on window. For the threshold controlling scale out or down, *Dynamic* uses its own setting in Elseidy *et al.* (2014) and other algorithms change the scheme when memory load is higher than eighty or lower than fifty percent of that configured for each task.

5.6.4.1 *Adaptivity on selectivity transmission*

To better understand our A-DSP as a flexible and adaptive join model that can adaptively change the dimensions of its processing architecture to satisfy the operational requirements, we disrupt the time series of *Social* data and do the *Social data query* with various selectivities. The different selectivities are generated by changing the correlative days ds. Specifically, the correlative days can be expressed as $|S1.date - S2.date| = ds$, and in Fig. 5.12, we use $ds = 0$, $ds = 3$ and $ds = \infty$ to denote the equivalent, range and full join operation, respectively. Figure 5.12(a) shows the task consumption of different approaches under the above situational settings. Regardless of the join type, *Square* and *Dynamic* always consume the most tasks. This is because they are both based on a fixed matrix architecture. Conversely, *Bi* and *Readj* consume the least tasks, as they do not need to store the copy of the incoming data stream. However, the complicated routing strategies and broadcast action of these methods will inevitably be an obstacle for the system's throughput performance, as shown as Fig. 5.12(b). As shown in Fig. 5.12(a), our adaptive dimensional space processing model can require resource on demand according to the specific join operation type. Furthermore, in spite of A-DSP consuming less tasks, it can guarantee a system with high performance of throughput.

5.6.4.2 *Adaptivity on relative stream volume change*

In Fig. 5.13(a), we adjust ϱ every three minutes. Accordingly, the migration volumes for each algorithm are displayed in Fig. 5.13(b). *Bi* and *Bi_6* algorithms have less migration cost due to the less redundant storage. However, as per the discussion above, it may lead to a higher CPU cost which may lower throughput. *Dynamic* suffers from high migration cost in that it

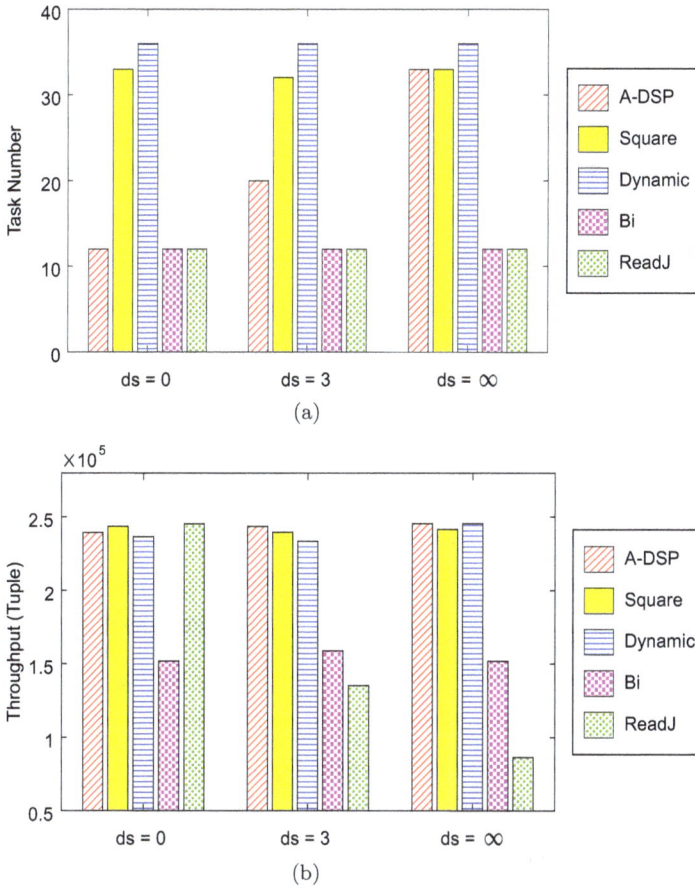

Fig. 5.12. Performance under various selectivities. (a) Task consumption and (b) through-put performance.

requires processing task number to be to the power of two, and it reduces the flexibility with dynamics. Our algorithm A-DSP explores the most appropriate processing scheme which has a relatively cheaper migration cost.

Our synthetic workload generator creates snapshots of tuples for discrete time intervals from an integer key domain K. The tuples follow Zipf distributions controlled by skewness parameter z, by using the popular generation tool available in Apache project. We use parameter f to control the rate of distribution fluctuation across time intervals. At the beginning of a

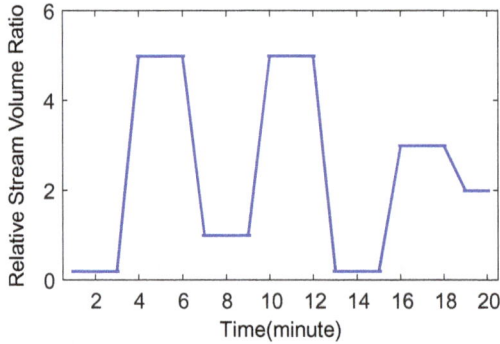

(a)

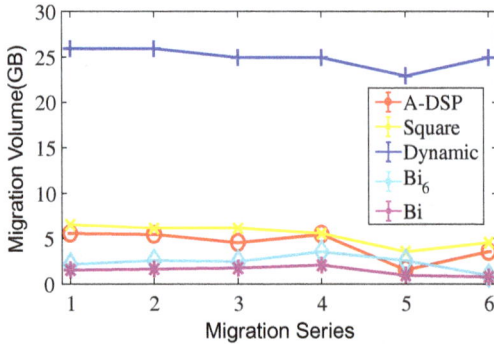

(b)

Fig. 5.13.   Performance with relative stream volume change. (a) Relative stream volume change ϱ and (b) migration volume.

new interval, our generator keeps swapping frequencies between keys from different task instances until the change on workload is significant enough, i.e., $\frac{|L_i(d)-L_{i-1}(d)|}{L} \geq f$.

Figure 5.14 shows the throughput and latency with varying distribution change frequency running on E_{Q_5} (Figs. 5.14(a) and 5.14(b)) and B_{MR} (Figs. 5.14(c) and 5.14(d)), respectively. In Fig. 5.14, we draw the theoretical limit of the performance with the line labeled as *Ideal*, for which the processing corresponding query using *Square* in the condition of adequate resources is available. Obviously, *Ideal* always generates a better throughput and lower processing latency than any other, but cannot be used in real-world applications due to its resource waste. When varying the distribution change frequency f, both the throughput and latency of Bi_6

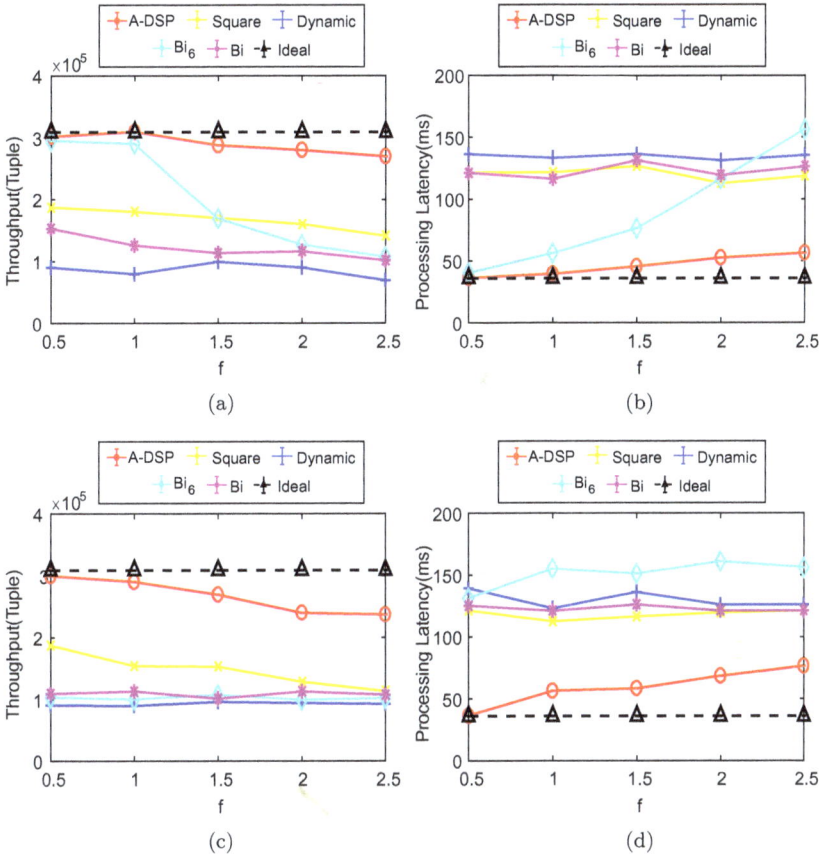

Fig. 5.14. Throughput and latency with varying distribution change frequency, where (a) and (b) Run on a E_{Q_5}, and (c) and (d) on B_{MR}. (a) Stream dynamics vs. throughput, (b) stream dynamics vs. latency, (c) stream dynamics vs. throughput and (d) stream dynamics vs. latency.

change dramatically as shown in Figs. 5.14(a) and 5.14(b). In particular, Bi_6 works well only in the case with less distribution variance (f) as shown in Figs. 5.14(a) and 5.14(b). In the meantime, both Bi and *Dynamic* always have a low throughput and high processing latency as shown in Fig. 5.14 because of the broadcast action in Bi and the limit number of tasks using *Dynamic*. On the contrary, our A-DSP algorithm always performs well, with performance very close to the optimal bound set by *Ideal*.

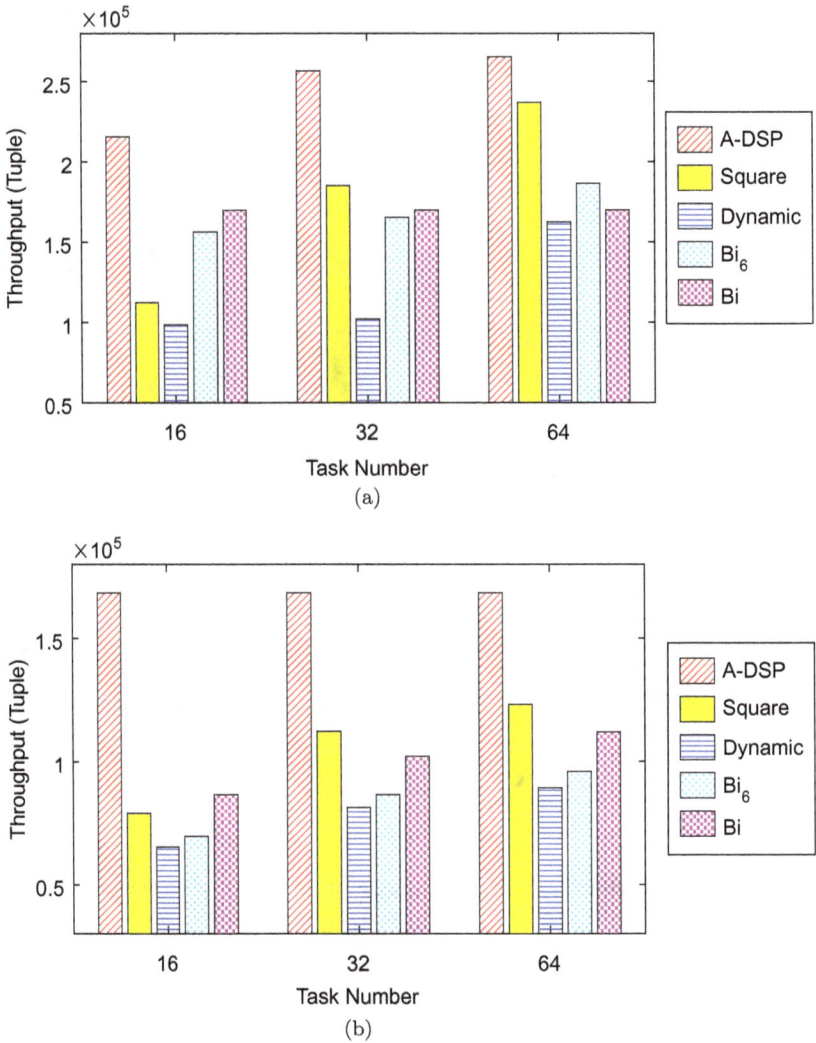

Fig. 5.15.   Performance under limit tasks. (a) Social data and (b) stock data.

5.6.5   *Performance on real data*

5.6.5.1   *Throughput under limited resources*

To better understand the performance of the approaches in action, we present the dynamics of the throughput on two real workloads, especially when the system is limited using the number of tasks. On Social data, we implement a band-join topology on Storm by distributing tuples to tasks for store and join on keywords. On Stock data, a self-join on the data over sliding window is implemented, which maintains the recent tuples based on the size of the window over intervals. The results are available in Fig. 5.15, showing that our method A-DSP always produces a higher throughput. Though *Dynamic* is content insensitive, it produces a lower throughput than A-DSP as the available resources cannot always meet its demand. On both *Social data* and *Stock data* with different available tasks, *Bi* and *Bi*$_6$ have little change in the performance of throughput because the biggest obstacle to their performance is the huge broadcast tuples for these queries. The throughput of *Dynamic* is only one-third of A-DSP when the limitation task number is 32, which leads to huge resource waste and is definitely undesirable for cloud-based streaming processing applications.

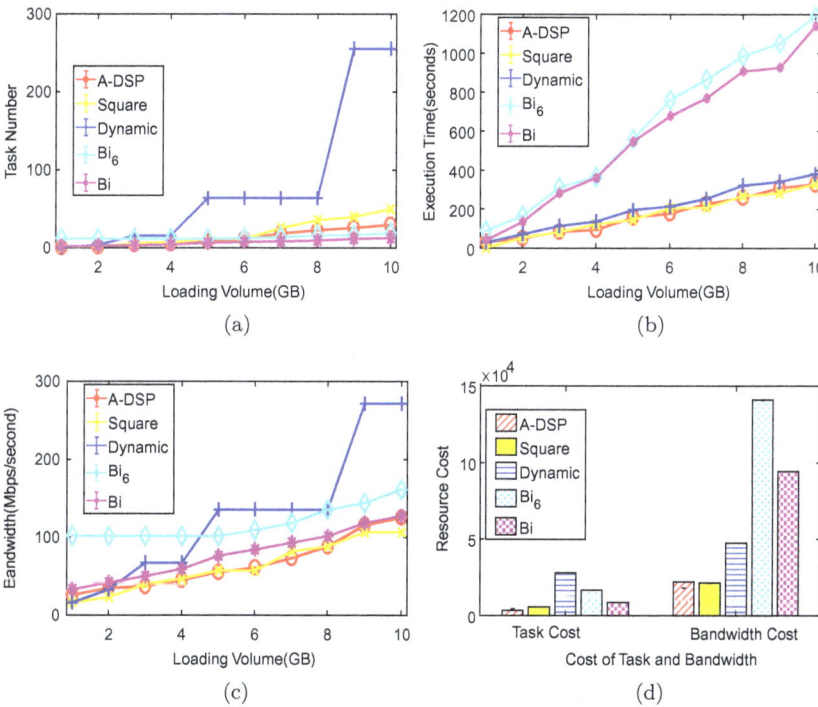

Fig. 5.16. Performance on real data. (a) Task consumption, (b) execution time, (c) bandwidth consumption and (d) resource consumption.

5.6.5.2 *Resource utilization efficiency*

To prove the usability of our algorithm, we do band-join *Social data query* on 10 GB Weibo datasets. We load the 10 GB dataset continuously, and measure resource consumption by different algorithms. In Fig. 5.16(a), bipartite-graph-based models Bi and Bi_6 use less tasks as they are mainly designed for memory optimization as explained in Fig. 5.10. Our method A-DSP provides a flexible matrix scheme which applies for new tasks according to its real load while *Dynamic* scales out in a generous way. Our algorithm is efficient in completing all the work while the bipartite-graph-based models are the slowest due to lack of CPU resources as shown in Fig. 5.16(b).

Figure 5.16(c) shows the bandwidth usage for each algorithm when loading data into the Storm system. Though Bi uses less tasks than A-DSP as shown in Fig. 5.16(a), its bandwidth usage is more than ours as it broadcasts the same amount of incoming tuples to all tasks in the other side of the bipartite graph. *Dynamic* costs the most bandwidth. Figure 5.16(d) provides the overall resource cost (task and bandwidth) by time duration, as computed by $RC = \sum_{r \in \mathbb{R}} r \cdot t_r$ and we consider cost by continuing occupation of resources. It confirms that A-DSP can deal with the band-join more economically.

Remarks: The bipartite-graph join model is more suitable for chapter scale join operations under a relatively stable data distribution of the incoming stream. Furthermore, since this model stores two candidate join streams separately, the join protocol has to be more complicated so as to ensure the completeness of join results regardless of the order of the incoming tuples, which is why Bi and Bi_6 generate a low throughput and high latency in Figs. 5.11, 5.14 and 5.15. *Dynamic* has poor performance in many results. This is because the matrix model incurs the following disadvantages: (1) The number of tasks is strictly decided by the number of cells in the matrix, which is equivalent to the product of the number of rows and columns (Figs. 5.10, 5.11(a), 5.11(c), 5.11(e) and 5.15); (2) In terms of the stream changes, including the increase or decrease of the stream volume and the addition or removal of the processing tasks, it must be consistent with matrix cells (Figs. 5.13(b), 5.14 and 5.16). Finally, since the A-DSP can adaptively change the dimensions of processing architecture to satisfy the operational requirements, it always achieves better performance in the above results.

5.7 Summary

This chapter focuses on how to handle parallel stream joins in a more flexible and adaptive manner, especially to address the demands on operational cost minimization over a cloud platform. Inspired by 1-DPS where tuples join according to a predefined routing strategy and the 2-DPS methods where tuples from different streams are guaranteed to meet with each other, we propose a A-DSP model to assure processing correctness together with efficient resource usage. A-DSP can realize resource allocation on demand. Additionally, we design algorithms with moderate complexity to generate task mapping schemes and migration plans to fulfill the objective of operational cost reduction. Empirical studies show that our proposal incurs the cheapest cost when the stream join operator is run under a pay-as-you-go scheme.

Chapter 6

Case Studies

To illustrate how to use our proposed methods to handle workload imbalance, we present some case studies in this chapter. Based on discussion and analysis of Chapters 3–5, we can summarize the challenges of using a DSPE as follows:

- **Computation mode:** In a DSPE, each incoming tuple is preserved for queries within a certain period. For this reason, a spatial index, which maintains the spatial entries of all trajectories, will inevitably incur a significant update cost. Furthermore, it is also challenging to maintain the existing indices to a distributed and parallel architecture with real-time update supported. It is obvious that a simple global centralized index will increase the query latency as all incoming tuples must be first directed to the index for routing and update.
- **Workload balance:** Dynamic workload imbalance is a unique feature of the distributed streaming system since the input stream is dynamic and continuous. Generally, the data dynamic is mainly shown in two aspects: (1) Dynamic data flow rate refers to the change of incoming data volume. It challenges the overall processing capacity, and the system needs to scale out by adding new nodes. (2) Dynamic data distribution refers to the uneven and fluctuating key distribution of incoming tuples. That is, some of the keys appear much more frequently than others, which leads to load imbalance among tasks. To solve the above challenges, it is necessary to create new transmission channels to redistribute data

streams with states (if any) to other underload tasks, so as to make full use of system resources.

The DSPE, which is designated for massive stream data processing with low latency, offers an effective solution for such workloads. However, the traditional solutions for Real-Time Trajectory Similarity cannot be directly extended to DSPE systems because of two main reasons: First, a two-tier state information including trajectories and their adjacency should be maintained in a DSPE, which should be designed differently to the standalone solution. Second, workload skewness and variance are common phenomena in DSPEs, which are not considered in a standalone system.

6.1   Challenges of Spatio-temporal Processing

In general, the basic operations on spatio-temporal graphs can be roughly divided into two types: aggregate and join. The aggregate operation can be described by giving the selected range and output statistical summary information of the characteristic objects within the limited range. The above description can be expressed as $R_1, \ldots, R_m \mathcal{G}_{F_1,\ldots,F_n}$. In the expression, $\mathcal{G}$ signifies that aggregation is to be applied, its subscript F_i specifies which aggregate operation is to be applied such as min or average on sets of values and the subscript R_i permits the range list of aggregate functions. Compared to the traditional join which is based on value matching, the join type based on spatio-temporal graph is more diverse, such as range join and similarity calculations. For definiteness without loss of generality, we use trajectory to identify each object which produces the continuous motion, namely an edge in the spatio-temporal graph. This is because trajectory as a series of ordered spatio-temporal sequence data can truly reflect the behavioral preferences of individuals or groups. During the execution of most applications, trajectory similarity is a basic operation to explore the relationship between moving objects.

In a DSPE, the computational states in each parallel processing slot are mutually imperceptible. However, operators based on spatio-temporal graph are typically stateful, since they always require two-tier state information including trajectory itself (edge in graph) and its adjacencies. As for the example shown in Fig. 6.1, there are two trajectories P and Q with points p_{1-3} and q_{1-3}, respectively. Those two trajectories are divided

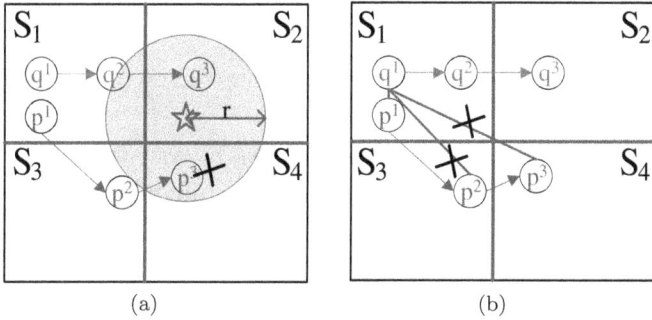

Fig. 6.1. Example of information loss in distributed computing environment. (a) Aggregation and (b) join.

into four parallel processing slots: q_1, q_2 and p_1 locate in S_1, q_3 locates in S_3, p_2 locates in S_3 and p_4 locates in S_4. For an aggregate operation as shown in Fig. 6.1(a), given a query point as a center of a circle and its radius, the aggregate operation outputs how many active objects are within the predefined boundaries. However, the processing framework as shown in Fig. 6.1(a) may generate an incorrect result since the active point p_3 and the query point are located in different processing slots. Similarly, Fig. 6.1(b) shows the state information loss problem after calculating the similarity of those two trajectories. Due to both p_2 and p_3 being located in different processing slots with q_1, the distances between q_1 and p_2, q_1 and p_3 are both lost. Based on this, in the rest of this chapter, we will use our proposed matrix model to maintain a state information guarantee strategy for such information loss phenomenon as shown in Fig. 6.1 to ensure the correctness of such a query in a DSPE.

6.2 Spatio-temporal queries on a DSPE

For ease of description, we use G to denote the universe query area and trajectories in G can be seen as different edges of spatio-temporal graph. A trajectory P consists of a sequence of spatio-temporal points, $P = \{p_1, p_2, \ldots, p_i, \ldots\}$, each of which is a three-dimensional vector expressed as (trajectory-id, timestamp, spatio-temporal point). Based on this, we summarize the ultimate goal as follows: Given a set of trajectories' stream $\tau = \langle T_1, T_2, \ldots, T_n \rangle$, the distance measure D and a configuration parameter K, our model outputs the K similar trajectories for the selected trajectory(set) in a real-time manner.

For definiteness and without loss of generality, we present three different measures for trajectory similarity. (a) We use LCSS that focuses on the adjacent stateful operation of trajectories. (b) We consider how to handle trajectory similarity by pairing points from different trajectories, called MaxM and MinM.

Q1:LCSS: Given the parameters time domain threshold γ and space domain threshold δ, the Longest Common Sub-Sequence Similarity $LCSS_{\gamma,\delta}(A, B)$ between two objects A and B is defined as

$$
\begin{aligned}
&LCSS_{\gamma,\delta}(A, B) \\
&= \begin{cases}
0, & if\ A\ or\ B\ is\ empty; \\
1 + \mathbf{LCSS}_{\gamma,\delta}(\mathbf{Tail(A)}, \mathbf{Tail(B)}), & if\ d(P_1^A, P_1^B) < \gamma \\
& and\ t(P_1^A, P_1^B) < \delta; \\
\mathbf{Max(LCSS}_{\gamma,\delta}(\mathbf{Tail(A)}, \mathbf{B}), & \\
\quad \mathbf{LCSS}_{\gamma,\delta}(\mathbf{A}, \mathbf{Tail(B)})), & otherwise.
\end{cases}
\end{aligned}
$$

In the above expression, we use Euclidean distance [Haan *et al.* (2000)] to measure the distance of two points, and the γ and δ are the thresholds defined by the user(s) that allow flexible matching in the time and space domain. Specifically, if the distance between two points is less than δ and the time difference is less than γ, they are usually considered to be matched.

Q2:MaxM: Given two trajectories P and Q, the distance of MaxM(P, Q) can be expressed as

$$
\text{MaxM}(P, Q) = \max_{p_i \in P} \left\{ \min_{q_i \in Q} \{ d(p_i, q_j) \} \right\}.
$$

Q3:MinM: Given two trajectories P and Q, the distance of MinM(P, Q) can be expressed as

$$
\text{MinM}(P, Q) = \min_{p_i \in P} \left\{ \max_{q_i \in Q} \{ d(p_i, q_j) \} \right\}.
$$

In the above expressions of Q2 and Q3, p_i and q_j are points of trajectories P and Q, respectively, and $d(p_i, q_j)$ is any metric between these points. For simplicity, we also define as Euclidean the distance between p_i and q_j in the following section. Furthermore, Q2 and Q3 are both the basic operations, which can be used for Hausdorff distance and Fréchet distance, respectively.

6.3 Matrix Model for Trajectory Similarity

As discussed in Section 6.2, different distance metrics for trajectory similarity operations require different state information. Without loss of generality, we need a basic state information structure that can support the mainstream trajectory distance measurement, named complete distance information table (CDIT) and defined as follows:

Definition 6.1. For the trajectories P and Q, we identify the table created by taking the Cartesian product of the distance of each point pair between trajectories as CDIT, denoted as CDIT $= \{d(p_i, q_j) | p_i \in P, q_j \in Q\}$.

Figure 6.2(a) shows the example of two trajectories P and Q which both have four points, and there are two windows w_1 and w_2 both covering three points. Corresponding to the trajectories in Figure 6.2(a), Fig. 6.2(b) shows the *CDIT*. Specifically, $\lceil (q_1, p_1), (q_3, p_3) \rfloor$ in Fig. 6.2(b) corresponds to w_1 in Fig. 6.2(b) and $\lceil (q_2, p_2), (q_4, p_4) \rfloor$ corresponds to w_2, where $\lceil (q_i, p_j), (q_{i'}, p_{j'}) \rfloor$ means the cells covered by the rectangle form the upper-left cell (q_i, p_j) to the lower-right cell $(q_{i'}, p_{j'})$.

In order to better demonstrate the versatility of our method, we take a more complex trajectory similarity metric *DTW* as an example to illustrate our design in the following portion. Specifically, each window must

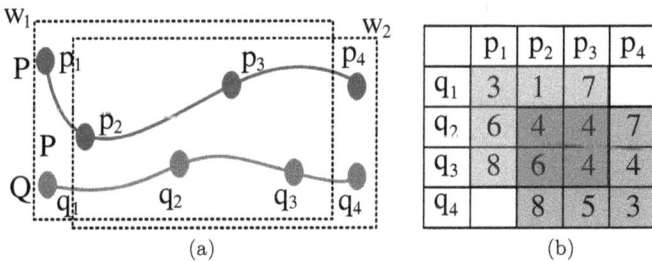

	p_1	p_2	p_3	p_4
q_1	3	1	7	
q_2	6	4	4	7
q_3	8	6	4	4
q_4		8	5	3

(a)   (b)

Fig. 6.2. Example of trajectories and their CDIT in different windows. (a) Trajectories and (b) CDIT.

recalculate the DTW result according to the current content of itself as DTW uses the iterative method to measure its distance. For instance, the pair result of DTW in w_1 is $(\langle q_1, p_1 \rangle, \langle q_1, p_2 \rangle, \langle q_2, p_3 \rangle, \langle q_3, p_3 \rangle)$, and it is $(\langle q_2, p_2 \rangle, \langle q_3, p_3 \rangle, \langle q_4, p_4 \rangle)$ in w_2, which is totally different. CDIT as a basic information table contains all the calculation basis of trajectories' distance.

As described in Chapters 4 and 5, join-matrix is a high-performance model on distributed stream joins and supports arbitrary join predicates. It can handle data skew perfectly since it randomly routes tuples to cells with each stream corresponding to one side of the matrix. For the trajectory similarity, we put the query and basic trajectories set in the column and row directions, respectively. As the example shows in Fig. 6.3(a), stream P (or Q) is split into two substreams $\{P_1, P_4\}$ and $\{P_2, P_3\}$ (or $\{q_1, q_2\}$ and $\{q_3, q_4\}$). Therefore, the join between P and Q is decomposed into four sub-tasks, each of which takes a pair of substreams and calculates the join result. In other words, the union of join results of those four sub-tasks constitutes the CDIT.

In the process of trajectory similarity using the above matrix model, our proposed algorithms can determine the number of rows and columns of the join-matrix and ensure that there are no repeated results when an existing tuple is sent to both the row and column directions. Based on the complete state set provided by the matrix model, all distance measures can be calculated. Furthermore, the performance of trajectory distance computation is susceptible to the number of trajectories and points. Additionally,

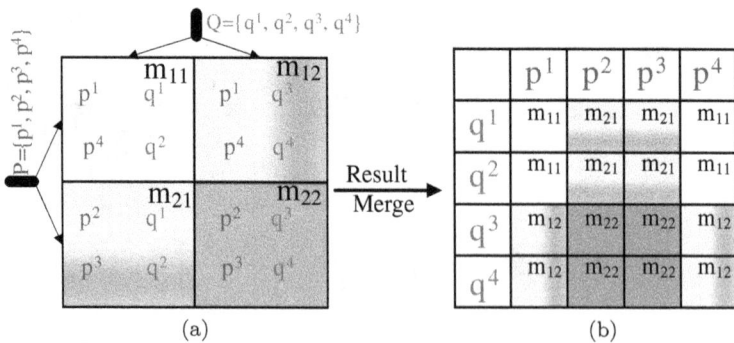

Fig. 6.3. Example of computational model. (a) Computational model and (b) complete state set.

the similarity operator is usually performed on millions of trajectories and points in real-world applications. To alleviate the above problem, workload shedding [Fang *et al.* (2019); Xie *et al.* (2017)] can be implemented on our matrix model directly, which focuses on how an entire trajectory can be pruned by just examining individual segments given a distance threshold for the trajectory distance. Applying the workload shedding strategies, we can reduce the broadcast volume of tuples greatly from the headstream. In other words, we only need to assign tuples to their adjacent task group(s).

6.4 Summary

In this chapter, we studied our proposed methods in a realistic application scenario. First, we presented how the dynamic workload distribution mechanism works for intra-operator load balancing in distributed stream processing engines. Then, we focused on how to handle the dynamic spatio-temporal join in a real-time manner. Our matrix model provides an easy-to-use and lightweight processing scheme enabling the system's high flexibility to handle the dynamic trajectory input.

Chapter 7

Conclusion

This book focuses on how to design the workload balance strategies for a DSPE to process continuous streams so as to achieve real-time performance with low latency and high throughput. We first present a new dynamic workload distribution mechanism for intra-operator load balancing in distributed stream processing engines. It is a new key-based workload partitioning framework, with practical algorithms to support dynamic workload assignments for stateful operators. The framework combines hash-based and explicit key-based routing strategies for workload distribution, which specifies the destination worker threads for a handful of keys and assigns the other keys with the hashing function. When short-term distribution fluctuations occur in the incoming data stream, the system adaptively updates the routing table containing the chosen keys in order to rebalance the workload with minimal migration overhead within the stateful operator. We formulate the rebalance operation as an optimization problem, with multiple objectives on minimizing state migration costs, controlling the size of the routing table and breaking workload imbalance among the worker threads. Furthermore, inspired by the idea of "Split keys on demand and Merge keys as far as possible", we introduce a novel cost model to guide designing of balance schedules. To satisfy requirements that the availability and efficiency are the main concern of the DSPE system, we proposed a new dynamic workload distribution mechanism for intra-operator load balancing and fault tolerance which achieved a lower resource consumption compared to the previous methods.

As for the increase of data volume and the change of data distribution, the adaptive load balance algorithm on keys for the dynamic stream is important to improve the performance of the distributed stream process system. In this book, we also present a general framework to support dynamic workload assignments for stateful operators. In order to balance load with relative small migration costs, we formulate it as an optimization problem and propose an adaptive balance adjustment algorithm. We order the keys by loads and then segment those keys into levels by considering the distance compensation for reducing the balance deviation. Through both theoretic analysis and extensive experimental verification, it is proved that our algorithm can achieve load balance with the requirement of limited routing table size efficiently and effectively. In this book, we also focus on designing flexible and adaptive θ-join algorithms to handle distributed join processing on the stream system. Inspired by the matrix-based method which can ensure the correctness of the join result and be immune to data skewness, we propose a new scheme change algorithm based on the matrix model which inherits all advantages of traditional methods but improves them on scalability and effectiveness. We implement our design on Storm and compare it with the other state-of-art work to verify our idea.

In the future, we will investigate the theoretical properties of the algorithms to better understand the optimality of the approaches under general assumptions. We will also try to design a new mechanism to ensure the correctness of processing results when there exist extremely hot keys with which the total workload associated exceeds the computing power of a single task instance. Furthermore, the exploring directions of our further research is listed as follows: (1) We will continue to design algorithms for θ-join which may break through the matrix model aiming to make full use of system resource. (2) We will continue seeking a more comprehensive cost model and more flexible and adaptive load adjustment strategies to improve system performance. (3) We will explore the possibility of more flexible and scalable mapping and migration strategies with smaller migration costs. We will also try to design a new mechanism to ensure the correctness of processing results when there exist extremely dynamic keys.

Bibliography

Abadi, D., Ahmad, Y., Balazinska, M., *et al.* (2005). The design of the borealis stream processing engine, in *CIDR*, Vol. 5, pp. 277–289.

Abadi, D. J., Carney, D., Çetintemel, U., Cherniack, M., Convey, C., Lee, S., Stonebraker, M., Tatbul, N., and Zdonik, S. B. (2003). Aurora: A new model and architecture for data stream management, *VLDBJ* **12**(2), pp. 120–139.

Ahmad, Y. and Cetintemel, U. (2004). Network-aware query processing for stream-based applications, in *VLDB (VLDB Endowment)*, pp. 456–467.

Ananthanarayanan, R., Basker, V., Das, S., Gupta, A., Jiang, H., Qiu, T., Reznichenko, A., Ryabkov, D., Singh, M., and Venkataraman, S. (2013). *Photon: Fault-tolerant and Scalable Joining of Continuous Data Streams* (ACM), pp. 577–588.

Aniello, L., Baldoni, R., and Querzoni, L. (2013). Adaptive online scheduling in storm, in *DEBS* (ACM), pp. 207–218.

Anis Uddin Nasir, M., De Francisci Morales, G., *et al.* (2015). The power of both choices: Practical load balancing for distributed stream processing engines, in *ICDE*, pp. 137–148.

Balazinska, M., Balakrishnan, H., Madden, S. R., and Stonebraker, M. (2008). Fault-tolerance in the borealis distributed stream processing system, *ACM Transactions on Database Systems (TODS)* **33**(1), p. 3.

Balkesen, C., Teubner, J., Alonso, G., and Zsu, M. T. (2012). Main-memory hash joins on multi-core cpus, *Eth Zurich*.

Bellavista, P., Corradi, A., Kotoulas, S., and Reale, A. (2014). Adaptive fault-tolerance for dynamic resource provisioning in distributed stream processing systems, in *EDBT*, pp. 85–96.

Blanas, S., Li, Y., and Patel, J. M. (2011). *Design and Evaluation of Main Memory Hash Join Algorithms for Multi-core Cpus* (ACM), pp. 37–48.

Bruno, N., Kwon, Y., and Wu, M.-C. (2014). Advanced join strategies for large-scale distributed computation, *Proceedings of the VLDB Endowment* **7**(13), pp. 1484–1495.

Castro Fernandez, R., Migliavacca, M., Kalyvianaki, E., and Pietzuch, P. (2013). Integrating scale out and fault tolerance in stream processing using operator state management, in *Proceedings of the 2013 ACM SIGMOD International Conference on Management of Data* (ACM), pp. 725–736.

Chen, L., Özsu, M. T., and Oria, V. (2005a). Robust and fast similarity search for moving object trajectories, in *Proceedings of the 2005 ACM SIGMOD International Conference on Management of Data* (ACM), pp. 491–502.

Chen, T. P., Haussecker, H., Bovyrin, A., Belenov, R., Rodyushkin, K., Kuranoc, A., and Eruhimov, V. (2005b). Computer vision workload analysis: Case study of video surveillance systems. *Intel Technology Journal* **9**, 2.

Cheng, L., Kotoulas, S., Ward, T., and Theodoropoulos, G. (2014). Robust and skew-resistant parallel joins in shared-nothing systems, in *CIKM*, pp. 1399–1408.

Cherniack, M., Balakrishnan, H., Balazinska, M., Carney, D., Cetintemel, U., Xing, Y., and Zdonik, S. B. (2003). Scalable distributed stream processing, in *CIDR*, Vol. 3, pp. 257–268.

Coffman Jr, E. G., Garey, M. R., and Johnson, D. S. (1984). Approximation algorithms for bin-packing—An updated survey, in *Algorithm Design for Computer System Design* (Springer), pp. 49–106.

Cormode, G. and Muthukrishnan, S. (2005). An improved data stream summary: the count-min sketch and its applications, *Journal of Algorithms* **55**(1), pp. 58–75.

Dewitt, D. and Gray, J. (1992). Parallel database systems: The future of high performance database systems, *Communications of the ACM* **35**(6), pp. 85–98.

Ding, J., Fu, T., Ma, R., Winslett, M., Yang, Y., Zhang, Z., and Chao, H. (2015). Optimal operator state migration for elastic data stream processing, *Mccarthy*.

Dittrich, J. P., Seeger, B., Taylor, D. S., and Widmayer, P. (2002a). Progressive merge join: A generic and non-blocking sort-based join algorithm, in *Vldb*, pp. 299–310.

Dittrich, J. P., Seeger, B., Taylor, D. S., and Widmayer, P. (2002b). Progressive merge join: A generic and non-blocking sort-based join algorithm, in *VLDB* (VLDB Endowment), pp. 299–310.

Elseidy, M., Elguindy, A., Vitorovic, A., and Koch, C. (2014). Scalable and adaptive online joins, *VLDB* **7**(6), pp. 441–452.

Epstein, R. S., Stonebraker, M., and Wong, E. (1978). Distributed query processing in a relational data base system, in *SIGMOD*, pp. 169–180.

Fang, J., Wang, X., Zhang, R., and Zhou, A. (2016). Flexible and adaptive stream join algorithm, in *Asia-Pacific Web Conference* (Springer), pp. 3–16.

Fang, J., Zhang, R., Fu, T. Z., Zhang, Z., Zhou, A., and Zhu, J. (2017). Parallel stream processing against workload skewness and variance, in *Proceedings of the 26th International Symposium on High-Performance Parallel and Distributed Computing* (ACM), pp. 15–26.

Fang, J.-H., Zhao, P.-P., Liu, A., Li, Z.-X., and Zhao, L. (2019). Scalable and adaptive joins for trajectory data in distributed stream system, *Journal of Computer Science and Technology* **34**(4), pp. 747–761.

Frentzos, E., Gratsias, K., and Theodoridis, Y. (2007). Index-based most similar trajectory search, in *ICDE*, pp. 816–825.

Fu, T. Z. J., Ding, J., Ma, R. T. B., Winslett, M., Yang, Y., and Zhang, Z. (2015). Drs: dynamic resource scheduling for real-time analytics over fast streams, in *ICDCS* (IEEE, Columbus), pp. 411–420.

Fu, T. Z. J., Ding, J., Ma, R. T. B., Winslett, M., Yang, Y., and Zhang, Z. (2017). DRS: auto-scaling for real-time stream analytics, *IEEE/ACM Transactions on Networking* **25**(6), pp. 3338–3352.

Gedik, B. (2014). Partitioning functions for stateful data parallelism in stream processing, *VLDBJ* **23**(4), pp. 517–539.

Gedik, B., Schneider, S., Hirzel, M., and Wu, K. (2014). Elastic scaling for data stream processing, *IEEE Transactions on Parallel Distribution System* **25**(6), pp. 1447–1463.

Ghanbari, H., Simmons, B., Litoiu, M., and Iszlai, G. (2011). Exploring alternative approaches to implement an elasticity policy, in *2011 IEEE International Conference on Cloud Computing (CLOUD)* (IEEE), pp. 716–723.

Gonzalez, J. E., Xin, R. S., Dave, A., Crankshaw, D., Franklin, M. J., and Stoica, I. (2014). Graphx: Graph processing in a distributed dataflow framework, in *11th {USENIX} Symposium on Operating Systems Design and Implementation ({OSDI} 14)*, pp. 599–613.

Graefe, G. (1993). Query evaluation techniques for large databases, *ACM Computing Surveys (CSUR)* **25**(2), pp. 73–169.

Haan, H., Streb, J., Bien, S., and Rösler, F. (2000). Individual cortical current density reconstructions of the semantic n400 effect: Using a generalized minimum norm model with different constraints (l1 and l2 norm), *Human Brain Mapping* **11**(3), pp. 178–192.

Heath, T., Martin, R. P., and Nguyen, T. D. (2002). Improving cluster availability using workstation validation, in *ACM SIGMETRICS Performance Evaluation Review*, Vol. 30 (ACM), pp. 217–227.

Heinze, T., Zia, M., Krahn, R., Jerzak, Z., and Fetzer, C. (2015). An adaptive replication scheme for elastic data stream processing systems, in *Proceedings of the 9th ACM International Conference on Distributed Event-Based Systems* (ACM), pp. 150–161.

Hwang, J.-H., Balazinska, M., Rasin, A., Cetintemel, U., Stonebraker, M., and Zdonik, S. (2005). High-availability algorithms for distributed stream processing, in *ICDE 2005. Proceedings of the 21st International Conference on Data Engineering, 2005* (IEEE), pp. 779–790.

Hwang, J.-H., Cetintemel, U., and Zdonik, S. (2008). Fast and highly-available stream processing over wide area networks, in *IEEE 24th International Conference on Data Engineering, 2008. ICDE 2008.* (IEEE), pp. 804–813.

Hwang, J.-H., Xing, Y., Cetintemel, U., and Zdonik, S. (2007). A cooperative, self-configuring high-availability solution for stream processing, in *IEEE 23rd International Conference on Data Engineering, 2007. ICDE 2007.* (IEEE), pp. 176–185.

Ives, Z. G., Florescu, D., Friedman, M., Levy, A., and Weld, D. S. (1999). *An Adaptive Query Execution System for Data Integration* (ACM), pp. 299–310.

Jacques-Silva, G., Gedik, B., Andrade, H., Wu, K.-L., and Iyer, R. K. (2011). Fault injection-based assessment of partial fault tolerance in stream processing applications, in *Proceedings of the 5th ACM International Conference on Distributed Event-Based System* (ACM), pp. 231–242.

Ji, S., Mittal, P., and Beyah, R. (2017). Graph data anonymization, de-anonymization attacks, and de-anonymizability quantification: A survey, *IEEE Communications Surveys & Tutorials* **19**(2), pp. 1305–1326.

Ji, Y., Nica, A., Jerzak, Z., Hackenbroich, G., and Fetzer, C. (2016). Quality-driven disorder handling for concurrent windowed stream queries with shared operators, in *Proceedings of the 10th ACM International Conference on Distributed and Event-based Systems* (ACM), pp. 25–36.

Jiang, Y., Li, G., Feng, J., and Li, W.-S. (2014). String similarity joins: An experimental evaluation, *VLDB Journal* **7**(8), pp. 625–636.

Karger, D., Lehman, E., Leighton, T., Panigrahy, R., Levine, M., and Lewin, D. (1997). Consistent hashing and random trees: Distributed caching protocols for relieving hot spots on the world wide web, in *STOC*, pp. 654–663.

Katsipoulakis, N. R., Labrinidis, A., and Chrysanthis, P. K. (2017). A holistic view of stream partitioning costs, *VLDB* **10**(11), pp. 1286–1297.

Khandekar, R., Hildrum, K., Parekh, S., Rajan, D., Wolf, J., Wu, K.-L., Andrade, H., and Gedik, B. (2009). Cola: Optimizing stream processing applications via graph partitioning, in *Middleware* (Springer), pp. 308–327.

Kulkarni, S., Bhagat, N., Fu, M., *et al.* (2015). Twitter heron: Stream processing at scale, in *SIGMOD*, pp. 239–250.

Kutare, M., Eisenhauer, G., Wang, C., Schwan, K., Talwar, V., and Wolf, M. (2010). Monalytics: Online monitoring and analytics for managing large scale data centers, in *ICAC*, pp. 141–150.

Kwon, Y., Balazinska, M., *et al.* (2012). Skewtune: Mitigating skew in mapreduce applications, in *SIGMOD*, pp. 25–36.

Li, L., Kim, J., Xu, J., and Zhou, X. (2018). Time-dependent route scheduling on road networks, *SIGSPATIAL Special* **10**(1), pp. 10–14.

Lin, Q., Ooi, B. C., Wang, Z., and Yu, C. (2015). Scalable distributed stream join processing, in *SIGMOD*, pp. 811–825.

Liu, B., Zhu, Y., Jbantova, M., *et al.* (2005). A dynamically adaptive distributed system for processing complex continuous queries, in *VLDB*, pp. 1338–1341.

Mokbel, M., Lu, M., and Aref, W. (2004). Hash-merge join: Non-blocking join algorithm for producing fast and early join results, in *ICDE*, pp. 251–263.

Nasir, M. A. U., Morales, G. D. F., García-Soriano, D., Kourtellis, N., and Serafini, M. (2015). The power of both choices: Practical load balancing for distributed stream processing engines, *ICDE*.

Nasir, M. A. U., Serafini, M., *et al.* (2016). When two choices are not enough: Balancing at scale in distributed stream processing, in *ICDE*.

Noghabi, S. A., Paramasivam, K., Pan, Y., Ramesh, N., Bringhurst, J., Gupta, I., and Campbell, R. H. (2017). Samza: stateful scalable stream processing at linkedin, *VLDB* **10**(12), pp. 1634–1645.

Okcan, A. and Riedewald, M. (2011). Processing theta-joins using mapreduce, in *SIGMOD*, pp. 949–960.

Qian, Z., He, Y., Su, C., Wu, Z., Zhu, H., Zhang, T., Zhou, L., Yu, Y., and Zhang, Z. (2013). Timestream: Reliable stream computation in the cloud, in *Proceedings of the 8th ACM European Conference on Computer Systems* (ACM), pp. 1–14.

Rupprecht, L., Culhane, W., and Pietzuch, P. (2017). Squirreljoin: Network-aware distributed join processing with lazy partitioning, *Proceedings of the VLDB Endowment* **10**(11), pp. 1250–1261.

Salama, A., Binnig, C., Kraska, T., and Zamanian, E. (2015). Cost-based fault-tolerance for parallel data processing, in *Proceedings of the 2015 ACM SIGMOD International Conference on Management of Data* (ACM), pp. 285–297.

Schneider, F. B. (1990). Implementing fault-tolerant services using the state machine approach: A tutorial, *ACM Computing Surveys (CSUR)* **22**(4), pp. 299–319.

Schroeder, B. and Gibson, G. (2010). A large-scale study of failures in high-performance computing systems, *IEEE Transactions on Dependable and Secure Computing* **7**(4), pp. 337–350.

Shah, M., Hellerstein, J. M., Chandrasekaran, S., Franklin, M. J., *et al.* (2003). Flux: An adaptive partitioning operator for continuous query systems, in *ICDE* (IEEE), pp. 25–36.

Shang, S., Chen, L., Wei, Z., Jensen, C. S., Wen, J.-R., and Kalnis, P. (2016). Collective travel planning in spatial networks, *TKDE* **28**(5), pp. 1132–1146.

Shang, S., Chen, L., Wei, Z., Jensen, C. S., Zheng, K., and Kalnis, P. (2017). Trajectory similarity join in spatial networks, *Proceedings of the VLDB Endowment* **10**(11), pp. 1178–1189.

Shang, S., Chen, L., Wei, Z., Jensen, C. S., Zheng, K., and Kalnis, P. (2018). Parallel trajectory similarity joins in spatial networks, *VLDB Journal* **27**(3), pp. 395–420.

Shang, S., Ding, R., Yuan, B., Xie, K., Zheng, K., and Kalnis, P. (2012). User oriented trajectory search for trip recommendation, in *Proceedings of the 15th International Conference on Extending Database Technology* (ACM), pp. 156–167.

Shang, S., Ding, R., Zheng, K., Jensen, C. S., Kalnis, P., and Zhou, X. (2014). Personalized trajectory matching in spatial networks, *VLDB Journal* **23**(3), pp. 449–468.

Stamos, J. W. and Young, H. C. (1993). A symmetric and replicate algorithm for distributed joins, *IEEE Transactions on Parallel and Distributed Systems* **4**(12), pp. 1345–1354.

Su, H., Zheng, K., Huang, J., Wang, H., and Zhou, X. (2015). Calibrating trajectory data for spatio-temporal similarity analysis, *VLDB Journal* **24**(1), pp. 93–116.

Su, H., Zheng, K., Wang, H., Huang, J., and Zhou, X. (2013). Calibrating trajectory data for similarity-based analysis, in *SIGMOD*, pp. 833–844.

Su, L. and Zhou, Y. (2016). Tolerating correlated failures in massively parallel stream processing engines, in *ICDE*, pp. 517–528.

Su, L. and Zhou, Y. (2017). Passive and partially active fault tolerance for massively parallel stream processing engines, in *TKDE*.

Sun, J., Xu, J., Zhou, R., Zheng, K., and Liu, C. (2018). Discovering expert drivers from trajectories, in *ICDE*, pp. 1332–1335.

Tao, Y., Yiu, M. L., Papadias, D., Hadjieleftheriou, M., and Mamoulis, N. (2005). Rpj: Producing fast join results on streams through rate-based optimization, pp. 371–382.

Toshniwal, A., Taneja, S., Shukla, A., Ramasamy, K., Patel, J., Kulkarni, S., Jackson, J., Gade, K., Fu, M., Donham, J., *et al.* (2014). Storm@ twitter, in *SIGMOD*, pp. 147–156.

Trasarti, R., Pinelli, F., Nanni, M., and Giannotti, F. (2011). Mining mobility user profiles for car pooling, in *SIGKDD*, pp. 1190–1198.

Tsourakakis, C., Gkantsidis, C., Radunovic, B., and Vojnovic, M. (2014). Fennel: Streaming graph partitioning for massive scale graphs, in *Proceedings of the 7th ACM International Conference on Web Search and Data Mining* (ACM), pp. 333–342.

Gufler, B., Augsten, N., Reiser, A., and Kemper, A. (2012). Load balancing in mapreduce based on scalable cardinality estimates, in *ICDE*, pp. 522–533.

Upadhyaya, P., Kwon, Y., and Balazinska, M. (2011). A latency and fault-tolerance optimizer for online parallel query plans, in *Proceedings of the 2011 ACM SIGMOD International Conference on Management of Data* (ACM), pp. 241–252.

Urhan, T. and Franklin, M. (2001). Dynamic pipeline scheduling for improving interactive query performance, in *VLDB*, pp. 501–510.

Urhan, T. and Franklin, M. J. (2000). Xjoin: A reactively-scheduled pipelined join operator, p. 2000.

Vishwanath, K. V. and Nagappan, N. (2010). Characterizing cloud computing hardware reliability, in *Proceedings of the 1st ACM Symposium on Cloud Computing* (ACM), pp. 193–204.

Vitorovic, A., ElSeidy, M., and Koch, C. (2016). Load balancing and skew resilience for parallel joins, in *ICDE*.

Vlachos, M., Kollios, G., and Gunopulos, D. (2002). Discovering similar multidimensional trajectories, in *ICDE*, pp. 673–684.

Walton, C., Dale, A., and Jenevein, R. (1991). A taxonomy and performance model of data skew effects in parallel joins, in *VLDB*, pp. 537–548.

Wang, H., Su, H., Zheng, K., Sadiq, S., and Zhou, X. (2013). An effectiveness study on trajectory similarity measures, in *Proceedings of the Twenty-Fourth Australasian Database Conference-Volume 137* (Australian Computer Society, Inc.), pp. 13–22.

Wilschut, A. and Apers, P. (1993). Dataflow query execution in a parallel main-memory environment, *Distributed and Parallel Databases* **1**(1), pp. 103–128.

Wolf, J., Bansal, N., Hildrum, K., Parekh, S., Rajan, D., Wagle, R., Wu, K.-L., and Fleischer, L. (2008). Soda: An optimizing scheduler for large-scale stream-based distributed computer systems, in *Middleware* (Springer), pp. 306–325.

Wu, Y. and Tan, K. (2015). Chronostream: Elastic stateful stream computation in the cloud, in *ICDE*, pp. 723–734.

Xie, D., Li, F., and Phillips, J. M. (2017). Distributed trajectory similarity search, *Proceedings of the VLDB Endowment* **10**(11), pp. 1478–1489.

Xing, Y., Hwang, J., Cetintemel, U., and Zdonik, S. (2006). Providing resiliency to load variations in distributed stream processing, in *VLDB* (VLDB Endowment), pp. 775–786.

Xing, Y., Zdonik, S., and Hwang, J. (2005). Dynamic load distribution in the borealis stream processor, in *ICDE* (IEEE), pp. 791–802.

Xu, Y., Kostamaa, P., Zhou, X., and Chen, L. (2008). Handling data skew in parallel joins in shared-nothing systems, in *Proceedings of the 2008 ACM SIGMOD International Conference on Management of Data* (ACM), pp. 1043–1052.

Yanagisawa, Y., Akahani, J.-I., and Satoh, T. (2003). Shape-based similarity query for trajectory of mobile objects, in *International Conference on Mobile Data Management*, pp. 63–77.

Yin, H., Zhou, X., Cui, B., Wang, H., Zheng, K., and Nguyen, Q. V. H. (2016). Adapting to user interest drift for poi recommendation, *IEEE Transactions on Knowledge and Data Engineering* **28**(10), pp. 2566–2581.

Ying, R., Pan, J., Fox, K., and Agarwal, P. K. (2016). A simple efficient approximation algorithm for dynamic time warping, in *SIGSPATIAL*, p. 21.

Zaharia, M., Das, T., Li, H., Hunter, T., Shenker, S., and Stoica, I. (2013). Discretized streams: Fault-tolerant streaming computation at scale, in *Proceedings of the Twenty-Fourth ACM Symposium on Operating Systems Principles* (ACM), pp. 423–438.

Zheng, K., Zheng, Y., Yuan, N. J., and Shang, S. (2013a). On discovery of gathering patterns from trajectories, in *ICDE*, pp. 242–253.

Zheng, K., Zheng, Y., Yuan, N. J., Shang, S., and Zhou, X. (2013b). Online discovery of gathering patterns over trajectories, *IEEE Transactions on Knowledge and Data Engineering* **26**(8), pp. 1974–1988.

Index

East China Normal University Scientific Reports
Subseries on Data Science and Engineering

Published (continued from page ii)

www.ingramcontent.com/pod-product-compliance
Lightning Source LLC
Chambersburg PA
CBHW050552190326
41458CB00007B/2013